D1483393

Brain Dysfunction in
Aggressive Criminals

Coauthors

George U. Balis, M.D.
Professor of Psychiatry

J. David Barcik, Ph.D.
Clinical Assistant Professor of Psychiatry (Psychology)

Barbara Hulfish, M.D.
Assistant Professor of Psychiatry (Neurology)

John R. Lion, M.D.
Professor of Psychiatry

Duncan McCulloch, E.E.
Research Associate Psychiatry (Neurobiology)

Matthew McDonald, Ph.D.
Clinical Assistant Professor of Psychiatry (Psychology)

David A. Paskewitz, Ph.D.
Assistant Professor of Psychiatry (Psychology)

Jeffrey S. Rubin, B.A.
Research Associate (Psychiatry)

All coauthors are in the Department of Psychiatry, University of Maryland School of Medicine, Baltimore.

Brain Dysfunction in Aggressive Criminals

Russell R. Monroe, M.D.
University of Maryland
School of Medicine

Lexington Books
D.C. Heath and Company
Lexington, Massachusetts
Toronto

Library of Congress Cataloging in Publication Data

Main entry under title:
    Brain dysfunction in aggressive criminals.

    Includes indexes.
    1. Violence. 2. Brain—Diseases. 3. Criminal psychology. I. Monroe, Rus-
sell R.
    RC569.5.V55B73   616.8'58   78-4402
    ISBN 0-669-02349-3

International Standard Book Number: 0-669-02349-3

Library of Congress Catalog Card Number: 78-4402

Contents

List of Tables

List of Figures

Preface

This is a sequel to my monograph, *Episodic Behavior Disorders: A Psychodynamic and Neurophysiologic Analysis,* published by Harvard University Press in 1970. The data collected in that study on over seven hundred subjects, including psychiatric inpatients, outpatients, and normal contrast groups was a hypothesis finding rather than a hypothesis testing project. The investigations reported in the current monograph, however, are hypotheses testing, although concurrently, much new empirical data will be reported.

In the original study I commented on the apparent sex reversal of episodic disorders in children and adult groups—that is, during childhood more males than females were hospitalized with characteristic symptoms of episodic behavioral disorders, while serial admissions to an acute adult psychiatric service showed more females than males meeting these diagnostic criteria. A detailed examination of the clinical records revealed that adult females showing episodic dyscontrol were likely to be hospitalized as the result of their dyscontrol acts, while adult males were more likely to be handled by the criminal justice system and incarcerated. For this reason aggressive prisoners were selected as the target population in the present study. The research subjects in this study are recidivist aggressors judged as defective delinquents under Maryland law.[a] A defective delinquent was defined "as an individual who by the demonstration of persistent aggravated, antisocial or criminal behavior evidences a propensity towards criminal activity and is found to have either such intellectual deficiency or emotional unbalance or both as to clearly demonstrate an actual danger to society so as to require such confinement and treatment, when appropriate, as may make it reasonably safe for society to terminate the confinement and treatment." The prediction of episodic disorders was confirmed to the extent that over 50 percent of the prison subjects we studied manifested episodic dyscontrol as defined in the original monograph and an equal number were found to have a significant neurophysiologic dysfunction. Thus, the medical model with specific diagnostic, prognostic, and therapeutic implications provides an heuristic framework for evaluating a significant group of criminals.

Research on prisoners as illustrated in this study is justified in the sense that the projected findings may help the individuals studied. This is true only as long as other medical-ethical considerations are kept in mind, such as informed consent, confidentiality, provision of continuing medical follow-up, and lack of coercion. These factors are discussed in detail in Chapter 4.

My interest in the episodic behavioral disorders has spanned twenty years of clinical practice. During this time I have been joined by a number of colleagues who both independently and collaboratively have developed similar interests.

---

[a]The defective delinquent law, an indeterminant sentence, under which these prisoners were incarcerated has since been repealed.

George U. Balis, M.D., Professor of Psychiatry, first collaborated with me in 1961 as a postresident fellow and throughout the intervening years has contributed a number of unique ideas to the concept of the episodic behavioral disorders. John R. Lion, M.D., Professor of Psychiatry, studied the relationships of epilepsy and aggression while a resident and fellow at the Massachusetts General Hospital. In 1971 he joined our faculty to continue these studies, founding a violence research center. Barbara Hulfish, M.D., Assistant Professor of Psychiatry (Neurology), independently developed an interest in limbic system dysfunction. Matthew McDonald, Ph.D., Instructor of Psychiatry (Psychology), did his graduate thesis on impulsiveness in children and again independently came to many conclusions that fit nicely with the concept of episodic behavioral disorders. These four individuals, with myself as principal investigator, formulated a research project which was funded by the Crime and Delinquency Section of the National Institute of Mental Health under the direction of Saleem Shah (MH 21035). It was this group, with the help of Jeffrey S. Rubin, B.A., Research Associate in the Department of Psychiatry, who collected the data for this study. Mr. Rubin was the only individual assigned full-time to the project, and his interpersonal skills in dealing with such diverse groups as the prisoners, the security personnel, professional staff of the Patuxent Institution, as well as the research project staff, was crucial in the success of this endeavor. Towards the end of the data collection process, David Barcik, Ph.D., Assistant Professor of Psychiatry (Psychology), then Director of Psychological Services in the State of Maryland, Department of Corrections, joined the research team. His early animal studies on the limbic system and his statistical knowledge made him an ideal addition to this team. David A. Paskewitz, Ph.D., Assistant Professor of Psychiatry (Psychology) was instrumental in formulating a method of computer analysis whereby the effects of the primidone administration could be analyzed. Finally, Duncan McCulloch, Biomedical Engineer and Research Associate in the Neurobiology Laboratories of Robert Grenell, Ph.D., contributed significantly to the "machine" analysis of the EEG data.

Aside from this research team others both within and without the Department of Psychiatry, University of Maryland School of Medicine, have contributed to this study, including Michael Plaut, Ph.D., Assistant Professor in Child Psychiatry (Research), Edward K. Knoblock, M.S., Department of Clinical Pathology, and John Overall, Ph.D., Professor of Psychiatry (Psychology), University of Texas Medical Branch, Galveston, all of whom provided invaluable advice, although responsibility for the published data rests with the authors alone. The electroencephalographic reports were submitted by Curtis Marshall, M.D., EEG Consultant to the Patuxent Institution, although extrapolation from the written records and interpretation of the data is again the sole responsibility of the authors. Dr. Marshall's electroencephalographic technician at the Patuxent Institution was Patrick Gerahty.

There were two lines of authority within the Patuxent Institution at the time of this study: the security officers under the direction of Forrest Calhoun and the medical staff under the direction of Michael Boslow, M.D., Medical Director. Final authority rested with Dr. Boslow who directed the entire staff. Thus, the Patuxent Institution was a unique prison-hospital facility. The Patuxent staff did not contribute directly to the study, except that the group therapists rated behavior of subjects in therapy sessions and we did extrapolate data from the diagnostic work-up in the prisoners' files which consisted of social histories, psychiatric evaluations, psychologic test data, as well as prison infractions. We would like to thank all concerned for the thoroughness of these reports as well as their wholehearted cooperation in this study. Finally, we thank the prisoners themselves for the candidness with which they discussed their problems. Their veracity was confirmed again and again even though some of us with prior experience in correctional systems were originally dubious about reported data. Sometimes these doubts were justified but confrontation quickly clarified matters in most instances.

Alfreda Honigfeld, who edited my monograph on Episodic Behavioral Disorders, also provided invaluable editorial assistance. Her expertise not only as an editor but in psychological testing, electroencephalographic technology, and psychopharmacology provided the necessary background for this difficult task. Thanks must be expressed to the Commonwealth Fund for its support in the preparation of the final manuscript. Recognition must also be given to the Maryland Psychiatric Research Center which on January 1, 1977 became affiliated with the Department of Psychiatry, University of Maryland School of Medicine. Under the direction of William Carpenter, M.D., the Center provided resources for the final analysis of the data. During the period 1972-1975, when part of this work was done, we received the unequivocal support of Eugene B. Brody, M.D., Professor of Psychiatry, at that time Chairman of the Department of Psychiatry, University of Maryland School of Medicine.

Russell R. Monroe, M.D.
Professor of Psychiatry
Chairman, Department of Psychiatry and
Director, Institute of Psychiatry
    and Human Behavior
University of Maryland School of Medicine

1

Episodic Dyscontrol: Definitions, Descriptions, and Measurement

George U. Balis and
Matthew McDonald

The literature on episodic behavioral disorders was thoroughly reviewed by Monroe in his monograph (1970) in which he described the concept, based on clinical, electroencephalographic, neurophysiological, psychological, and psychoanalytic considerations. The following is a brief review of the major theoretical constructs of the concept of episodic behavior disorders.

Monroe defined episodic behavioral disorders (EBD) as "precipitously appearing, maladaptive behavior that interrupts the life style and life flow of the individual"; the behavior "is out of character for the individual and out of context for the situation." He further postulated that the intermittent, abrupt, and precipitous quality of the disordered behavior must have specific etiologic, dynamic, and therapeutic implications. Figure 1-1 is a summary of Monroe's classification of episodic behavioral disorders which includes (1) *episodic inhibitions* including narcolepsy, catalepsy, akinetic mutism, periodic catatonia, and petit mal status; and (2) *episodic disinhibitions* which he further classified into two smaller subgroups designed as *episodic dyscontrol* and *episodic reactions*. The major criterion differentiating these two subgroups is the duration of the episode. The episodic dyscontrol is characterized by an interruption in life style and life flow which is represented "by an abrupt act or short series of acts with a common intention, carried through to completion with either relief of tension or gratification of a specific need." Monroe pointed out that these acts are motivated by intense feelings of fear and rage with no or limited foresight and result in serious antisocial acts. On the other hand, the episodic reactions are described as "more sustained interruptions in the life style and life flow, often characterized by multiple dyscontrol acts with varied intentions as well as other symptoms of a neurotic, psychotic, sociopathic, or physiologic nature." Monroe felt it was important to differentiate the episodic behavior disorders not only from chronic, insidious psychopathology but also from the "dyscontrol way of life" of the pure psychopathic individuals.

Monroe used a homeostatic model of personality functioning to conceptualize the underlying psychodynamic mechanisms responsible for the development of episodic behavioral disorders. In general, he conceptualizes motivated behavior as being the outcome of a homeostatic or transactional equilibrium between environmental demands and internal integrative mechanisms. Gratification of drives that motivate behavior is accomplished through a process of negotiation between the two systems, in such a manner that homeostasis is

1

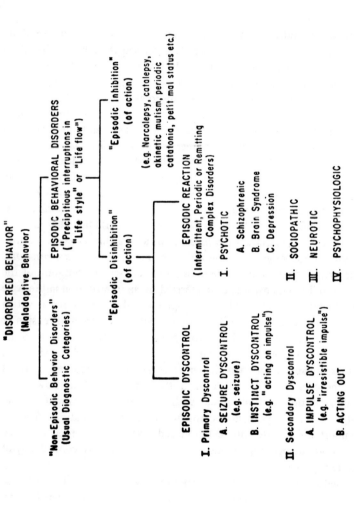

Figure 1-1. Disordered Behavior

Source: Russell R. Monroe, *Episodic Behavioral Disorders*. © 1970 by Harvard University Press, Cambridge, Massachusetts, p. 3. Reprinted by permission.

maintained. In that regard, drives with their need for gratification are balanced by reality testing and control. The adaptive value of a behavioral response is judged on the basis of its capacity to maintain the "steady state" of the transaction between the individual and his social and physical environment. This process is dependent not only upon the perception and apperception of the objective reality and the coordination of the motor act, but also upon varying degrees of integration, referred to as "reflection," or "thought as trial action." The latter is carried out through various cognitive processes of reasoning, memory, and anticipatory awareness of future consequences, as well as conscience (superego) mechanisms, that allow a choice of alternatives, in such a manner that drive gratification and its associated relief of tension is accomplished, while, at the same time, the homeostatic state of the transaction is maintained (Figure 1-2).

Within this homeostatic framework, Monroe conceptualized episodic dyscontrol as the result of an imbalance in the urge-control mechanisms, in which either intense urges (drives) overwhelm normal control mechanisms, or normal urges are left unrestrained by inadequately developed or secondarily compromised control mechanisms. When there is inhibition or deficiency in the integrative processes (impairment of the reflective delay), the resulting maladaptive behavioral response is labeled "seizure" or "instinct" dyscontrol, both of which are referred to as "primary dyscontrol" (Figure 1-3). In primary dyscontrol episodes, the deficient control is related to a lack of integrative reflection, usually manifested by the lack of delay between the environmental stimulus and the response act to that stimulus. This lack of reflection results in both an obliteration of reflective delay that allows choice among alternatives and "choice delay" (postponement of immediate gratification for long-term rewards as determined by the "reality principle"). Therefore, according to Monroe's theorizing, the sine qua non of the group of disorders he has labeled seizure or instinct dyscontrol (primary dyscontrol) must be an inhibition or deficiency in reflective delay with consequent failure in "choice" delay (Figure 1-2). Deficiency in reflective delay mechanisms resulting in primary dyscontrol is due to some neuronal dysfunction (faulty equipment), such as epileptic or organic disturbances of the central nervous system. On the other hand, "distortions" in reflective delay, attributed to "faulty learning," result in what he has labeled "impulse dyscontrol" and "acting out," both of which are referred to as "secondary dyscontrol" (Figure 1-3). In these instances there is a varying period of reflective delay between the original stimulus and the act itself, during which tension mounts until it reaches a breaking point when the urges overwhelm the controls and trigger the explosive act with its release of tension. The difference between acting out and impulse dyscontrol is that in acting out, the delays, both reflective and choice, are to a significant degree unconscious. Impulse dyscontrol is similar to instinct dyscontrol, differing in that in the former there is conscious premeditation to varying degrees preceding the act itself. In impulse dyscontrol

4

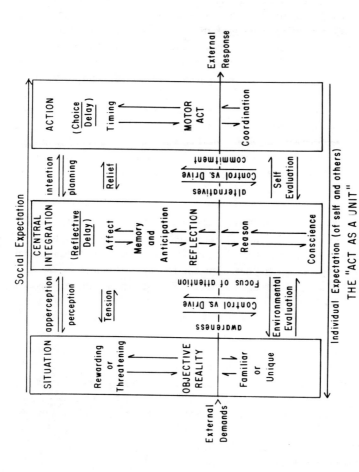

Figure 1-2. The Act as a Unit

Source: Russell R. Monroe, *Episodic Behavior Disorders*. ©1970 by Harvard University Press, Cambridge, Massachusetts, p. 154. Reprinted by permission.

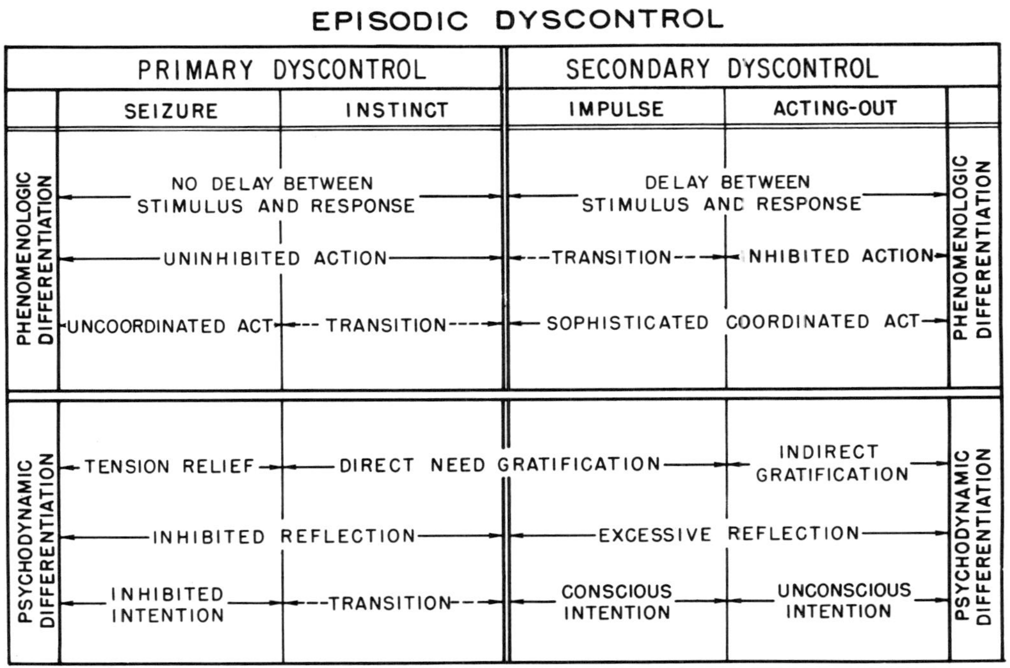

EPISODIC DYSCONTROL

	PRIMARY DYSCONTROL		SECONDARY DYSCONTROL	
	SEIZURE	INSTINCT	IMPULSE	ACTING-OUT
PHENOMENOLOGIC DIFFERENTIATION		NO DELAY BETWEEN STIMULUS AND RESPONSE	DELAY BETWEEN STIMULUS AND RESPONSE	
		UNINHIBITED ACTION	---TRANSITION---	INHIBITED ACTION
		UNCOORDINATED ACT---TRANSITION---	SOPHISTICATED COORDINATED ACT	
PSYCHODYNAMIC DIFFERENTIATION		TENSION RELIEF	DIRECT NEED GRATIFICATION	INDIRECT GRATIFICATION
		INHIBITED REFLECTION	EXCESSIVE REFLECTION	
		INHIBITED INTENTION	---TRANSITION--- CONSCIOUS INTENTION	UNCONSCIOUS INTENTION

Figure 1-3. Episodic Dyscontrol

Source: Russell R. Monroe, "Episodic Behavior Disorders: An Unclassified Syndrome," in *American Handbook of Psychiatry*, second edition, edited by Silvano Arieti, volume 3, edited by Silvano Arieti and Eugene B. Brody © 1974 by Basic Books, Inc., New York, p. 241. Reprinted by permission.

the basic mechanism is thought to be relatively weak control over intense or intolerable urges. In acting out there is an unconscious misuse of the reflective delay, called a misuse because the present situation is related to and inappropriately connected with a past situation, the inappropriate connection in turn being related to the affectively charged memories of unresolved conflicts. By conceptualizing episodic dyscontrol as an outcome of both "faulty learning" and "faulty equipment" (a nature-nurture interplay), Monroe further presented clinical and electroencephalographic evidence that purports to infer an epileptoid mechanism underlying all episodic behavioral disorders, although in varying degree. This epileptoid mechanism is most prominent in the primary dyscontrol group of episodic dyscontrol and least prominent in the secondary dyscontrol group of episodic dyscontrol.

In determining the importance of epileptoid ("faulty equipment") versus motivational ("faulty learning") factors underlying episodic behavioral disorders, Monroe compared clinical and electroencephalographic data phenomenologically. It appeared that epileptoid mechanisms, in contrast to motivational mechanisms, play an increasingly significant role when the following criteria were met: (1) the dyscontrol acts are primitive and diffuse, (2) the eliciting situation is neutral or ambiguous, (3) the secondary gains are slight or absent, (4) the perceptive-apperceptive capacity at the time of the act itself is impaired, although subtly, and (5) the patient experiences the behavior as "driven" or ego-alien. In such instances, EEG abnormalities are presumed to reflect excessive neuronal discharges deep in the brain, even though typical epileptic seizures are not prominent symptoms. After a review of the available neurophysiologic and psychologic evidence, Monroe made the following generalizations:

1. The frequent absence of specific EEG abnormalities in patients with episodic dyscontrol or episodic reactions does not preclude the assumption of an underlying epileptoid mechanism. This is based on the observation that routine scalp EEGs may be normal in known epileptics; also data from implanted electrode studies indicate that excessive neuronal discharges can occur in subcortical areas without any reflection in the routine scalp recordings.

2. The epileptic mechanism underlying episodic dyscontrol and episodic reactions may be associated with localized excessive neuronal discharges in subcortical structures, especially limbic structures. These discharges may be sustained for considerable periods without spread to the cortex and without typical epileptic behavior. Often such localized excessive neuronal discharges are accompanied by marked behavioral changes, not usually identified as epilepsy, such as dysphoria, depression, mounting irritability, slightly altered levels of awareness, impulsivity, depersonalization, and overt hallucinations or delusions characterized by precipitous onset and equally precipitous remission.

3. The diagnostic process in the identification of the epileptic nature of these disorders can be facilitated through use of EEG activating procedures, especially by alpha chloralose activation, which seems to reduce the number of

false negative findings without significantly increasing the incidence of false positives. Alpha chloralose has elicited two types of "activation patterns": a "specific" response characterized by focal hypersynchrony and/or slow waves and a "nonspecific" pattern characterized by high amplitude rhythmic delta-theta activity, which is bilaterally synchronous and symmetrical, with a frontal preponderance. The nonspecific pattern occurs in approximately 15 percent of the general population, thus indicating that the pattern itself, whether reflecting a true propensity for excessive neuronal discharge or perhaps a maturational lag, is not a sufficient indicator of the episodic behavioral disorder. Monroe suggested that this nonspecific pattern may be indicative of an underlying central nervous instability which may play an important role in the mechanism behind the dyscontrol acts.

Psychological Measurement of Dyscontrol Behavior

A review of the literature concerning impulsivity and aggressive acting out indicates many differing assessment approaches. The results of these investigations have been contradictory and confusion exists concerning the utility of psychological test instruments in assessing this construct. This confusion seems to be more the result of an inadequate appreciation of the multidimensionality of the construct than of a faulty selection of test instruments. For example, McDonald (1971), using a factor analytic approach to the study of impulsive control in children, found no less than three orthogonal factors emerging with the use of a wide variety of psychological test instruments. These factors were labeled (1) CNS integration, (2) cognitive control, and (3) behavioral control. He presented a conceptual model of impulse control integrating these factors (Figure 1-4).

Within McDonald's integrative model, physiological maturity as assessed by measures of perceptual motor control occupies a fundamental position. The basic assumption is that physiological maturity or central nervous system integration appears necessary but should not be considered sufficient to account for controlled responding in situations requiring prolonged concentration, deliberation, and ability to delay gratification. Such complex behaviors also require the development and integration of cognitive structures. Although the exact nature of such elements is still poorly defined, Luria's (1961) concept of the internalization of verbal commands that guide and direct behavior seems relevant here. However, the cognitive elements that facilitate the development of impulse control are much more complex in adults than the internalization of verbal commands. It is through the development and successful integration of physiological and cognitive structures that it becomes possible for nonimpulsive behavioral control to develop and manifest itself.

Since impulse control is a multidimensional construct, the psychological test

8

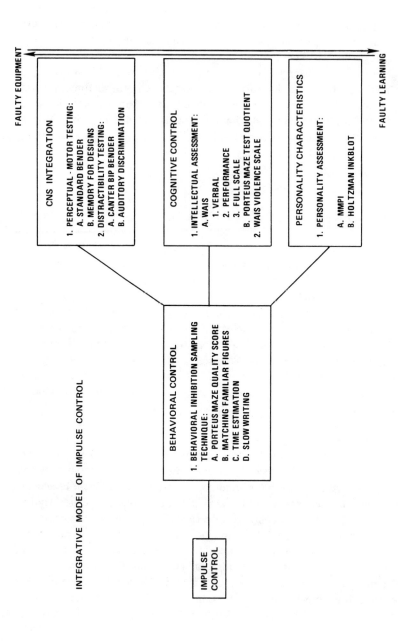

Figure 1-4. Integrative Model of Impulse Control

instruments chosen to measure impulse control attempt to assess each of the three dimensions outlined earlier. Furthermore, since the present investigation involves the study of impulsiveness and acting out in an adult population, personality characteristics were also considered to play a major role in the behavioral manifestation of impulse control. Consequently, a fourth theoretical dimension was added to the model of impulse control that was used for the selection of psychological-test instruments in the present investigation. In this model of impulse control in adults, behavioral manifestations of controlled reflective responding are seen as the result of an integration of personality characteristics, cognitive control, and central nervous system integration.

The "faulty learning versus faulty equipment" continuum as it relates to the construct of episodic dyscontrol lends itself to empirical investigation using the present integrative model. Here we see that questions involving CNS integrity fall toward the faulty equipment end of the continuum, whereas personality characteristics fall toward the faulty learning end of the continuum and cognitive control appears as a combination in the center of the continuum. When we look at the present model (Figure 1-4) in terms of abnormality or dyscontrol we become interested in localizing, through accurate diagnosis, which segment along this continuum is dysfunctional or deficient. Appropriate treatment intervention would differ depending upon our ability to localize the level of dysfunction or deficiency within a given individual. Thus, differential diagnosis and specific treatment interventions should be facilitated by appropriate psychological testing. Appendix B presents the psychological instruments used to assess the various dimensions of impulse control. A brief rationale for this selection follows.

Behavioral Inhibition: Sampling Technique

Typically, a wide variety of behavioral sampling techniques have been used in studies of impulse control. The Porteus Maze Quality Score, historically one of the earliest measures of impulse control, was intended by Porteus to reveal any "haphazard, impulsive or over-confident habit of action" (Porteus, 1960, p. 161). This score is composed of a weighted sum of particular errors made while traversing a series of paper mazes. This score differs from the Test Quotient (TQ) determined by the number of mazes correctly traversed, which is considered by Porteus as a measure of intelligence. The Quality Score has been shown to discriminate reliably between institutionalized delinquent and noninstitutionalized nondelinquents even when the groups were matched for intelligence (Porteus 1942, 1950, 1960). In addition, LaBarba (1965), extending this line of research, found that even the population of institutionalized delinquent boys judged independently as being "impulsive" and "acting out" scored significantly higher on the Quality Score than did a matched group of nonimpulsive institutionalized delinquents. Porteus developed the Quality Scoring System in 1941 as a result of his dissatisfaction with the Test Quotient's ability to differentiate between psychopathic delinquent children (a group traditionally felt to be lacking in impulse control) and normal children of the same intellectual level. The Quality Score, then, is a weighted sum of those critical errors of performance that allowed him to make the desired distinction.

In recent years Jerome Kagan (1965, 1966) has worked in the area of impulse control with a somewhat different perspective. His approach is similar to Porteus's in that he assesses impulsiveness by the use of a behavioral sampling technique, yet differs from Porteus's on several important dimensions. Kagan's approach involves giving the subject a series of matching tasks (Matching Familiar Figures Task) in which the child is asked to match a stimulus picture with one of six response pictures of high similarity (one identical) to the original standard stimulus. Measures of reaction time and errors provide indices of impulsiveness. Although Kagan's Matching Familiar Figures Task has been used primarily with children in the study of impulse control, it was included in the present study as a potentially useful instrument for determining the characteristic style of slow or fast reactions in situations of high response uncertainty.

Two additional brief behavioral sampling techniques of impulse control or delaying capacity were included in the present study. These were a Time Estimation Task and a Slow Writing Task. In the Time Estimation Task, described by Davis (1969), the subject is shown a stopwatch and is told to estimate a sixty-second passage of time. The watch is started by the examiner and hidden from the subject's view and stopped when the subject indicates verbally that a minute has passed. The amount of lapsed time is used as a score in the Time Estimation Task. In the motor inhibition task (Slow Writing Task also described by Davis 1969), the subject is asked to trace a simple diamond maze as slowly as possible, but without stopping the movement of his pencil. The amount of time that lapses during the completion of the maze is recorded and used as an indication of motor inhibition. Davis found that the Time Estimation Task and the Slow Writing Task could be used to differentiate between a population of normal elementary school children and a population of institutionalized emotionally disturbed children. We also introduced a test to evaluate distance estimation, asking subjects to draw a line one inch long.

Central Nervous System Integration

Historically, tests of perceptual motor control or competence have been used diagnostically to detect the presence or absence of organic brain dysfunction for both children and adults. Inability to reproduce successfully basic geometric designs has been associated with problems of perception, sensory processing, and motoric execution. It is the breakdown of the integration of these processes that has been associated with organic brain dysfunction. The two most widely used tests of perceptual motor competence are the Bender Visual Motor Gestalt Test (Bender Gestalt) and the Graham-Kendall Memory for Designs Test (MFD). Both tests require the subject to reproduce a series of complex geometric designs using paper and pencil. The two tests differ in that the MFD requires the subject to draw from memory the previously presented geometric figure. This test is considered by some to be a more sensitive detector of organic brain dysfunction than the Bender Gestalt since it requires a more complex integration of skills: perceptual motor integration and memory.

Episodic dyscontrol presupposes excessive neuronal discharges in subcortical areas usually involving the limbic system. Traditional perceptual motor tests have not been sensitive to such disturbances although they are generally considered sensitive to higher cortical dysfunctions. However, some recent work has suggested that traditional methods of testing perceptual motor control can be made more sensitive to CNS dysfunction by incorporating a distractibility component to the perceptual motor task. Canter (1966) has developed a procedure for administering and scoring the Bender Gestalt that adds this distractibility component. Here a second Bender Gestalt is administered on a sheet of test paper that contains a network of random lines printed on the paper. Thus the subject must "censor out" these distracting lines and draw the geometric designs on the test paper. Canter has found that by using this "Background Interference Procedure" (BIP) he is able to render the Bender Gestalt Test a more sensitive diagnostic instrument for detecting organic brain damage. Using the Background Interference Procedure, the following scores were obtained and used in the present study. These are (1) a total deviation score on the standard administration of the Bender Gestalt; (2) a total deviation score on the Background Interference Administration; (3) a BIP difference score which is obtained by subtracting the total number of deviations on the standard mode from those obtained on the BIP mode; (4) the number of "positives" which is an index of the number of designs showing a significantly positive BIP effect, that is, where the total deviations on the BIP mode exceeded the total deviations on the standard mode by at least two points; (5) a design overlap score which is derived by recording design overlaps in each of the two modes and subtracting the number of design overlaps in the standard mode from the number in the BIP mode; (6) a base level score which is an index of the general level of performance under standard conditions; and (7) an overall class score which is a one to three scale indicating an increasingly organic component to performance.

A second distractibility measure, the Goldman, Fristoe, Woodcock Test of Auditory Discrimination (ADT), was added to the test battery. Although no previous research has demonstrated the ability of this test to detect CNS dysfunction, it was included in the present battery to further investigate performance deficits that result from an inability to "censor out" irrelevant distracting stimuli. This test required the subject to identify the correct word-picture association under two separate conditions: the first in a quiet subtest and the second in a noise distraction subtest. Scores were derived in terms of errors on each of the two subtests.

Cognitive Control

Assessment of the cognitive control dimension of our model consisted of a general measure of intelligence: the Wechsler Adult Intelligence Scale. This test yields three major scores—a Verbal IQ, a Performance IQ, and a Full Scale IQ. These scores are composed of eleven subscale scores. Since the construct episodic dyscontrol is considered to be relatively independent of general intellectual functioning, no significant correlation between the WAIS full scale IQ and episodic dyscontrol was anticipated. In general, previous research has failed to demonstrate a unique WAIS subtest pattern that is correlated with violent behavior. However, a recent study by Kunce (1976) was able to demonstrate the effectiveness of a simple ratio of the similarities score to the total of all eleven subtest scores as a predictor of group membership (prisoners arrested for violent crimes versus prisoners arrested for nonviolent crimes). This is theoretically significant in that the similarities subtest is considered a measure of abstract reasoning ability, and previous studies (McFie 1960; and Reitan 1964) have noted the relationship between deficits in abstract reasoning and temporal lobe dysfunction. The present study afforded an opportunity to attempt to replicate the findings of Kunce as well as to specify further the relationship between episodic behavioral dyscontrol and particular patterns of cognitive functioning.

Personality Characteristics

Two general measures of personality were included in the present test battery: one an objective measure, the other a projective measure. The Minnesota Multiphasic Personality Inventory (MMPI) and the Holtzman Inkblot Technique were chosen. Many attempts have been made to isolate the particular MMPI configurations useful in predicting violent behavior. Sines (1966) noted the relationship between Highpoint 4-3 Code and violent behavior. This relationship was also noted by Persons and Marks (1971). Thus the relationship between MMPI Highpoint Code and violent behavior is at this point unclear. One serious drawback to the use of the MMPI in the present study was the limited reading ability of a significant number of the subjects. Consequently, the MMPI was administered orally to each subject by means of a tape recording. This technique proved successful in avoiding the problems of reading deficit.

The Holtzman Inkblot Technique was chosen as the projective personality instrument to be used in the present investigation instead of the Rorschach since the former is superior as a research instrument because of its quantification of responses. The Holtzman Inkblot Technique allows only one response per card whereas the Rorschach has no such limitation.

There is one serious flaw in attempting to develop a psychometric battery for identifying individuals with episodic dyscontrol. Inasmuch as the CNS dysfunction is intermittent, defects might only be obvious during the episode itself. And even if the transitory episode of dysfunction behavior is observed, the individual is so intractable that testing is impossible. The psychological battery would be more appropriately used on the group with prolonged episodic reactions. This latter group was not present in our prison sample. For a more detailed description of the psychometric instruments, the reader is referred to Appendix B and for a discussion of the results of psychological testing, to Chapter 5. In many of the analyses described in this book, the psychometric data are presented along with the psychiatric and neurologic data in appropriate tables.

References

Bender, L. 1938. *A visual motor Gestalt Test and its clinical use.* Research Monograph No. 3. The American Orthopsychiatric Association.
Canter, A. 1968. "The BIP-Bender Test for the detection of organic brain disorder: Modified scoring method and replication." *J. of Cons. Clin. Psycho.*, 32:522-526.
Carroll, J.L., and Fuller, G.B. 1971. "An MMPI comparison of three groups of criminals." *J. Clin. Psycho.*, 27:240-242.
Davis, A. 1969. "Ego functions in disturbed and normal children: Aspiration, inhibition, time estimation, and delayed gratification." *J. of Cons. Clin. Psycho.*, 33:61-70.
Goldman, R., Fristoe, M., and Woodcock, R. 1970. *Test of auditory discrimination.* Minnesota: American Guidance Service.
Graham, F.K., and Kendall, B.S. 1946. *Memory for designs test.* St. Louis: Washington University Press.
Hathaway, S.R., and McKinley, J.C. 1951. *Manual: Minnesota multiphasic personality inventory.* New York: Psychological Corporation.
Holtzman, W.H., Thorpe, J.S., Swartz, J.D., and Herron, W.E. 1961. *Inkblot perception and personality.* Austin: University of Texas Press.
Kagan, J., Pearson, L., and Welsh, L. 1966. "Conceptual impulsivity and inductive reasoning." *Child. Dev.*, 37:583-594.
Kagan, J. 1965. "Impulsive and reflective children: Significance of conceptual tempo," in Krumboltz, J. (Ed.), *Learning and the educational process.* Chicago: Rand-McNally.
Kunce, J.T., Bryan, J.J., and Eckelman, C.C. 1976. "Violent behavior and differential WAIS characteristics." *J. of Cons. Clin. Psycho.*, 44:(1)42-45.

LaBarba, R.C. 1965. "Relations of color responses on the Rorschach to qualitative scores on the Porteus Maze Test." *Perc. Mot. Sk.,* 21:61-62.

Luria, A.R. 1961. *The role of speech in the regulation of normal and abnormal behavior.* New York: Liveright.

McDonald, M. 1971. "A Multiple measurement approach to the study of impulse control in children." Unpublished doctoral dissertation, University of Maryland.

McFie, J. 1960. "Psychological testing in clinical neurology." *J. of Nerv. and Ment. Dis.,* 131:383-393.

Monroe, R.R. 1970. *Episodic behavioral disorders.* Cambridge: Harvard University Press.

Persons, R.W., and Marks, P.A. 1971. "The violent 4-3 MMPI personality type." *J. of Cons. Clin. Psycho.,* 36:(2)189-196.

Porteus, S.D. 1942. *Qualitative performance in the Maze Test.* Vineland: Smith.

Porteus, S.D. 1950. *The Porteus Maze Test and intelligence.* Palo Alto: Pacific Books.

Porteus, S.D. 1960. *The Maze Test and clinical psychology.* Palo Alto: Pacific Books.

Reitan, R.M. 1964. "Psychological deficits resulting from cerebral lesions in man," in Warren, J.M. and Akert, K. (Eds.), *Prefrontal granular cortex and behavior.* New York: McGraw-Hill.

Rorschach, H. 1942. *Psychodiagnostics.* Berne: Hans Huber.

Sines, J.O. 1966. "Actuarial methods in personality assessment," in Maher, B.A. (Ed.), *Progress in experimental personality research.* Vol. III. New York: Academic Press.

Wechsler, D. 1958. *The measurement and appraisal of adult intelligence.* 4th edition. Baltimore: Williams and Wilkins.

2

Review of Current Research
Russell R. Monroe
and *John R. Lion*

Monroe's monograph *Episodic Behavioral Disorders* (1970) reviews the American and English literature up to 1969 and establishes criteria at a descriptive, neurophysiologic, and psychodynamic level to distinguish between those patients whose episodic disorder was predominantly motivated and those whose disorder was predominantly epileptoid. It also describes specific pharmacologic regimens and psychotherapeutic techniques for treating patients with episodic behavioral disorders. The present chapter updates the bibliography through 1977, adding a few significant papers published prior to 1969 that were not included in the original monograph. Also included here is an evaluation of the influence that the concept of episodic behavioral disorders has had on the medical profession.

The Concept of Episodic Behavioral Disorders

Although Monroe further describes his concepts in the 1974 edition of the *Handbook of American Psychiatry* and Lion's text on *Personality Disorders* (1974), the term "episodic behavioral disorder" has not otherwise appeared in an article title during the intervening years. There has been more acceptance of the label "episodic dyscontrol," with three articles (Bach-y-Rita 1971; Maletsky 1973, 1974) using this terminology in their titles. However, the concept has been used by many others not only in the field of psychiatry but also in psychology, neurology, and neurosurgery. These reports will be discussed in the appropriate later sections.[a]

Professional and lay recognition of the dyscontrol syndrome was undoubtedly promoted most by Mark and Ervin in their popular book *Violence and the Brain* (1970). Their thesis views most violence as a manifestation of the dyscontrol syndrome and holds that many violent acts have a neurologic basis. They imply that large numbers in the general population show some type of brain dysfunction or brain abnormality which can be remedied through manipulation of the central nervous system, either by drugs or surgery. These points are discussed later in the chapter.

Freides (1976) clearly makes the essential differentiation, as Monroe had

---

[a]In the 1968 edition of the *American Psychiatric Association Diagnostic and Statistical Manual* (DSM II), the term "explosive personality" represents the entity most closely related to episodic dyscontrol. The most recent draft of DSM III (1978) contains the term "intermittent explosive disorder" as one of several disorders of impulse control.

suggested, between the nonepisodic and the episodic disorders, coining respectively the words "aphoria" and "diaphoria" for these disorders. He identifies "diaphoria" as including but not limited to seizure states and uses this model much as Monroe did in describing his "epileptoid" mechanism. Freides is aware of both psychologic and physiologic precipitating mechanisms, stating that this group "does not receive systematic consideration in most of the literature on psychopathology." He goes on to mention that "unpredictability or inconsistency is a prime symptom." He also notes both the value and the limitation of the EEG in aiding in this diagnosis. Freides differentiates as Monroe did between faulty learning and faulty equipment, referring to the "equipment versus the experience" polarity which is important for treatment planning.

Most observers recognize the complex interaction between intrapsychic, family, social, genetic, perinatal, and CNS insult, in contributing to the episodic behavioral disorders. Maletsky (1973) describes the episodic dyscontrol syndrome but does not acknowledge the similarities between his findings and Monroe's. Maletsky notes the significance of family conflicts in the manifestation of episodic behavior. Of his 22 patients, 19 had fathers who were prone to act aggressively and 16 had fathers who were alcoholic. Similar to the findings of Mitsuda (1967), Maletsky reports that 15 patients had a family history of epilepsy although their own symptoms were more characteristic of either atypical psychosis or the dyscontrol syndrome. Maletsky reports that all 22 subjects showed hyperactivity during childhood, a factor indicative of possible brain dysfunction. Twelve subjects had a history of febrile convulsions, important in view of the studies reported by Falconer (1972) that febrile convulsions can lead to mesial sclerosis in the temporal lobe. Seven patients had a history of head trauma with loss of consciousness; 11 subjects had some findings that suggested neurological deficit and 14 had EEG abnormalities. However these EEG abnormalities, as well as those described by Bach-y-Rita (1971), were different from those reported by Monroe (1970) as 6 subjects of the 14 showed spiking in the temporal region and the remaining had nonspecific rhythmic abnormalities, which did not include the theta rhythm that Monroe found in his activated records of patients with dyscontrol syndrome. It is worthwhile emphasizing that in Maletsky's series of 22 subjects, 18 had consulted a physician and 11 had had psychotherapy, showing that these patients were concerned about losing control and did seek help.

Twelve of Maletsky's subjects described some kind of aura or at least a premonition that attacks were eminent and 11 percent has postattack symptoms of headaches and drowsiness. Maletsky mentions that altered states of consciousness frequently occurred in 12 of his subjects and there was a driven quality to the actions, eliciting such comments from the patients as "I just couldn't help what I was doing even though I knew that it was wrong." Similarly, many of Monroe's subjects expressed extreme remorse for their action but the remorse did not inhibit future attacks. In Maletsky's series, 8 of the 22 subjects made suicidal gestures, again indicating that in any study of aggression, aggression towards self must be considered. Also, as Monroe (1970) and Lion (1973) also reported, Maletsky notes that alcohol was occasionally a precipitating or activating agent.

Most observers report symptoms suggesting an ictal phenomenon, minimal brain dysfunction, or hyperactivity as associated with episodic behavioral disorders. Small (1973) and Elliott (1976) emphasize that it is essential for the psychiatrist to evaluate neurologic signs and symptoms for evidence of minimal brain dysfunction or the less obvious forms of epilepsy and mental retardation. Clinical vignettes describe patients with episodic symptoms of anxiety, hysteria, depression, fugues, as well as episodic physiologic symptoms such as diabetes or high blood pressure. Both Small and Elliott relate these to an epileptoid mechanism and stress the value of this concept as an indication for the effective use of anticonvulsive medications in the treatment of these patients.

Lion (1969a, 1969b) estimates that there are "half a million people suffering from cerebral palsy, 6 million from mental retardation, 2 million from convulsive disorders and somewhere between 5 and 10% of all children from a hyperkinetic behavioral disorder." These figures, plus the unavailable ones on number of individuals who have sustained severe head injuries or suffer from genetic, metabolic, or nutritional destruction, suggest that a large percentage of the population have some disordered central nervous system function. Such estimates may shed light on the magnitude of the problem of brain dysfunction but cannot be used to make any simple statements relevant to treatment or prevention.

There has been less recognition of the more prolonged episodic disorders which Monroe labels "episodic reactions." An older report overlooked in Monroe's original monograph is a report by Davison (1964) on the subject of episodic depersonalization. He describes 7 patients who had such depersonalizations lasting from several hours to several months, which he characterized as a "dream state." It was noted that events began "in a split second" and disappeared equally rapidly, a characteristic emphasized by Monroe for all episodic reactions. Davison tends to minimize EEG abnormalities, but in looking at the details of his report it would seem that his patients had some excessive theta rhythm, a finding that coincides with Monroe's.

In another early report by Shearer (1964) on periodic organic psychosis associated with herpes simplex, the author reports that fever associated with herpes simplex preceded psychotic behavior by twelve to thirty-six hours. In the prodromal period there was lethargy, drowsiness, irritability, often accompanied by stomachaches, headaches, or both. The psychosis generally cleared within seven to twelve days. Not only were these patients psychotic but they were also hyperactive, impulsive, and irritable. Their attention span was reduced and they showed symptoms of perseveration and confusion as well as inability to perform complex tasks. All of these typify what Monroe refers to as the episodic organic brain syndrome, one form of episodic reaction.

Bellak (1976) discusses a subgroup of the schizophrenias that he believes have some degree of minimal brain dysfunction as an etiologic mechanism resulting in problems of spatial orientation and language development, and low stimulus barriers. These difficulties, in turn, lead to problems in establishing ego boundaries, poor coordination, and difficulties with written and spoken words, as well as with abstract conceptualization. He mentions that poor impulse control also characterizes this group, but tends to overlook the episodic nature of the disorder.

Many of the prolonged episodic reactions as defined by Monroe are reported in the literature under other diagnostic labels. One of the most common is the acute schizophrenic reaction. Connolly (1971) reports an association between delusions about one's sexual identity and olfactory and gustatory hallucinations in schizophrenic patients. In view of the frequency of these gustatory and olfactory disturbances in temporal lobe epilepsy, and the change of libido associated with temporal lobe epilepsy, the question arises whether this group of "schizophrenic" patients might be related to patients with temporal lobe or limbic system dysfunction. Apparently the authors were aware of this possibility and cite the reports of Delgado (1959), who found that electrical stimulation of the temporal lobe induces doubt about the subject's own sexual identity.

Another such example of unrecognized episodic disorders is in the report of Guggenheim (1974), who points out that catatonic schizophrenia has a variable prognosis. The author found that catatonic schizophrenics who seem to have a relatively good prognosis tended to be those showing a sudden onset either of purely hyperkinetic behavior or pure akinetic symptoms. Those with mixtures of these symptoms responded poorly. He reports, as have others, that excited catatonics most often have a rapid onset and an equally precipitous improvement. Such patients were not only likely to show good symptomatic remission but also to make a good social adjustment after discharge from the hospital. It is this type of patient that Monroe feels should be more properly diagnosed with episodic psychotic reaction for it is probably the epileptoid mechanism rather than the schizophrenic predisposition that is the basis for a good prognosis. Other reports suggesting episodic behavioral disorders without specifically identifying them as such are those by McCabe (1975, 1976). In the latter study the author proposes that although atypical psychoses may be a heterogenous entity, they are not just misdiagnosed schizophrenic disorders which should have been diagnosed as affective psychoses. It has been proposed by Mitsuda (1974) and Belford (1976) that a "third" psychosis (other than schizophrenia and affective disorders) be considered as part of the diagnostic nomenclature.

Violence and Episodic Dyscontrol

Monroe points out that dyscontrol acts are usually motivated by intense primitive affects of fear, rage, or displeasure. Furthermore, what he designated as primary dyscontrol is a true "short circuit" between the stimulus and the action. Such behavior is not modified by "thinking as trial action," nor is primary dyscontrol behavior modulated by concern over future consequences, either to the actor himself or to the individual or object acted upon. For this reason the dyscontrol acts are usually maladaptive and often, but not always, are extremely destructive and result in bizarre crimes.

The political assassinations of the Kennedys as well as a number of dramatic homicidal acts such as those of Richard Speck, who wantonly killed several hospital nurses in Chicago, and Charles Whitman, who inexplicably shot several people on the University of Texas campus, revived an interest in the study of violence. This in turn led to a rash of publications in the neurologic, psychologic, and sociologic literature on the causes and prevention of violent behavior. Foremost among these was the twelve-volume National Commission's Report on Violence, with one chapter by Ervin and Lion on the subject of organic aspects of violent behavior (1970). Most publications, however, emphasize the social and cultural aspects of violence; very few give significant attention to impulsive violence or the dyscontrol syndrome particularly as it might be related to some central nervous system dysfunction. One of the first books published on violence, *Violence and the Struggle for Existence,* edited by Daniels, Guilila, and Ochberg (1970), has one chapter on the biological basis of aggression and devotes little more than a page to the limbic system dysfunction and the dyscontrol symptoms. Likewise, Bandura's *Aggression: A Social Learning Analysis* (1973) devotes less than two pages to the possibility of a neurological deficit as a crucial explanation for aggressive behavior. In Fawcett's *The Dynamics of Violence* (1971), two chapters are devoted to the possibility of neurophysiologic dysfunction, one by Lion and another by Gross, the latter reporting that 55 percent of consecutive admissions to a child guidance clinic had EEG abnormalities and soft neurologic signs representing evidence for a possible organic brain disorder. Gross felt that the neurophysiologic dysfunction was important because of the response of these children to anticonvulsant medication. The report edited by Garattini and Sigg entitled *Aggressive Behavior* (1969) includes several pertinent chapters devoted to the treatment of aggression with anticonvulsant medications, or possible psychosurgical intervention for the uncontrollably aggressive individual with brain dysfunction.

For the purpose of this review, the classification of aggression by Chandler (1973) as either instrumental aggression or expressive aggression is useful. The aggression characteristic of the dyscontrol syndrome, particularly the more primitive primary dyscontrol, is usually expressive. Chandler's article is useful in further describing how aggression becomes legitimized or delegitimized, pointing out that the characteristics that make aggression illegitimate are unpredictability and direct actions of short duration with tangible destruction. This is the crucial characteristic of the dyscontrol syndrome. Lorimer (1972) states "there exists in some people who commit acts of violence a medical condition, a malfunction of the brain, particularly the limbic system, that is as much a medical disease as diabetes."

Shah (1974) in his chapter on biological and psychological factors in criminology recognizes the dyscontrol syndrome as a distinct entity and proposes the following clinical observations that would suggest organic involvement of the limbic system:

1. objectively verifiable history of personality change without environmental explanation
2. behavior, particularly aggression, in a person epidemiologically unlikely to be commencing or continuing a criminal career, for example, mature women and older persons
3. recent history of unexplained "spells"
4. fluctuating emotions including self-destructive thoughts
5. aggression directed at least initially toward friends and relatives rather than strangers
6. presence of organic mental signs such as memory loss

However, it is our opinion that although these criteria have a certain validity, they are not inclusive or specific enough in themselves adequately to reflect the complexities of identifying the dyscontrol syndrome.

Bach-y-Rita (1971) presents data on 130 violent patients with episodic dyscontrol. He found that these patients demonstrated aggressive outbursts of a paroxysmal nature with prodromal symptoms and postictal features. Alcohol and other drugs such as amphetamines played a prominent role in the production of the violent outbursts. Almost all had sought psychiatric help and over half of their sample had prior psychiatric hospitalizations. A total of 53 patients had made suicidal gestures or attempts, usually impulsively. In their histories, 29 patients reported hyperactivity and 72 reported one or more episodes of unconsciousness from head injury or illnesses; 25 patients reported childhood febrile convulsions, or adult seizures. A total of 79 patients received EEG examination; 37 showed spikes in the temporal lobe region and the rest asymmetries or other rhythmic changes. It must be noted that the high incidence of temporal lobe spike findings was due to a skewed patient population, as 23 patients were known to be epileptic. It is of interest that X-ray contrast studies done on 22 patients revealed two positive findings indicative of ventricular atrophy. The contrast studies included arteriograms and pneumoencephalograms. Psychological tests given to 43 patients showed 12 to have subnormal intelligence and 9 others to have signs of organic impairment. Mark (1970) states that the "early warning test" of limbic brain dysfunction may be seen in those individuals who have a low threshold for impulsive violence. Again, this statement has conceptual validity but does not reflect the complexities of applying such a test in a clinical situation. Symptoms that he reports as identifying this limbic brain dysfunction or what is called dyscontrol behavior are soft neurological signs, abnormal EEG, childhood history of hyperactivity, fighting, temper tantrums, enuresis, and nail biting. Morrison (1975), in discussing the explosive personality as a sequel to the hyperactive child syndrome, reports findings appropriate for the episodic dyscontrol syndrome. The salient historical features that characterized the early years of his patients were hyperactivity and decreased ability to concentrate. He suggests that as the hyperactivity decreases during maturation it is replaced by aggressiveness and hair-trigger temper with the individual showing destructive impulsive behavior.

Less has been written about the dyscontrol syndrome and violence turned on one's self. Trautman (1961) reports on suicidal "fits." He describes the suicidal act as following a period of severe and painful emotional excitement with mounting tension, a description suggesting an epileptoid phenomenon within the limbic system. When this excitement reached a climax, the patients then acted impulsively in a self-destructive way. If they survived the incident, the patients reported, "I suddenly lost control of myself" or "I suddenly lost my mind" or "my mind went blank" or "I could not think anymore" or "I did not realize what I was doing." Trautman emphasizes that these patients seemed to be out of contact with reality and acted as if they were in a trance, a description similar to the acute confusional state that Monroe correlated with primary dyscontrol symptoms or episodic brain syndrome.

Planansky (1977), reporting on a group of schizophrenics who showed homicidal aggression, found that the characteristic symptoms are confusion and impulsiveness, and that these symptoms, leading to misperception compounded by a loss of control, are an ominous sign among schizophrenics who may become homicidal. Furthermore, he states, "at times the patient's behavior during the attack and his own perception of the inner pressures are suggestive of a discharge-like neural event." He also states that "one has an impression that the self-destructive as well as the homicidal urges are features of a unitary psychotic development which might be designated as destructive dyscontrol, possibly underlying all or most of the aggression against the self and other people." He does not feel that it is aggressive delusions alone that lead to the overt aggression, but rather a clinical picture that "featured a blend of delusional, catatonic, affective and anxiety components at the times of overt aggression." What the author overlooks are the episodic quality of the reactions and the confusional state in these violent patients which would suggest that they are not typical schizophrenics, but patients with an episodic psychotic reaction—with elements suggesting an acute brain syndrome.

MacMurray (1973) points out that behavioral disorders divide themselves into two fairly distinct groups, those characteristic of fright reactions and those of rage reactions. He suggests that episodic fright reactions such as arctic hysteria, kayak-angst, latah, and imu are found in cultures having a high gratification of dependency needs and occur predominantly in female populations, whereas the rage reactions such as the witiko psychosis, amok, and Gururumbu occur mainly in male populations of cultures with severe denial of dependency needs. He also assumes that rage reactions are most characteristic, but not limited to, epilepsy; and fear reactions are more characteristic, but not limited to, schizophrenia. Cross-cultural studies, then, must consider both the inverse correlations between epilepsy and schizophrenia as well as the inverse correlations between denial of dependency needs and gratification of such needs. He suspects that some of the cross-cultural differences in aggression may be grounded in the difference between the epilepsy-schizophrenia ratio, and others in the way dependency needs are managed, while still other cases of cross-cultural differences will be based on the complex interaction of these factors.

Investigating the phenomenon of "running amok" in cultural aspects of violence, Westemeyer (1973) draws attention to the fact that after World War II in Thailand, "running amok" increased and that a similar picture occurred in Laos from 1959 to 1966. He feels that the amok syndrome reflects the projection of rage on a reference group—an altered form of suicide in areas where suicide is not approved—and is a behavior common to "shame cultures" as opposed to "guilt cultures." Epidemics of amok occur during periods when traditional ways are giving way to new influences so that the old values are being undermined.

Climent (1973) states that maternal loss correlates highly with violence in the women studied, and Felthouse (1977) finds that the typology of assaultive females is more similar to that of assaultive males than had heretofore been reported. Tupin (1973) shows that physical aggression of father toward son and early separation from one or both parents correlates with the habitually violent criminal as compared with the nonviolent criminal or those who had been violent on only one occasion.

Neurophysiologic and Neuroanatomic Considerations in the Episodic Behavioral Disorders

Some investigators prefer to use the term "limbic system disorder" rather than "episodic behavioral disorder." The former implies that there is an excessive neuronal discharge limited to the limbic system that is a frequent occurrence because of the low seizural threshold of the limbic system and the vulnerability of this system to anoxic damage resulting from traumas. The few subcortical studies in the literature give direct evidence that the limbic system often shows a storm of electrical activity that correlates roughly with maladaptive behavior. The lack of knowledge regarding the role of excessive neuronal discharges in other subcortical areas, such as the hypothalamus, in the development of episodic disorders suggests caution in labeling the episodic disorders as a limbic system dysfunction (Monroe 1970).

Recent studies showing evidence for and against the concept that limbic dysfunction is crucial for the manifestation of the dyscontrol symptoms are summarized here. Stevens (1964) reports that amygdala seizures initiated by carbachol implanted in cats induces "violent delirium" within fifteen minutes. There is also the famous patient, Julia, of Mark (1970) in whom radio-stimulation of the amygdala induced violent rage attacks. Kling (1975) notes the effect of amygdalectomy on the social behavior of nonhuman primates in the natural state and reports a deficit in the emotional expression of these animals, including aggression. The one contradictory report regarding the amygdala and aggression is that of Gloor (1975) who has never observed a rage response to stimulation of the temporal lobe or the temporal subcortical structures in epileptic patients. This is unusual in view of the stimulation studies reported by Hitchcock (1973), who found that 10 of 18 patients receiving electrical stimulation of the amygdala showed some kind of aggressive behavior, while three expressed "flight" response. Other emotions elicited on stimulation were anxiety, guilt, embarrassment, and jealousy. The authors report that these emotions usually were associated with periods of confusion. Amygdala stimulation also elicited other symptoms associated with episodic disorders, such as disorientation, incoherent speech, visual distortions, diplopia, as well as typical and atypical seizures.

In view of the considerable areas of the brain devoted to pleasurable or "start" responses, it is surprising that seldom does stimulation in the limbic system induce a pleasurable response (Hitchcock 1973), although Heath (1972) reports pleasurable responses to septal stimulation.

Gloor (1975) in his studies of temporal lobe epileptics states that the temporal-neocortex is important not only for auditory and visual perceptual functions, but also for the evocation of past memories and for the matching of present and past experiences. This matching with the past gives the present motivational significance. What is primarily affective is activated through the limbic system. That is, the subjective experience of fear connects the information storehouse of the neocortex with the fundamental motivational drive mechanisms centered in the hypothalamus. Monroe (1970) emphasizes the importance of associative connections between the present event and past experience as being an essential part of the reflective delay or "thought as trial action" essential for the considered adaptive act and usually lacking or significantly distorted in dyscontrol behavior.

Falconer (1972) believes that asphyxial episodes responsible for Ammon's Horn sclerosis follow severe febrile convulsions in infancy. In a further study (1973) on 250 patients who had temporal lobectomy including the hippocampus and the lateral amygdala, 50 percent had mesial temporal sclerosis, 25 percent had hamartomas, and 10 percent had miscellaneous lesions such as scars and infarcts.

Epilepsy and Episodic Behavioral Disorders

Stevens (1970) objects to calling behavioral disorders "epilepsy" no matter how characteristic they are of an ictal phenomenon, unless the patient demonstrates typical grand mal seizures, simple automatism, petit mal or focal epileptic attacks. Yet it is clinically apparent that one can identify behavioral changes associated with a circumscribed excessive neuronal discharge which Hughlings Jackson conceives as the fundamental ictal process characteristic of all epilepsy. When one observes precipitous onset of dyscontrol behavior preceded by a premonition or aura and followed by some kind of sequelae such as lethargy, headache, or a partial amnesia, and when this is coupled with a subjective feeling of behavior beyond one's control, then the behavior seems to be an ictal process (Monroe 1970).

Nevertheless, Rodin (1971), reporting on the psychomotor seizure patterns and behavior of known temporal lobe epileptics, is skeptical of correlating violent outbursts with the seizure state. He states that violence is more often associated with the confusion occurring in the postictal state. Bloomer (1974b) discusses the ictal and interictal aspects of violent behavior, and Lion (1976) describes the accompanying EEG abnormalities in a group of paroxysmally impulsive and aggressive patients without comment. Scientific controversy surrounding the question of whether or not violence is an ictal or interictal phenomenon remains unsettled and is in large measure dependent upon brain recording sites. These issues have been reviewed by Goldstein in an NINDS-sponsored workshop (1974) on violence and brain dysfunction.

It is difficult to conceive of the prolonged episodic reaction as an ictal rather than an interictal response, but these reactions do have ictal characteristics, such as precipitous onset and remission. Hess (1971) describes several patients with prolonged seizural activity of several months duration as measured by EEG. However, both Monroe and Hess find a lack of correlation between the cortical activity and behavioral dysfunction, explaining this on the basis that scalp recordings are not a true reflection of an ictal phenomenon in subcortical structures. A finding of Goddard (1972) in studying animals following amygdala stimulation is interesting in this regard. Although continued stimulation rapidly leads to exhaustion or habituation with the stimulation no longer capable of inducing seizural activity, repeated intermittent stimulation tends to reduce seizural thresholds. Goddard calls this the "kindling" effect. As it is known that stressful situations can induce focal seizural activity in the amygdala (Monroe 1970), Goddard's finding suggests that such intermittent stress-induced seizural activity may reduce seizural threshold. Pinel (1975) shows that even subthreshold amygdala stimulations have a kindling effect. This offers a possible explanation for long-term continuous behavioral disturbances that may be correlated with intermittent but rapidly recurring seizural activity in an amygdala with a lowering of seizural threshold. This point of view is supported by Post (1976) who suggests that the kindling mechanism provides a critical conceptual link which helps explain (1) the occurrence of late psychosis in chronic temporal lobe epileptics, (2) the sensitivity of former amphetamine addicts to recurrence of delusions after months of abstinence, (3) the mechanism by which environmental events might sensitize patients to acute exacerbations of their illness, (4) the acute onset of some affective psychosis, and (5) the criterion for "functional" psychosis of these disorders in that there is an episodic neurophysiologic alteration without structural change.

Mark (1975) reports what he calls the "long latency effects"–behavioral changes resulting from brain stimulation that outlast after-discharges. These behavioral changes often resemble psychosis and persist minutes, hours, and even days. Thus, Mark (ignoring the kindling effect) proposes that the episodic reactions, while not truly ictal, result from a previous ictus. He suggests that the ictal phenomenon results in modification of neurotransmitters which in turn causes the prolonged behavioral deviation.

Glowinski (1973) uses the concept of subictal discharge to explain the disturbance of memory functioning in temporal lobe epileptics. He compares temporal lobe epileptics with centrencephalic epileptics and finds in both a high level of distractability. While distraction tests do not discriminate between the two groups, the temporal lobe subjects have particular difficulty in integrating and memorizing meaningful verbal material. Glowinski proposes that there are frequent minimal electrical discharges of significant magnitude to influence behavior detectable on psychological tests and that these electrical discharges interfere with the registration and consolidation of sensory input particularly if the discharge occurs in close proximity to the presentation of the new information.

Stevens (1973) says that the inundation of extraneous stimuli characteristic of early schizophrenia is similar to epileptic attacks but still maintains that there is a real difference between schizophrenia and epilepsy. During the height of the hallucinatory episodes, the EEG demonstrates low voltage fast activity in schizophrenics rather than the spiking that one would expect in the psychomotor epileptic. She does mention that 5-7 cycle per second activity occurs in the temporal regions in schizophrenics, and that these individuals are sensitive to photic stimulation, respond with myoclonic jerks, and show a low seizural threshold. The distinction between seizures and schizophrenia seems less clear as she describes these episodes in more detail. For example, "loss of consciousness, characteristic electroencephalographic changes, and relative uninterruptibility of the individual attacks are important in distinguishing psychomotor seizures from schizophrenic blocking episodes. However the similarity of mental and motor content and the stereotypies suggests that both disorders (schizophrenia and epilepsy) may use closely related anatomical structures. . . ." We would agree that there is a difference between the classical schizophrenia and relatively clear-cut simple automatism, but Monroe's point is that there is an episodic psychotic reaction that has characteristics of both states which is erroneously called either psychomotor seizure or schizophrenia. His proposal is that this intermediate group is clearly distinguishable from either of the other two and should be distinctively labeled. Thus, if one clearly identifies schizophrenia, episodic psychotic states, and simple automatisms, one can determine the appropriate pharmacologic regimen. Stevens (1973) rightly points out that the different therapeutic responses may indicate different biochemical mechanisms despite involvement of identical or closely related neurophysiologic systems.

Reynolds (1968) proposes the idea that the difference between epilepsy and schizophrenia can be found in folic acid metabolism and that the explanation for the inverse relation between schizophrenia and epilepsy will be explained by further study in this area. He suggests that the findings of Slater (1965) of the late developing schizophrenia in chronic epileptics might be due to anticonvulsants blocking the folic acid and B-12 metabolism with concomitant low serum levels of folic acid, which in turn leads to psychotic symptoms. While treatment with folic acid may relieve these psychotic symptoms, it interferes with the anticonvulsant regimen. He also proposes that this explains the response of schizophrenics to electroshock treatment since the seizure elevates serum folic acid, a fact demonstrated by several reports in the literature of some schizophrenics responding to folic acid and B-12 regimen (Reynolds 1968). Levi (1975) believes that this inverse relationship between schizophrenia and epilepsy is the result not of folic acid deficiency alone but also of a methionine deficiency.

The argument about the inverse relationship between "fits" and psychosis may be clarified by the following. Flor-Henry (1969) suggests that the abnormal activity in the depth of the temporal region is inversely correlated with seizure frequency but directly correlated with psychotic manifestations. The validity of this statement without many more observations on patients with chronically implanted subcortical electrodes remains questionable, but the author does correctly emphasize that the type of EEG abnormality recorded by routine scalp recordings is not a true reflection of what is going on in the subcortical areas. Also, it is obvious that the disparity in results among investigators depends on the source of patients studied and the measuring scales utilized for evaluating behavioral disorders, as well as the semantic confusion regarding a standard definition of seizure or epilepsy. The crux of the matter for the clinician, however, is not so much whether there is a relationship between epilepsy and many behavioral disorders but whether certain episodic behavioral disorders will respond to drugs that elevate seizural threshold. In this study (Chapter 7) we show that a precise association of deviant behavior with temporal spikes is not as frequent in this experimental group as has been reported in other studies. In fact, we find that such episodic behavioral disorders are more likely to correlate with activated bilateral generalized theta activity with a frontal predominance. We maintain that it is simplistic to think of a correlation of episodic dyscontrol with temporal lobe epilepsy, whether this is defined by EEG or behavioral criteria, or even with epilepsy in general, because of inadequate techniques for monitoring electrical activity in subcortical structures.

Standage (1975), utilizing the Present State Examination (PSE) which is a clinical interview providing a symptom profile for the preceding month, and the Eysenck Personality Inventory, finds little difference in mental status between temporal lobe epileptics and those showing grand mal or other seizures. He also finds little difference between the epileptics and a control group of outpatients attending the physical medicine clinic. All subjects scored positively on depressive mood, somatic symptoms, irritability, low self-opinion, psychomotor retardation, muscle tension and symptoms of anxiety, subjectively impaired memory and concentration, and mild paranoid symptoms. Thus, he feels that these symptoms represent a characteristic response to sustained chronic illness.

Sigal (1976), studying 1,728 hospitalized psychotics over a four year period, finds only 28 epileptics, 12 of whom showed a temporal lobe EEG abnormality. Four of the patients present a chonic psychosis, all having schizoid or otherwise abnormal premorbid personalities, but none have a temporal focus. Five are diagnosed as "compensation demand syndrome" and four of these five have an epileptic focus in the dominant temporal lobe. Ten patients are diagnosed as behavioral disorders who also have clinical symptoms of grand mal or petit mal epilepsy but none have temporal lobe epilepsy. Nine cases have a periodic psychosis. In 4 of these the psychoses followed a grand mal seizure and were accompanied by a confusional state with marked aggressiveness. Two of the four show a dominant temporal lobe focus; one, nondominant temporal lobe focus and one, no temporal lobe focus. Three of the patients suffer from periodic affective states and in two of the three, the lesion was in the nondominant temporal lobe; in the third, the EEG foci was bilateral. Two suffer from paranoid psychotic states, both of them having bilateral temporal foci. None of these patients are considered to have a schizoid or paranoid premorbid personality.

Bruens (1971) in a study of 19 subjects with psychosis and epilepsy suggests that the psychotic status can be divided into 4 syndromes:

1. paranoid syndrome with delusions (9 patients)
2. psychosis with mental regression (5 patients)
3. schizophrenic-like psychosis with thought disorder (2 patients)
4. confusional states of relatively short duration (3 patients).

He reports that 15 of the 19 have delusions and hallucinations that are not typically schizophrenic; that is, not as "hard" as true schizophrenic delusions. The hallucinations and delusions in those with psychoses and epilepsy involved everyday life, not the "world of archetypes." In these patients there is no "praecox" feeling and their affect tends to remain warm and appropriate. In Bruens's series the type of seizure varies but 13 did have psychomotor attacks. Five have the combination of both temporal focus and bilaterally synchronous spike and wave complexes with petit mal absences. In only 5 of the 19 subjects did epileptic activity diminish during the psychosis. Thus, Bruens's data do not support the inverse relationship between psychosis and epilepsy.

Mignone (1970) did a prospective study of 38 clearly established epileptics and a retrospective study of 113 unquestionable epileptics. Looking for possible MMPI profile differences between psychomotor epileptics and nonpsychomotor epileptics, he was interested in such parameters as psychosis, schizophrenia, aggressiveness, impulsivity, sexual dysfunction, and affective disorders. He breaks down these groups by EEG findings into bilateral foci, unilateral dominant foci, and unilateral nondominant foci. He also divides subjects into those who had psychomotor seizures associated with grand mal and those with psychomotor seizures without grand mal. In general, his findings are negative as to the predominance of psychiatric symptoms in the psychomotor group as opposed to other epileptics. However epileptics in general show more morbidity than would have been predicted in the general population. He reports slightly higher MMPI "schizophrenic" scores in the psychomotor epileptics than in those with generalized fits or those without any fits at all, and deviant scores are higher if the temporal lesion is in the dominant hemisphere. "Social introversion" is higher in those with generalized seizures and dominant hemisphere temporal foci, while "depression" and "hypochondriasis" is higher for late onset seizures. "Hypochondriasis" is also higher in those with more frequent fits. In view of Monroe's (1970) findings of frequent physiologic disorders of an episodic nature, as well as those of Mitsuda (1967) that episodic physical symptoms are often associated with activated EEG abnormalities, Monroe proposes that what seems to be hypochondriasis may actually be a physiologic disturbance due to the subcortical seizural activity, particularly in the hypothalamic region.

Flor-Henry (1972, 1973) and Yeudall (1977) feel that laterality of the focus may be important with regard to behavioral symptomatology. For instance, they state that schizophrenic and paranoid symptomatology is related to dominant temporal lobe-limbic system dysfunction and that affective psychosis is correlated with nondominant temporal lobe-limbic system dysfunction. They also feel that psychopathic symptoms are more likely to occur with a dominant lobe dysfunction. Further elaborating the laterality concept, they say that in females the dominant hemisphere is functionally more efficient than the nondominant one, while the reverse is true in males. This is the reason that females show a superiority in language acquisition while males are more effective in visual-spatial tasks, exploratory drives, and aggressivity. Also they believe that in females the nondominant hemisphere is more vulnerable to pathology while in males it is the dominant hemisphere that is vulnerable. Thus, more males exhibit infantile autism with language defects as well as dyslexia while females are more likely to show affective disorders. The dominant hemispheric vulnerability characteristic of males, they believe, explains the aggressive psychopathic predominance in males and the diminished verbal ability as compared to performance IQ seen in males. Falconer (1973) believes the right hemisphere is more likely impaired by febrile convulsions that occur during the first two years of life and that more females have febrile convulsions during this early period. On the other hand, males are more likely to have febrile convulsions after age two with left (dominant) hemisphere involvement. He offers no suggestion as to why girls are more likely to have febrile convulsions earlier than boys.

Glowinski (1973) in a comparison between temporal lobe and centren-cephalic epileptics demonstrates that although performance deteriorated equally in the two groups with distracting tasks, temporal lobe epileptics show significantly greater memory impairment. He notices no significant relationship between laterality of the temporal lobe epileptogenic lesions and impaired verbal or nonverbal memory test. He explains his findings on the basis that there is a minimal irregularly occurring subictal electrical discharge in temporal epileptics which disturbs memory functioning by directly interrupting consolidation, even though it is not sufficient to lead to seizures. Temporal lobe epileptics are particularly deficient in tasks regarding integration of meaningful verbal material suggesting that the immediate registration of a limited amount of simple new information is satisfactory, but if the amount of information or its complexity exceeds the temporal lobe memory span the subject cannot code and retain it.

In view of the above findings there are interesting anecdotal case reports by Waxman (1975) discussing the chronic behavioral changes in temporal lobe epilepsy. He notes alternations in sexual behavior and religiosity, and also found a new symptom, compulsive writing and drawing. The patients stated that they write so they will not forget, or draw a picture to maintain some memory of important events. The author, however, does not feel this is a complete explanation for the compulsive writing. The author also discusses the problems in discriminating ictal from interictal behavioral disorders, saying, "while clinical observations have compelled the classical characterization of ictal and interictal states in the patient with epilepsy, the dichotomy is less clear at the level of the electrophysiologic process, where frank seizure activity may be superimposed on frequently recurring minimal paroxysmal discharges."

Jensen (1975b) reviews the genetic studies on epilepsy, contributing a new study of 74 patients. He finds the family prevalence of epilepsy in his study to be 2.9 percent or five to six times higher than expected when compared to a general population. He also discovers a high incidence of patients with cerebral neurologic heredity, but only if there was a multiple genetic burden afflicting one or more first degree relatives is this inheritable "taint" prognostically unfavorable. He also notes a very high prevalence of psychiatric disorders in the families of his epileptic subjects but most of these patients had been referred from a psychiatric hospital for temporal lobectomy.

From the time of Monroe's original article, "Episodic Disorders: Schizo-phrenia or Epilepsy" (1959), the question has arisen whether episodic psychotic reactions should be considered as schizophrenic or epileptic. Later, Monroe (1970) emphasizes that the weight of evidence would seem to lean towards considering many of the episodic disorders as significantly determined by an epileptoid phenomenon, particularly in view of the frequent therapeutic response to anticonvulsant medication. Monroe points out, however, that there was not necessarily a relationship between the episodic disorders and typical seizures nor typical epileptic EEG patterns. In other words, the episodic disorders have to be considered a distinct clinical entity. Also Monroe repeatedly emphasizes that there is a complex interaction between the environment and the central nervous system dysfunction which determines the specific manifestation of the dyscontrol syndrome. He says that a conservative way to state the complex interrelations between "faulty equipment" and "faulty learning" is the following: "If an individual is destined to become neurotic, psychotic, psychopathic or otherwise deviant, the behavior is more likely to be episodic if there is a dysfunction in the central nervous system of a type generally involving paroxysmal excessive neuronal discharges within the limbic system."

Episodic Behavioral Disorders with Abnormal EEGs

To determine the contribution of "faulty equipment" versus that of "faulty learning" one can either investigate patients with typical seizural disorders and see how many show concomitant behavioral disturbances as compared to matched control groups, as in the studies mentioned earlier, or one can look at specific behavioral disorders such as the episodic behavioral disorders and see whether EEG abnormalities are more frequent in this group than would be predicted in the general population.

Shagass (1976) reviews the electrophysiologic data on schizophrenia. Certain points in that review are pertinent for our current consideration, particularly those studies that suggest some CNS instability in schizophrenics or subgroups of schizophrenia. The interesting finding is that process schizophrenics are liable to have hyperstable, hypernormal records while other groups show more unstable records or lowered seizural thresholds. Examples are lowered Metrazol thresholds in catatonics (Lieberman 1954), "B-Mittens" mainly in reactive schizophrenia (Struve 1972a), and 14 and 6 positive spikes in suicidal assaultive cases (Struve 1972b). Our suggestion would be that there are a group of patients routinely designated as reactive schizophrenics that would be considered as manifesting an episodic psychotic reaction with an underlying "epileptoid" mechanism, and hence more likely to have an abnormal EEG. Shagass (1976) points out that in evoked potential findings there is also a dichotomy between reactive and process schizophrenia.

Wells (1975) points out that there are transient psychotic episodes that may mimic depressive, hysterical, schizophrenic, and acute organic psychoses, which are accompanied by ictal recordings on scalp EEGs. He reports two such cases of his own and five others in the literature and suggests characteristic symptoms of these ictal psychoses very similar to the episodic behavioral disorders as defined by Monroe, namely, the abrupt onset with a relatively healthy premorbid personality, delirium, a history of similar episodes with abrupt spontaneous exacerbations and remissions, and a history of fainting or falling spells.

Small (1976) reviews the electroencephalograms of 766 patients who received a diagnosis of schizophrenia. Fourteen percent of this group have distinctly abnormal EEGs and are mainly patients who did not meet the criteria for definitive schizophrenic diagnosis and were reclassified as affective or schizo-affective disorders. We feel that these patients would be more appropriately diagnosed as episodic psychotic reaction with epileptoid mechanisms. We concur with Small that the EEG is a valuable diagnostic instrument in giving data that has precise therapeutic implications with respect to treatment with drugs that raise the seizural threshold.

Stevens (1973) argues that "all that spikes is not fits" but limits the concept of "fits" to a classic form of epilepsy. Nevertheless, she reports that 40-50 percent of children hospitalized for psychiatric reasons have abnormal EEGs, most commonly in the temporal lobes and usually bilaterally. This is particularly true for psychotic children but not as true for hyperactive behavioral disorders. She also admits that some children have "epileptic-looking" EEGs but do not have seizures, yet their behavior does benefit from phenytoin. She is still reluctant to call this epilepsy. As Monroe has repeatedly pointed out, there is heuristic value in referring to such disorders as epileptoid in that it calls a clinician's attention to the fact that a pharmacologic regimen that includes anticonvulsant drugs is likely to be beneficial. Stevens finds, as Monroe (1970) does in his small group of children, that neurologic dysfunctions and environmental stress are cumulative rather than reciprocal.

Struve (1977) also reports a higher incidence of EEG abnormalities in patients with a history of suicidal acts or suicidal thoughts. He also finds increased abnormalities in the mixed depressive and aggressive group. Apparently these data do not support his earlier finding that the prevalence of EEG abnormalities are significantly higher in those who overtly act out their suicidal impulses (Struve 1972b). Williams (1969) finds abnormal EEGs, usually theta waves, in his aggressive patients. The EEG abnormality localizations are different from those of Monroe (1970) who finds, in activated EEGs, an anterior predominance of theta waves that become generalized. In Williams's study, the theta waves are found most frequently in the anterior temporal, then the fronto-temporal, and finally the posterior temporal areas. He does not find the prevalence of EEG abnormalities significantly changed even if he eliminates from his sample those patients with a history of typical epilepsy or those with mental retardation.

Some studies have suggested other EEG patterns that might correlate with episodic behavioral disorders. Lorimer (1972) notes an association with low seizural threshold and the high frequency band activity in the 30-40 Hz. range. He finds this type of activity in individuals whose violence can be classified as "senseless and animalistic." He observes a syndrome characterized not only by violence but also by a prodromal of headaches described as "bursting" or "piercing" followed by aggression that relieves the headache. Associated symptoms are disturbances of smell, vision, hearing, and taste, as well as strange pressures in the chest and gastrointestinal disturbances such as nausea and vomiting. These individuals are irritable, unpleasant, unpredictable, impulsive, and irrational. The spells range from mild blackouts to furor states or fight or flight patterns. Varying degrees of amnesia are associated with these spells and patients show personality changes such as a low tolerance to frustration, restlessness, and irritability. This 30-40 Hz. abnormality occurs in short one-fifth to two-fifths-second bursts, predominantly in the frontal areas, but is not always bilaterally synchronous nor is it clearly unilateral or focal. It is sporadic during waking records but increases in frequency during drowsiness or light sleep. It is not increased by hyperventilation but seems to be activated by photic and auditory stimulation.

In another group of subjects Lorimer finds relatively high amplitude sinusoidal waves in the 6-8 per second band, apparently similar to what Monroe elicits with alpha chloralose activation (1970). However, Lorimer finds that these individuals did not have the somatic symptoms described earlier and seem callously indifferent to the grotesquely brutal murders for which they were convicted. They show no anxiety following the act nor do they claim amnesia. However, in a penitentiary they are easy to manage. This particular group responds well to diazepam, which supports the findings of Monroe on the use of chlordiazepoxide (1965a, 1965b) for aggressive patients.

Olsen (1970) in studying 6 per second spike waves shows that his group of subjects have vegetative or dystonic complaints. Among his 310 female subjects, 163 have other EEG abnormalities as well. They are likely to have atypical epileptic symptoms and sometimes have headaches, gastrointestinal disturbances, dizziness, and syncope. Younger patients are more likely to have epilepsy, while the middle age group have psychiatric symptoms, and the older age group have vegetative symptoms. These papers, as well as those of Monroe (1970) and Mitsuda's collaborators (1967), emphasize the frequency of somatic complaints in episodic disorders.

Conflict over whether prisoners are more likely to show abnormal EEGs or to have epilepsy is discussed in detail in Monroe's original monograph (1970). The debate continues, with no consensus regarding this area of investigation. Nelson (1974) studying 194 prisoners classifies 100 as nonpsychopathic, 56 as aggressive psychopathic, and 38 as nonaggressive psychopathic. He reports 40 individuals (20 percent) showing paroxysmal EEG abnormalities and the aggressive psychopaths showing significantly more abnormalities than the other groups. On the other hand, Fenton (1974) in a study designed to confirm or refute the early studies of Hill (1944, 1952) is unable to support the latter's original findings which show that posterior temporal slowing is associated with aggressive behavior. Fenton has a matched control group, an acute group, and a chronic group. The latter two groups show this slow activity most frequently without any significant differences in symptoms, social-economic background, or aggressive behavior. Fenton's study finds slow activity more frequently than Hill's and most common in older subjects (average age about thirty); thus he questions Hill's suggestion that this posterior slowing is a maturational phenomenon.

Gunn (1969) finds the prevalence of epilepsy in prisoners to be 7.1 per 1,000 as compared with the prevalence of epilepsy in the general population of Iceland at 3.7 per 1,000 and the accepted British figure of 4.4 per 1,000. We wonder whether any differences might be explained by variations in diagnostic criteria. A total of 35.4 percent of Gunn's epileptics are labeled "ill defined." This may explain the high figure he reports in the prison population by contrast to those generally reported for the population as a whole. Although Gunn feels that there is no correlation between temporal lobe epilepsy and criminal aggression, he does feel that temporal lobe epileptics show significantly increased impulsivity. Gibbs (1972), in a study at an Indiana prison, is impressed by the total absence of epilepsy in that prison population. Our results reported in later chapters show very few criminals with either a history of epilepsy or manifesting typical epileptic EEGs, even after activation. However, 58 percent do show baseline abnormalities and even more show abnormalities after activation (Chapter 7).

Papatheophilou (1975), comparing homosexuals with a matched control group, focuses on the EEG build-up with hyperventilation. He finds that in the controls, 73 percent show no build-up of slow wave activity, while only 37 percent of the homosexuals show no build-up. In view of the importance of activated generalized theta activity in our current study and the correlation of this with build-up of slow activity during baseline hyperventilation, this finding may be of particular significance; the patients in our present study with activated abnormalities are more likely to show homosexual activity within the prison setting (see Chapter 8).

Correlations between EEG patients and objective psychological tests remain controversial. Milstein (1971) matches adults with EEG abnormalities to controls with normal EEGs. The psychological tests are pencil and paper self-evaluations, including the MMPI, Mood Scale, Cornell Medical Index, Institute for Personality and Ability Testing, Zung Self-Rating Depression Scale, and the Taylor Manifest Anxiety Scale. The 14 and 6 per second positive spike group are differentiated from comparison groups by the Cornell Medical Index in that the patients described themselves as angry and hostile, as well as having musculoskeletal symptoms. Otherwise, the individuals with normal EEGs show more psychopathology than those with abnormal ones. However, in view of such contradictory clinical observations, it is probable that this reflects the inadequacy of both psychological and neurophysiological measuring instruments rather than clinical reality. Satterfield (1974), studying hyperactive children, finds that a group of 22 with definite EEG abnormalities have significantly higher WISC (Wechsler Intelligence Scale for Children) performance scale scores, as well as higher WISC subtest scores (Picture arrangements and visual associations). There are also significantly fewer perseveration errors on the Bender Gestalt than in 35 children with borderline EEGs. Teachers rate this group with definite EEG abnormalities as fidgity and restless as opposed to the shy and overly sad group who do not show abnormal EEGs. Satterfield reports that the prognoses are not poor in the group with EEG abnormalities compared to those with normal EEGs. In fact, in many ways this group functions better, a finding similar to that reported by Stevens (1970).

Activated Electroencephalography in Episodic Behavioral Disorders

Monroe (1970) discusses the frequency of false-negative (normal) EEGs even in the classical epileptic patient, not to mention those manifesting episodic behavioral disorders. Ajmone-Marsan (1970) examines this problem by studying 308 subjects with unquestionable epilepsy. He made 1,824 recordings, an average of six records per patient and finds 1,055 positive and 769 negative recordings. Positive records are obtained in only 55 percent of the subjects on first EEG examination. Repeated EEGs for at least one year reveal positive findings in 92 percent of the subjects, illustrating the value of repeated examinations if one is utilizing the EEG as a diagnostic tool. There is a predominance of negative records in patients over age forty, and in those patients whose seizures started after age thirty. This age differentiation is particularly dramatic in first record abnormalities in that 70 percent of patients aged ten or younger show positive first records, whereas only 30 percent over age forty show positive first records. Only 2 percent of the patients with temporal lobe epilepsy have persistently negative records. Fenton (1974) reviews the value and limitations of EEG evaluations of psychiatric patients, suggesting that depsite the frequency of "false" negatives, this procedure has important diagnostic value in the field of psychiatry.

In view of the chance of false-negative (normal) records when actual brain dysfunction exists, the question arises as to the effectiveness of the usual activating procedures such as hyperventilation and sleep recordings. Niedermeyer (1971) states that limbic spikes are not altered markedly by levels of awareness, but his data indicate that sleep elicits spikes in an occasional patient. Morgan (1970) reports that although hyperventilation is an undisputed aid in the diagnosis of petit mal epilepsy, it increases only slightly the number of positive findings in other forms of epilepsy. A significant group show augmentation in their already present baseline abnormalities but only 18 percent exhibit focal abnormalities for the first time during hyperventilation, while 7 percent develop new paroxysmal activity under similar conditions.

Stevens (1970) and Nelson (1974) report that photic stimulation is an effective activating procedure, as is hyperventilation, in eliciting abnormalities in prisoners whether they are labeled nonpsychopathic, aggressive psychopaths, or nonaggressive psychopaths, with 20 percent of the prisoners showing paroxysmal EEG abnormalities. Alcohol is also an effective activator which elicits paroxysmal bursts of slow activity in 52 percent of their prison subjects. Unfortunately, this report does not include a detailed description of the slow activity. Marinacci (1963) reports on the activation of psychomotor seizures with beverage alcohol, but Bach-y-Rita (1970) is unable to replicate this phenomenon when administering alcohol intravenously to patients complaining of rage outbursts associated with drinking—the so-called pathological intoxication.

Lorimer (1972) reports that both photic and auditory stimulation are helpful in eliciting 30-40 cycle per second EEG activity, which he believes correlates with dyscontrol behavior. This activation seems particularly effective if presented in a stressful manner, that is, with varying intensities and frequencies.

Methoxyhexital (Brevital) is a popular activating agent. Wilder (1971a, 1971b) summarizes previous animal studies suggesting that this drug causes suppression of inhibitory influences which, in turn, permits the synchronous discharge of hyperexcitable neurons characteristic of an epileptic focus. He feels that this is effective predominantly in the limbic system and temporal lobe because of the low threshold in these areas, and states that the drug activates only "epileptic tissue" and not normal brain tissue. In studying various techniques for locating the primary focus in the temporal lobe, Wilder and coworkers use an increasingly complex series of tests, including the routine EEG with nasopharyngeal electrodes, intravenous and intracarotid Brevital, recordings directly on the cortex, and subcortical recordings in the hippocampus and amygdala areas. They note an increased accuracy of localization with the utilization of increasingly complex procedures. The most significant increment in knowledge comes when they add intravenous Brevital to the routine EEG procedure. In patients suspected of centrencephalic epilepsy they find 0.4 mg. per kilogram, a sufficient activating dose, whereas 1.9 mg. per kilogram is required in patients with psychomotor seizures. In general these finds are supported by Musella (1971).

On the basis of studies on cats that show cocaine—induced seizural activities within the limbic system, Mark (1975) tries cocaine as an activating procedure for limbic dysfunction in humans. This is not effective, although it does induce high amplitude slow activity. In view of this finding and also of Heath's (1973) report of slow waves induced by marijuana in the septal region, one wonders whether the capacity of cocaine to induce slow activity in the limbic system might correlate with a drug-induced sense of euphoria.

Legg (1974) reports one individual who, on two separate occasions, shows an increased number of petit mal attacks and also a major seizure within a few hours after initiating treatment with imipramine. This patient has an abnormal baseline EEG and following administration of 12.5 mg. of imipramine there is considerable increase in EEG abnormality, that is, prolonged bursts of paroxysmal spike wave activity and scattered single spikes, as well as sharp waves and generalized paroxysmal theta waves. Thus, in susceptible persons, seizures apparently can be precipitated by the tricyclic antidepressants, a finding Monroe also corroborates (1970). As one of the most common episodic reactions is severe episodic depressive reaction, failure to identify this type of episodic disorder with its underlying limbic system dysfunction can have serious consequences. Such depressions should be treated with anticonvulsants rather than tricyclics.

One complexity in differentiating schizophrenia from the episodic disorders in terms of a neurophysiologic mechanism is Heath's (1962) finding that schizophrenics have spikes in the limbic system, particularly in the septal region. He differentiates between septal "schizophrenic spikes" and the "storms of electrical activity" that occur in the amygdala-hippocampal region in episodic disorders, which are comparable to what one sees on scalp recordings of epileptics during overt seizures. That is, the schizophrenic pattern is interictal (isolated spikes or spike slow waves). The limbic dysfunction in the amygdala-hippocampal area is more typical of an ictal EEG.

Another possibility for determining the neurophysiologic difference between classical schizophrenia and the episodic psychotic reaction exists on the basis of Hanley's (1972) finding which confirms Heath's earlier studies of spikes in the septal region (1954). However, Hanley reports that the best correlation between the bizarre behavior of the schizophrenic and the EEG is provided by an analysis in the 25-28 cycle per second band. This, plus Lorimer's (1972) studies cited earlier, suggest that more attention should be paid to the fast activity in the 20-40 cycle per second band and to behavior.

A strange but perhaps important form of activation is reported by Sweet (1969) who played a tape recording of a baby crying to an adolescent who had murdered her baby step-sibling while the baby was crying. The recording precipitated an abnormal EEG paroxysm. We also have seen one such patient in our clinic. Smith (1973), studying 34 parents who battered their children, finds that 8 had abnormal EEGs. Six of the 8 with abnormal EEGs were classified as aggressive psychopaths. The possibility of a baby's vocalization eliciting seizural discharge suggests an area that obviously needs further study. Feldman (1976) contributes to the ever-increasing group of subjects where the seizures are precipitated by emotional triggers. He presents five such individuals documented by videotape recordings. These studies underscore the fact that dyscontrol acts precipitated by emotional stress do not exclude a concomitant excessive neuronal discharge in the central nervous system.

There have been no reports on the use of alpha chloralose as an activating agent since the details of this procedure were reported by Monroe (1970). Undoubtedly, one reason for the disinterest in this drug lies in the administrative complication of its use, since under current FDA regulations it is still considered an experimental drug. Although alpha chloralose induces false-positives in 15-20 percent of subjects, it probably minimizes false-negatives, with the exception of chronic alcoholics and individuals on substantial doses of benzodiazepines who seem resistant to the procedure. In a large referral practice, Monroe finds alpha chloralose activation useful in that the positive findings it elicits encourage referring physicians to persist with an anticonvulsant regimen even though it takes time and effort to work out an effective therapeutic combination. Without an activated EEG abnormality most physicians will not persist with such a regimen.

Surgical Studies of Aggression

The surgical approach to the treatment of intractable pain, epilepsy, and mental disorders has been the outstanding source of knowledge regarding possible localization of function within the human central nervous system. Although animal studies are the basis for these surgical techniques, only in the humans can we see the complex relationships and collect the necessary introspective data for the full evaluation of either stimulation or ablation of specific nuclei or tracts within the central nervous system.

The many medical, ethical, philosophical problems associated with surgical brain procedures are well known. As society fears the potential abuse of brain manipulation it restricts these procedures. Brain manipulation, particularly psychosurgery, elicits an extremely negative reaction not only among professionals but also in the public at large, provoking a number of lay-oriented books such as those by Maya Pines, *The Brain Changers* (1973), and Marilyn Ferguson, *The Brain Revolution* (1973). Elliot Valenstein's more scientific treatise, *Brain Control: A Critical Examination of Brain Stimulation and Psychosurgery* (1973), rejects the idea that psychosurgery offers a possibility for authoritarian control of behavior and also minimizes the unrealistic hopes that many social problems can be solved by appropriate application of our current knowledge of the brain. He says, "it is very unlikely that any of the ablation or stimulation techniques or for that matter drugs presently being investigated are capable of reducing undesirable aggression in a normal population."

Perhaps we will be forced to rely on studies such as those of Kling (1975) who attempts to narrow the gap between human and animal studies by evaluating primates in their natural habitat before and after surgical ablations. Brown (1977) describes a combined surgical intervention in refractory patients, usually bilateral innomino-amygdalotomy and cingulate isolation, pointing out the effectiveness of this combined procedure, not only on psychotic symptom-otology but also on aggressiveness. He defends the value of such a procedure in a criminal population, reviewing briefly the current controversy of treating incarcerated individuals with psychosurgical techniques.

Early attempts to avoid the irreversible effect of nervous tissue destruction resulting from ablation or undercutting through the use of electrical stimulation have not proven clinically useful. Heath (1977) circumvents the relapses of the early stimulation treatment by introducing a "brain pacemaker" and believes it will be a treatment for intractable psychiatric illness. In 10 of 11 such subjects this has proven true at least for a short term follow-up. From our point of view it is important to note that 8 of his eleven subjects were violent.

Stimulation, however, may be used to pinpoint areas that will be subse-quently destroyed. Often an attempt to modify certain target symptoms, for example, seizures, compulsions, or aggressive behavior, results in temporary or sometimes permanent undesirable behavior patterns. Despite the supposedly irreversible nature of the destructive procedures, behavioral improvement seen after surgery sometimes turns out to be transitory. Attempts to improve these techniques have emphasized precise small lesions in specific subcortical areas, either nerve tracts or nuclei, with the hope of obtaining an amelioration of the undesirable behavioral traits without concomitant defects in the patient's intellect or character. When this is directed toward an identifiable epileptogenic focus it is, strictly speaking, a neurosurgical procedure; if it is destruction of normal brain tissue in an effort to modify behavior, it is a psychosurgical procedure. Unfortunately, it is not always clear whether the operation is neurosurgical or psychosurgical as here defined.

New techniques remain experimental until long-term follow-up ranging from five to ten years becomes available. While the older lobotomy studies offer a possibility for such long-term follow-up, unfortunately few such studies have been published. Follow-ups are imperative if the classical lobotomy procedure itself is to be considered a clinical rather than an experimental procedure. Many of the existing studies are relatively worthless for follow-up evaluation because they lack objective baseline evaluations. Authors' protests concerning the difficulty in obtaining presurgical psychological data sometimes seem to be a rationalization for poor experimental design. Another disconcerting aspect of the psychosurgery literature is that patients are usually described as intractable. However, from the data presented, it would seem that a more rigorous or persistent pharmacologic regimen should have been tried before surgical inter-vention.

The neurosurgeon deserves credit in the area of human subcortical studies which have revealed a low seizural threshold in the limbic system and the presence of circumscribed excessive neuronal discharges within this system, often without cortical or scalp reflection of this "storm of electrical activity." Such information has led the clinician to be more persistent in trying a pharmacologic regimen utilizing drugs that raise seizural threshold. The fact that individuals with circumscribed or "partial epilepsy" often do not have typical seizures but do have episodic behavioral disorders has widened the clinician's horizon as to the effectiveness of anticonvulsant drugs.

Temporal Lobotomy

The most significant follow-up on the conventional temporal lobotomy is Falconer's (1973) report on 100 subjects who were followed six to twenty years after temporal lobotomy. All these patients had epilepsy but only 13 were regarded as mentally normal, a total of 47 were considered psychopaths, most of whom had been institutionalized; 16 had been psychotic before surgery, and 27 demonstrated aggression. At follow-up, 14 of the 100 subjects showed no improvement while 34 were completely free of seizures. Concerning behavioral abnormalities, 55 had made continuing social adjustment with increased occupational performance and better interpersonal relationships, as compared to 22 who had made a satisfactory adjustment before operation. Aside from seizures, the most common symptom described is "interictal aggression"; that is, "unpredictable explosive outbursts in response to minor frustrating situations." Falconer finds that aggression is relieved most often in those patients where the identifiable pathology was mesial sclerosis (7 of 13 subjects). Patients who had been or were psychotic are more likely to have had hamartomas, and 7 of the 12 subjects with psychosis benefited from this operation. The psychotic patients that benefited most were those with episodic confusional states that Monroe would label episodic organic reactions. Jensen (1975a) presents data that he feels demonstrate the importance of a temporal lobectomy in reducing the long-term morbidity in severe epileptics. Falconer (1973) believes that if epilepsy is resistant to anticonvulsant drugs and if this can be established by the time the child is ten to twelve years of age, surgery should be performed as quickly as possible.

Kelly (1973, 1976) reviews the neurophysiology and neuroanatomy of the various subsystems within the limbic system and then evaluates the rationale for the more precise stereotaxic destruction of individual nuclei or tracts. Many of these studies focus on the effect of amygdalotomy.

Amygdalotomy

One of the earliest of such procedures was that of Narabayashi (1963, 1970, 1975), a neurosurgeon and psychiatrist, who performed bilateral amygdalotomies on 37 children, ages six to ten, who had at least two of the following symptoms: epilepsy, mental retardation, or aggressive behavior, and only after there had been prolonged attempts to treat these patients otherwise. In over fifteen years of active clinical practice only 37 children have been operated on, indicating a considerable degree of caution used by Narabayashi in selecting these patients. (The clinical records of these patients were reviewed by one of the present authors (R.M.).) Also he feels that he now has identified a technique that is particularly effective not only in eliminating seizures but also in modifying the destructive behavior, hyperactivity, and the short attention span that often resulted in these children being erroneously diagnosed as mentally deficient.

Narabayashi describes the amygdala nucleus as approximately 18 millimeters in diameter in the normal adult. The area 6-18 millimeters from the midline represents the medial nucleus while that 20-24 millimeters from the midline, the lateral nucleus. He can identify this area both radiologically and physiologically. The latter technique involves looking for distinctive injury discharges as the probe is put in place and identifying whether it is in the medial or lateral portion of the amygdala by olfactory stimulation with ether, the stimulus burst being larger in the lateral portion than in the medial portion. Under general anesthesia he further identifies the appropriate area by stimulation that induces pupillary dilation and transitory arrest of respiration in the inspiratory phase. He attempts to place a lesion at the medial aspect of the lateral nucleus through electrical coagulation 3-4 millimeters in diameter. He admits that he is not looking for an epileptogenic focus and because of the direct connections between the anygdalae, bilaterally, he has given up a unilateral procedure. Utilizing his technique he has not induced a single Kluver-Bucy syndrome. He reports dramatic therapeutic results in patients who were completely incapacitated prior to operation.

Heimburger (1966) has treated a number of patients with unilateral and bilateral destructions of the amygdala following a technique similar to Narabayashi's, and reports not only a significant improvement in seizure control, but also a modification of the aggressive behavior. As he is one of the earliest workers in this field, long-term follow-up of his patients is feasible and currently reported by Ivan Small (1977). Small feels that the procedure has been definitely effective in controlling seizures, but less so in modifying aggression.

Ramamurthi (1970) reports on the stereotaxic ablation of what he calls an irritable focus in 8 children with temporal lobe epilepsy, all of whom have "associated episodic behavioral disorders." The procedure was either unilateral or bilateral. Four of his patients were completely relieved of their epilepsy and two relieved of their episodic behavioral disorders. Drug dosage was reduced to one-third of the preoperative level in two others, while in two, fits were controlled but preoperative levels of medication had to be continued. In discussing this paper, Narabayashi says that in his experience unilateral procedures may alleviate generalized epileptic seizures but seldom lead to a sustained improvement in psychomotor seizures.

Kiloh (1974) reports on 18 patients, 15 of whom received bilateral amygdalotomy and 3 a unilateral procedure. The patients were treated for aggressive and self-mutilative behavior often with concomitant seizures. Only 5 of the group had significant EEG abnormalities and only 7 of the 18 had been tried on anticonvulsants or benzodiazepines. The author finds that self-mutilators who improved after the operation later relapsed. This is confirmed by other investigators such as Vernet (1970) and Hitchcock (1973). Kiloh suggests that on the basis of this observation the neurophysiologic mechanism for aggression directed towards self might be different from that for aggression directed outwardly, inasmuch as patients with aggression directed outwardly show some improvement after an amygdalotomy. However, in their series the self-mutilating patients were also mentally retarded; such patients are less likely to show improvement with amygdalotomy than are patients with normal intelligence. Kiloh has better results if there is a coexistent epilepsy. However, the results are not impressive since, of the 18 patients, only 4 showed sustained improvement for a significant follow-up period from two to four and a half years after operation.

Hitchcock (1973) also reports on 18 patients who had undergone amygdalotomy. He proposes an assessment scheme for evaluating this operation. In this series, 15 of the 18 patients had some kind of seizures, but again the operation was primarily for abnormal aggressive behavior. Other characteristics of his group are that 5 had severe subnormal mental functioning and as a whole the group is described as overactive, destructive, and rebellious. Four males had problems with aggression associated with excessive alcohol intake. Results are not impressive. However, what may be important is that his target area was the medial nucleus of the amygdala in contrast to Narabayashi's assertion that the most effective area for controlling aggression as well as seizures is the medial aspect of the lateral nucleus.

Other Procedures

Vernet (1970) reports on 12 patients with personality disorders or chronic schizophrenia in whom aggressive-destructive behavior remained a prominent feature, even though 7 of the 12 had had previous psychosurgery (two cingulotomies and five frontal lobotomies). In 11 of the 12 subjects who had an amygdalotomy following the Narabayashi technique, there was a disappearance or marked reduction in aggressive episodes. This would seem to support the idea that better results may be obtained from lesions in the more lateral rather than the medial aspect of the amygdala. Vernet also finds that the 2 subjects in his series who were self-mutilators did not respond to the amygdalotomy but did show improvement to subsequent frontal tractotomy.

Although amygdalotomy is usually the favored procedure, particularly for aggressive patients, other target areas are selected in the treatment of behavioral disorders. For instance, Schvarcz (1972) utilizes hypothalamotomy. The lesions were made at the site of maximum sympathetic response to stimulation inducing hypertension and tachycardia, which is the medial part of the posterior hypothalamus. He was particularly careful to avoid lesions in the ventral medial nucleus because animal studies show that such lesions produce savage behavior. In their follow-up period of six to forty-eight months, 7 patients showed no aggressive behavior at all; 3 patients had some aggressive behavior that was controlled by drugs, and only 1 patient was considered a failure. Unfortunately, their psychologic and psychiatric data is sparse.

Andy (1975, 1976) presents two case reports on amygdalotomy for bilateral temporal lobe seizures in severely disturbed individuals. What is striking about these detailed case reports is that they required multiple operations; that is, bilateral amygdalotomy and also orbitotomy in one and a repeat and enlarging operation on the left amygdala in the other. Although there was dramatic improvement in the behavior, both patients had to be continued on anticonvulsant medication.

Richardson (1972) reports on stereotaxic cingulotomy combined with prefrontal lobotomy, claiming that this combination reduces narcotic withdrawal symptoms and cancer pain. Ballantine (1967), in a study of 40 patients, reports good results with cingulotomy in "mental disease." Stimulation in the cingulum results in nonspecific, poorly described feelings of anxiety and discomfort in most subjects, and in 3 of the 10 there was a dramatic increase in the original clinical syndrome. Following the operation these patients are described as quiet, nonspontaneous, following commands without question. There was also urinary incontinence for two to six weeks, but the mental apathy and incontinence subsided. Kelly (1976) in his review article reports the increased effectiveness of stereotaxic procedures as compared to "free hand" operations.

It is apparent from these reports that most neurosurgical treatments of aggression have had limited success. With the possible exception of Narabayashi's lesions in the medial aspect of the lateral nucleus of the amygdala and the good results reported by Schvarcz on lesions in the medial part of the posterior hypothalamus, other procedures do not seem to be effective. To moderate the target symptom of aggression may require multiple destructive procedures. The deficiencies in data in published reports, particularly with regard to lack of psychological data and lack of long-term follow-up, leave even reported positive results unconvincing. With the development of the concept of episodic behavioral disorders and the effectiveness of a medical regimen utilizing anticonvulsants, it seems both logical and imperative that neurosurgeons operate only on patients whose symptoms have failed to respond to intensive long-term trials on anticonvulsant medication. Baseline behaviors require rigorous documentation to assess efficacy of therapy and possible indications for surgical interventions.

Pharmacologic Treatment of Episodic Behavioral Disorders

Phenytoin

Monroe (1970) suggests that the first regimen to try when an epileptoid mechanism is clearly established or strongly suspected is the anticonvulsant phenytoin (Dilantin). There have been many reports of both successes and failures in using phenytoin as a pharmacological regimen in the behavioral disorders. A difficulty in evaluating these reports involves the lack of differentiation of episodic from nonepisodic disorders. Monroe contends that phenytoin would be effective only in episodic disorders, and then only in those with an epileptoid mechanism. Maletsky (1973), relying on the concept of episodic dyscontrol, reports that 19 of 22 subjects achieved at least a 75 percent reduction in frequency and severity of violent outbursts with phenytoin. In a later paper, Maletsky (1974) reports, as Monroe does, that patients seem to flare up in anger less often, and, once angered, "did not go all the way" in producing a violent fit.

An example of an episodic syndrome, not recognized as such by the authors, is the report by Green (1974), of 10 patients with compulsive eating who were successfully treated with phenytoin. The rationale for treating them with phenytoin was an abnormal EEG. However, on reviewing clinical histories, a definite episodic quality to the patients' symptoms was apparent. Haward (1969) reports on using phenytoin in a group of severely psychotic aggressive patients. This is one of the few studies that comes close to replicating an early study by Monroe (1965b). Haward claims good results in these aggressive patients even after a two-week regimen on low doses (100 mg. twice a day).

When the patient sample is not clearly differentiated on the basis of episodic symptoms, but manifests heterogenous symptoms classified as "mental aberrations," the results, not unexpectedly, are mixed. Simopoulos (1974), after discontinuing phenothiazines, treated long-term regressed hospitalized male patients randomly assigned to either phenytoin or placebo. He used appropriate doses, increasing phenytoin from 325 to 625 mg. per day over an eight-week treatment program. As measured by the Brief Psychiatric Rating Scale, phenytoin had most influence on hostility and worked best on men with high initial hostility scores. At the high dose level there is retarded motor behavior and blunted affects; thus, he proposes a maximal dose of 500 mg. per day in patients who are particularly hostile. Pinto (1975), studying female patients with a combined phenothiazine-phenytoin combination, also finds that women show a reduction in irritable aggressive behavior. However, impaired social competence and thought disturbances became more evident. Uhlenhuth (1972) treated an unselected group of neurotic adult psychiatric outpatients over a period of eight weeks. Those patients who respond to phenytoin did so in terms of lessening irascibility, compulsiveness, and a possible significant reduction in their depression and anxiety. Connors's (1971) study on a treatment of delinquent boys with phenytoin and methylphenidate finds no significant differences between the drug and placebo group though their experimental design was limited. He analyzed a number of symptoms that reflect episodic disorders, but does not make such a distinction in any global way. His negative findings are surprising in view of a pilot study done by Hanlon (1973) at a girl's treatment center where there was a dramatic improvement in behavior with phenytoin.

Ifabumuyi (1976) discusses the psychedelic-drug-induced psychotic reaction, the acute stage often responding to "talking down." The author points out that there is another group of patients that have a more chronic course and respond uncertainly to major tranquilizers and/or ECT. This group of subjects do not present with the vivid symptoms but rather with loose associations, paranoid set, and a marked vagueness, as well as flat affect. His study is anecdotal. The author found that both the acute and the chronic type of drug psychosis responded to diphenylhydantoin whereas the group had not responded to other medication. Inasmuch as at least an acute form is often self-limiting, it is hard to evaluate how much of the improvement is due to the drug.

Other Anticonvulsants

Other anticonvulsants may ultimately prove to be more effective than phenytoin, but there is little in the literature on their use. Monroe (1965b) reports on the use of primidone (Mysoline) in treating aggressive behavior. There have been no subsequent reports utilizing this drug, except for the current study of Monroe et al. (see Chapter 11). Rim (1975) reports no appreciable difference in the anticonvulsant properties of primidone and carbamazepine (Tegretol), but the author concludes "psychological studies completed on 25 patients show a slight statistical difference in the level of arousal and attention in favor of carbamazepine."

Because carbamazepine is reported as particularly effective in a treatment of psychomotor seizures, it might be useful in the treatment of the episodic disorders. Using carbamazepine, Dalby (1971), in a study of 93 patients, reports complete control in 33 percent and partial control in 27 percent of patients with psychomotor seizures. He states that the antiepileptic effect is least pronounced in patients over twenty-five and those with dementia or mental retardation. He also adds that it is not useful in patients with psychiatric symptoms, except for improvement in those symptoms dependent upon seizure control. In his patients, 8 percent had adverse side effects and 7 percent an actual increase in symptoms. Unfortunately, Dalby does not give details regarding the psychiatric aspects of his sample.

Rodin (1976), comparing patients on a combination of phenytoin-primidone and phenytoin-carbamazepine in a double crossover study with each patient as his own control, concludes that those patients with no history of emotional or intellectual disturbances do better on primidone. On the other hand, those with emotional problems do better with carbamazepine. Livingston (1974), studying 255 anticonvulsant refractory patients, finds that carbamazepine is an exceedingly effective anticonvulsant, particularly in patients with temporal lobe seizures as well as those with major motor seizures. He considers this the drug of choice for psychomotor seizures. However, he does not discuss in detail any behavioral effects of such a regimen. Lion (1975a) points out that it is vital to distinguish which class of patients demonstrates violence that has at its basis some degree of brain dysfunction responsive to anticonvulsant regimens.

Tunks (1977) identifies the dyscontrol syndrome as a limbic system dysfunction which demands a medical regimen consisting of a drug that raises seizural threshold. She points out that carbamazepine is an anticonvulsant that has certain structural characteristics in common not only with imipramine but also with promazine, and in her studies finds improvement in subjects where there is only "a diffuse and nonspecifically abnormal EEG" without clinical evidence of epilepsy. She anecdotally reports case histories of several patients with a dyscontrol symptom who have responded to carbamazepine. A typical case report was an individual who at age thirteen began showing aggressive outbursts on the average of every four days, without discernible precipitating factors. Twelve to twenty-four hours prior to the outburst, the patient would "look different" and have a glazed or fixed appearance in her eyes. These episodes were followed by guilt and remorse, with statements to the effect that she couldn't help it. The EEG is described as "poorly organized" with slowing of activity on hyperventilation. Her treatment consisted of 600 mg. of carbamazepine per day with a blood level of 14 mg. per liter. She suggests that the iminodibenzl group of drugs might be a group to study seriously in developing a specific medication for the dyscontrol symptoms because of its common characteristics with imipramine and chlorpromazine.

Benzodiazepines

Monroe (1970) mentions that the benzodiazepines, by virtue of their anticonvulsant properties, are also effective in treating dyscontrol patients. The benzodiazepines are given either alone or in combination with the usual anticonvulsants. Lorimer (1972) also finds this to be the case with diazepam (Valium), and Rickels (1974) reports that chlordiazepoxide (Librium) is particularly effective in aggressive-impulsive women. Brazier (1975) demonstrates on the EEG-derived spectral data that diazepam has a rapid effect over a wide range of frequencies and also suppresses spiking in the limbic system, more so than does phenobarbitol. This finding is similar to that reported by Monroe for chlordiazepoxide

(1970). Clonazepam (Kick 1973) in doses ranging from 2-12 mg. per day is reported to be more effective in grand mal and psychomotor seizures than either diazepam or phenytoin, so that this drug might be effective in treating episodic disorders. Gastaut (1971) also finds it very effective at low doses for status epilepticus.

Neuroleptics

Hara (1971), in a brief report on 14 patients with schizophrenic-like symptoms but without a history of clinical seizures, notes poor response to phenothiazines and a good response to haloperidol or antiepileptic agents or combinations of the two. Monroe (1970) states that many of the episodic disorders tend to deteriorate when placed on phenothiazines. Davies's (1975) study confirms that phenothiazines augment paroxysmal EEG abnormalities and exacerbate the patients' symptoms. These patients are typical of what Monroe describes as episodic psychotic reactions; that is, the patients had not only auditory hallucinations but also visual, olfactory, and tactile hallucinations. The patients also reported feelings of depersonalization and showed irritability and poor impulse control with overt rage attacks. They showed more confusional symptoms and states of clouded consciousness. The symptoms occurred episodi-cally when compared with relatively continuous "core" symptoms more typical of schizophrenia.

Simpson (1976) also studies psychotic exacerbations produced by neuro-leptics. The psychotic symptoms include confusion, rambling speech, disorienta-tion, paranoid ideation, agitation, excitement, violent behavior, visual as well as auditory hallucinations, and depersonalization. In this group antiparkinson medication does not alter the symptoms but there is improvement with cessation of the neuroleptics. There is another group of subjects showing symptoms more characteristic of either inhibited or excited catatonics with clouding of con-sciousness but no amnesia. These episodes are controlled by adding antiparkin-son agents and decreasing neuroleptics.

Singh (1976) also describes a group of schizophrenics who developed psychotic symptoms similar to those described by Simpson, but whose main characteristic was a dysphoric subjective response to the neuroleptics. He suggests that this group is distinct from nuclear schizophrenia and as described by Langfeldt (1969) is a uniquely different "schizophreniform" psychosis. Monroe (1970) points out that Langfeldt's schizophreniform psychoses have many characteristics of the episodic disorders. Stevens (1970) reports that in adults and children with behavioral abnormalities accompanied by epileptic-looking EEGs, anticonvulsants are effective, but otherwise phenothiazines are to be preferred. It would seem that there are continuing reports in the literature that suggest a group of disorders of an episodic nature often misdiagnosed as schizophrenia which are exacerbated by the usual antipsychotic medications.

Tricyclics

Monroe (1970) reports several patients treated by the tricyclic antidepressants in whom the drug exacerbated symptoms or precipitated convulsions. It is his thesis that episodic depressive reactions are important to identify as they respond well to anticonvulsants and not the tricyclics. In view of this, a report by Morrison (1975) on a group of subjects with "explosive personality" as a sequel to the hyperactive syndrome who did respond to the tricyclics is interesting. He identifies the uniqueness of this syndrome and says that whatever development or constitutional brain defects are present in explosive personalities, are also responsible for some of the hyperactive child syndromes. His rationale for utilizing the antidepressants is that they are useful for treating some hyperactive children.

Lithium

Altshuler (1977) reports on 9 patients treated with lithium. Two acting-out adolescents and 5 of 6 schizophrenics responded to the treatment. One patient with a personality disorder was discontinued because of side reactions. The lithium seems to affect the target symptoms of impulsivity and aggressiveness. If there were other symptoms, for instance, schizophrenia, they required supplementary medication with the phenothiazines although often at lower levels than were necessary before the addition of lithium.

Tupin (1972) also utilizes the concept of the episodic behavioral disorders. In a literature review of lithium he finds that often patients described as episodic and aggressive with periodic phasic, or recurrent, symptoms respond to lithium. Tupin notes that the symptoms were organic or hysterical, and that the patients were unmanageable, abusive, noisy, and confused. All of these characteristics are typical of Monroe's dyscontrol syndrome or his episodic-psychotic reactions. Two other reports on the effect of lithium in impulsive-aggressive individuals are those by Sheard (1971) and Lion (1975b). Lithium, however, has no clear anticonvulsant effect, although it is reported to raise seizural thresholds in limbic systems and this may be the basis of its potential usefulness in treating episodic disorders. Also, it may be, as Lion (1974c) suggests that some of these disorders of impulsivity and aggression are equivalents of affective or mood disorder and hence respond to lithium.

Stimulants

Central nervous system stimulants such as amphetamine and methylphenidate are used to treat hyperkinetic patients who have some degree of brain dysfunction. Many of these patients can be considered to have episodic behavioral disorders; hence, research on this regimen should be pursued.

Other Agents

The data and theories concerning the use of hormonal agents and other psychotropic drugs to treat aggression, are presented by Lion (1975a). Several articles in the current literature identify the schizo-affective disorders as representing a unique syndrome to be differentiated from both schizophrenia and affective disorders (McCabe 1976). Dempsey (1975) reports on the positive response of such patients to electroconvulsive therapy (ECT) and/or lithium. In view of the frequent clinical observation that some of the episodic disorders seem to be alleviated by frank seizures, this finding is important and suggests that a careful investigation of ECT as a treatment modality for the episodic dyscontrol and episodic-psychotic reactions should be considered. Elliot (1977) has found propranolol useful for controlling aggressive behavior following brain damage.

Psychotherapy of Episodic Disorders

Monroe (1970) reviews the psychotherapeutic literature regarding the treatment of patients with episodic behavioral disorders. This literature is largely psychoanalytic in nature and pertains to "acting out" problems in treatment. The problems of impulsivity in the psychoanalytic literature relate to the patient's tendencies to translate affective issues into unpremeditated and impulsive acts which the patient cannot otherwise express in therapy because certain feelings are unacceptable. The term "acting out" has largely been a transference-related term, and Monroe (1970) draws attention to the fact that many impulsive acts that appear to the clinician as "acting out" in quality may be epileptoid acts, or may reflect epileptoid mechanisms which place the potential treatment process in a different light.

This is not to say that patients with epileptic disturbances do not have relevant underlying psychodynamic conflicts which play a role in their behavioral disturbances. On the other hand, patients with documented grand mal epilepsy are shown to have their seizures triggered by repetitive and psychodynamically significant variables which act as stressors for the epileptic state (Feldman 1976). Patients with psychomotor epilepsy seem particularly vulnerable to certain psychological issues, and the entire topic of the epileptic personality is reviewed by Blumer (1974a). He describes the frontal lobe personality and the temporal lobe personality, and lists certain clinical characteristics that are typical of the personalities afflicted with these disorders. Bach-y-Rita (1971) describes the fact that many of his patients with episodic dyscontrol problems are psychodynamically vulnerable to abandonment and in this regard are quite homogeneous. Monroe (1970) stresses that psychotherapy is an important treatment modality for patients afflicted with episodic behavioral disorders, whether those disorders have a clear epileptic basis or not. Since these patients are liable to act without foresight and appear to have diminished capacity to premeditate the consequences of their acts, they require psychotherapeutic enlightenment with regard to the sequelae of their actions and the affective state accompanying their behavior in order more carefully to monitor what they do. Monroe (1970) speculates that there may be a physiologic short circuit between the stimulus and the response in patients with episodic behavioral disorders. That is, an adverse stimulus such as a verbal threat or insult impinging upon the patient, becomes translated into aggressive behavior without any cognitive awareness on the patient's part regarding the quality, nature, significance, or outcome of the act. This "epileptoid" short circuit precludes effective control of behavior. It is Lion's (1972) contention that the effective therapy of impulsive patients entails two processes. First, there is the need to teach such patients to fantasize effectively and to think about all aspects of their act from beginning to end. Many patients who are impulsive show an impoverished ability to fantasize, and do not cogitate on events within themselves, but translate any kind of adverse emotional state into detrimental behavior, be that behavior drinking, driving recklessly, or hitting the nearest available person. It thus becomes incumbent on the therapist to teach these patients how to fantasize and how to think about events and feelings in a way conducive to a full appreciation of the range of emotions; thus a necessary aspect of therapy is to teach patients afflicted with episodic behavioral disorders to become aware of their inner affective states. Many patients with episodic dyscontrol do not know when they are angry, and cannot identify the precursors to anger or the accompanying physical sensations, such as a pounding in the chest, tachycardia, sweating, "knot in the stomach," or other signs and symptoms indicative of rage. The failure of such patients to appreciate the accompanying physical sensations leads them to misidentify their own anger or perceive it only in a dimly global way. This in turn leads to steps, such as drinking or drug-taking, designed to squelch or suppress the unpleasant affective state. Sudden and impulsive overdoses for example, are described by Lion (1974a, 1974b, 1974c) as representative not of actual suicidal threats or gestures, but of sudden attempts to suppress unpleasant affective states. The patient with an episodic behavioral disorder must be taught to identify and tolerate adverse emotional states, as well as the conditions that give rise to them, as a prerequisite for verbal expression and a more effective means of coping with his environment.

Maletsky (1974) points out that the more complex problems of anxiety, chronic depression, marital conflict, and employment difficulties, which usually accompany aggressive outbursts, often persist after psychopharmacologic control of dyscontrol acts. For this reason, extensive psychotherapeutic intervention is a necessary adjunct to the medical regimen.

Summary

Although the label *episodic behavioral disorders* has not received general acceptance, there is an increasing distinction made between nonepisodic and episodic behavioral abnormalities. Neither has the subcategory of the episodic behavioral disorders, *episodic reactions* (neurotic, psychotic, psychophysiologic, and so on) found favor, but the other subcategory, namely *episodic dyscontrol* (dyscontrol behavior, dyscontrol acts) has become widely used.

In regard to the etiology of the episodic disorders it is accepted that these syndromes represent a complex interaction between intrapsychic, family, and social factors on the one hand and genetic, perinatal trauma, and CNS instability or seizural activity on the other.

Not only have the ictal characteristics of episodic behavioral symptoms been emphasized, but there is increasing recognition of signs or symptoms of minimal brain dysfunction as well as a history of childhood hyperactivity.

Many observers raise the issue of whether the more prolonged episodic reactions should be considered a "third" psychosis, that is one distinct from both schizophrenia and affective disorders. These prolonged episodic psychotic reactions are associated with confusional states with elements suggesting an acute brain syndrome.

There is increasing recognition that the dyscontrol acts are often aggressive outbursts towards others or towards the self, thus resulting in criminal behavior.

The current neurophysiologic data suggest that these episodic disorders reflect a focal or circumscribed ictal phenomenon in the limbic system. It remains unclear whether other systems are involved, but it is clear that this limbic dysfunction is usually not correlated with scalp EEG abnormalities. If there are scalp abnormalities, these are not limited to the temporal lobe. Those individuals with limbic dysfunctions usually do not give a history of typical epileptic seizures.

The episodic symptoms may be physiologic dysfunctions leading to perplexing somatic complaints often misdiagnosed as hypochondriasis, somatic delusions, or malingering, when in fact there is a real physiologic disequilibrium.

Long-term follow-up of neurosurgical procedures to modify episodic behavioral disorders, particularly aggression, have rarely indicated persisting clinical improvement. It is important, then, that individuals selected for such a drastic therapy should have a prolonged trial on medication with little or no clinical improvement before surgery is considered.

No single pharmacologic agent is ideally effective for this disorder but anticonvulsants including phenytoin, primidone, and carbamazepine have been reported as useful, as well as the benzodiazepines, particularly chlordiazepoxide and diazepam. It is also reported that lithium is useful. In some instances the tricyclics may be effective and in other instances by virtue of lowering the seizural threshold they will aggravate behavioral abnormalities and even precipitate overt epilepsy. The neuroleptics or major tranquilizers often aggravate symptoms in these individuals.

Chronic difficulties associated with episodic symptoms such as anxiety, depression, marital conflicts, and employment difficulties require psychotherapeutic intervention even if there is psychopharmacologic control of the episodic symptoms.

References

Ajmone-Marsan, C., and Zivin, L.S. 1970. "Factors related to the occurrence of typical paroxysmal abnormalities in the EEG records of epileptic patients," *Epilepsia,* 11:361.

Altshuler, K.Z., Abdullah, S., and Rainer, J.D. 1977. "Lithium and aggressive behavior in patients with early total deafness," *Dis. Nerv. Syst.,* 38:521.

Andy, O.J., Jurko, M.F., and Hughes, J.R. 1975. "Amygdalotomy for bilateral temporal lobe seizures," *Southern Med. J.,* 68:743.

Andy, O.J. 1976. "Psychomotor-psychic seizures treated with bilateral amygdalotomy and orbitotomy," *Southern Med. J.,* 69:88.

Bach-y-Rita, G., Lion, J.R., and Ervin, F. 1970. "Pathological intoxication: Clinical and electroencephalographic studies," *Amer. J. Psychiat.,* 127:698.

Bach-y-Rita, G., Lion, J.R., Climent, C., and Ervin, F.R. 1971. "Episodic dyscontrol: A study of 130 violent patients," *Amer. J. Psychiat.,* 127:1473.

Ballantine, H.T., Jr., Cassidy, W., Flanegan, N., and Morino, P. 1967. "Stereotaxis anterior cingulotomy for neuropsychiatric illness and intractable pain," *J. Neurosurg.,* 26:488.

Bandura, A. 1973. *Aggression: A social learning analysis.* Englewood Cliffs: Prentice-Hall.

Belford, B. 1976. "Electrophysiological basis for dichotomy in schizophrenia," *Psychological Reports,* 39:591.

Bellak, L. 1976. "A possible subgroup of the schizophrenic syndrome and implications for treatment," *Amer. J. Psychother.,* 21:194.

Blumer, D. 1974a. "Organic personality disorders," in Lion, J.R. (Ed.). *Personality Disorders: Diagnosis and Management.* Baltimore: Williams & Wilkins.

Blumer, D.P., Williams, H.W., and Mark, V.H. 1974b. "The study and treatment, on a neurological ward of abnormally aggressive patients with focal brain disease," *Confin. Neurol.,* 36:125.

Brazier, Mary A.B., Crandall, P.H., and Lieb, J.P. 1975. "Effects of diazepam and phenobarbitol on cortical limbic system EEG in temporal lobe epileptics," *Neurol.,* 4:396.

Brown, M.H. 1977. "Multi-target neurosurgery in the treatment of schizophrenia and violence," *The Psychiatric Journal of the University of Ottawa,* 2:29.

Bruens, J.H. 1971. "Psychoses in epilepsy," *Psychiat. Neurol. Neurochir.,* 4:175.

Chandler, D.B. 1973. "Towards a classification of violence," *Sociological Symposium*, 9:69.

Climent, C., et al. 1973. "Epidemiological studies of women prisoners. I: Medical and psychiatric variables related to violent behavior," *Amer. J. Psychiat.*, 130:985.

Conners, C.R., et al. 1971. "Treatment of young delinquent boys with diphenylhydantoin sodium and methylphenidate," *Arch. Gen. Psychiat.*, 24:156.

Connolly, F.H., and Gittleson, N.L. 1971. "The relationship between delusions of sexual change and olfactory and gustatory hallucinations in schizophrenia," *Brit. J. Psychiat.*, 119:551.

Dalby, M.A. 1971. "Antiepileptic and psychotropic effects of carbamazepine (Tegretol) in the treatment of psychomotor epilepsy," *Epilepsia*, 14:105.

Daniels, D.N., Guilila, M.F., and Ochberg, F.M. 1970. *Violence and the struggle for existence.* Boston: Little, Brown.

Davies, R.K., Neil, J.F., and Himmelhoch, J.M. 1975. "Cerebral dysrhythmias in schizophrenics receiving phenothiazines: Clinical correlates," *Clin. Electr.*, 6:103.

Davison, K. 1964. "Episodic depersonalization observations on 7 patients," *Brit. J. Psychiat.*, 110:505.

Delgado, J.M.R. 1959. "Modification of social behavior induced by remote-controlled electrical stimulation of the brain," *Abstracts 21st Intern. Physiol. Congress Aviation.*

Dempsey, G.M., Tsuang, M.T., Struss, A., and Dvoredsky-Wortsman, A. 1975. "Treatment of schizo-affective disorder," *Compr. Psychiat.*, 16:55.

Diagnostic and Statistical Manual of Mental Disorders: Draft (January 15, 1978), Task Force on Nomenclature and Statistics, American Psychiatric Assoc., Washington, D.C.

Elliott, F.A. 1976. "The neurology of explosive rage. The dyscontrol syndrome," *Practitioner*, 217:51.

_____. 1977. "Propranolol for the control of belligerent behavior following acute brain damage," *Ann. Neurol.* 1:489.

Ervin, F.R., and Lion, J.R. 1970. "Clinical evaluation of the violent patient," in *Crimes of violence.* Washington, D.C.: National Commission on the Causes and Prevention of Violence, Vol. 11-13, Staff Study Series. U.S. Government Printing Office.

Ervin, F.R. 1973. "Violence and brain disease," *JAMA*, 226:1463.

Falconer, M.A. 1972. "Place of surgery for temporal lobe epilepsy during childhood," *Brit. Med. J.*, 2:631.

_____. 1973. "Reversibility by temporal lobe resection of the behavioral abnormalities of temporal lobe epilepsy," *New Eng. J. Med.*, 289:451.

Fawcett, J. 1971. *Dynamics of violence.* Chicago: American Medical Association.

Feldman, R.G., and Paul, N. 1976. "Identity of emotional triggers in epilepsy," lecture delivered at the University of Maryland School of Medicine.

Felthouse, A.R. and Yudowitz, B. 1977. "Approaching a comparative typology of assaultive female offenders," *Psychiatry*, 40:270.

Fenton, G. 1974. "Straightforward EEG in psychiatric practice," (Review of bibliog.), *Proc. Roy. Soc. Med.*, 67:911.

Ferguson, M. 1973. *The brain revolution.* New York: Taplinger.

Flor-Henry, P. 1969. "Psychosis and temporal lobe epilepsy: A controlled investigation," *Epilepsia*, 10:363.

_____. 1972. "Ictal and interictal psychiatric manifestations in epilepsy: Specific or non-specific?" *Epilepsia,* 13:773.

Flor-Henry, P., and Yeudall, L. 1973. "Lateralized cerebral dysfunction in depression and in aggressive criminal psychopathy: Further observations," *Int. Res. Com. System,* July.

Flor-Henry, P. 1974. "Psychosis, neurosis and epilepsy," *Brit. J. Psychiat.,* 124:144.

Freides, D. 1976. "A new diagnostic scheme for disorders of behavior, emotions, and learning based on organism environment interaction," Part I and II, *Schizo. Bull.,* 2:218.

Garattini, S., and Sigg, E.B. 1969. *Aggressive behavior.* Proceedings of the International Symposium on the Biology of Aggressive Behavior, Instituto Di Ricerche Farmacologiche "Mario Negri," Milan, 2-4 May. New York: John Wiley and Sons.

Gestaut, H., Courjon, J., Poire, R., and Weber, M. 1971. "Treatment of status epilepticus with a new benzodiazepine more active than diazepam," *Epilepsia,* 12:197.

Gibbs, F., Heimberger, R., Lorier, F., and Stevens, J. 1972. "Roundtable discussion: Violent behavior and the electroencephalogram," *Clin. Electr.,* 3:180.

Gloor, P. 1975. "Electrophysiological studies of the amygdala," in Fields, W.S., and Sweet, W.D. (Eds.). *Neural Bases of Violence and Aggression.* St. Louis: Warren H. Green.

Glowinski, H. 1973. "Cognitive deficits in temporal lobe epilepsy," *J. Nerv. Ment. Dis.,* 157:129.

Goddard, C.U. 1972. "Long term alteration following amygdala stimulation," in Eleftheriou, B.E. (Ed.). *Neurobiology of the Amygdala.* New York: Plenum Publishing.

Goldstein, M. 1974. "Brain research and violent behavior," *Arch. Neurol.,* 30:1.

Green, R., and Rau, J. 1974. "Treatment of compulsive eating disturbances with anticonvulsant medication," *Amer. J. Psychiat.,* 131:428.

Guggenheim, F.G., and Haroutin, M.B. 1974. "Catatonic schizophrenia: Epidemiology and clinical course," *J. Nerv. Ment. Dis.,* 158:291.

Gunn, J., and Fenton, G. 1969. "Epilepsy in prisons: A diagnostic survey," *Brit. Med. J.,* 4:326.

Hanley, J., et al. 1972. "Automatic recognition of EEG correlates of behavior in a chronic schizophrenic patient," *Amer. J. Psychiat.*, 128:1524.

Hanlon, T. 1973. Personal communication.

Hara, M., Yamaguchi, T., Takahashi, K., Kanno, O., Ishida, T. Norma, I., Kajiwara, A., and Imamura, I. 1971. "Schizophrenic-like symptoms with seizure discharges." *Electroenceph. Clin. Neurophysiol.*, 31:188.

Haward, L.R.C. 1969. "Differential modifications of verbal aggression by psychotropic drugs," in Garattini, S., and Sigg, E.B. (Eds.). *Aggressive behavior.* New York: John Wiley and Sons.

Heath, R.G. 1954. *Studies in schizophrenia.* Cambridge: Harvard University Press.

_____. 1962. "Common characteristics of epilepsy and schizophrenia: Clinical observation and depth electrode studies," *Amer. J. Psychiat.*, 118:11.

_____. 1972. "Pleasure and brain activity in man," *J. Nerv. Ment. Dis.*, 154:3.

_____. 1973. "Marijuana: Effects on deep and surface electroencephalograms of rhesus monkeys," *Neuropharm.*, 12:1.

_____. 1977. "Modulation of emotion with a brain pacemaker." *J. Nerv. Ment. Dis.*, 165:300.

Heimburger, R.F., et al. 1966. "Stereotaxic amygdalotomy for epilepsy with aggressive behavior," *JAMA*, 198:741.

Hess, R., Scollo-Lavizzari, C., and Wyss, F.E. 1971. "Borderline cases of petit mal status," *Eur. Neurol.*, 5:137.

Hill, D. 1944. "Cerebral dysrhythmia: Its significance in aggressive behavior," *Proc. Roy. Soc. Med.*, 37:317.

_____. 1952. "The EEG in episodic, psychotic, and psychopathic behavior," *Electroenceph. Clin. Neurophysiol.*, 4:419.

Hitchock, E., and Carins, V. 1973. "Amygdalotomy," *Postgrad. Med. J.*, 49:894.

Ifabumuyi, O.I., and Jeffries, J.D. 1976. "Treatment of drug-induced psychosis with diphenylhydantoin," *Can. Psychiatric Assoc. Journal,* 21:565.

Jensen, I. 1975a. "Temporal lobe epilepsy. Late mortality in patients treated with unilateral temporal lobe resections," *Acta Neurol. Scand.*, 52:374.

_____. 1975b. "Genetic factors in temporal lobe epilepsy," *Acta Neurol. Scand.*, 52:381.

Kelly, D. 1973. "Psychosurgery and the limbic system," *Postgrad Med. J.*, 49:825.

_____. 1976. "Psychosurgery in the 1970's," *Brit. J. Hosp. Med.*, 8:165.

Kick, H., and Dreyer, R. 1973. "Clinical procedures with clonazepam under particular conditions of psychomotor epilepsy," (abstract) *Acta Neurol. Scand.*, 49:54.

Kiloh, L.G., et al. 1974. "Stereotactic amygdaloidotomy for aggressive behavior," *J. Neurol. Neurosurg. Psychiat.*, 37:437.

Kling, A. 1975. "Brain lesions and aggressive behavior of monkeys in free living groups," in Fields, W.S., and Sweet, W.D. (Eds.). *Neural Bases of Violence and Aggression.* St. Louis: Warren H. Green.

Langfeldt, G. 1969. "Schizophrenia: Diagnosis and prognosis," *Behav. Sci.,* 14:173.

Legg, N.J., and Swash, M. 1974. "Clinical note: Seizures and EEG activation after trimipramine," *Epilepsia,* 15:131.

Levi, R.N., and Waxman, S. 1975. "Schizophrenia, epilepsy, cancer, methionine, and folate metabolism. Pathogenesis of schizophrenia," *Lancet,* 2:11.

Lieberman, D.M., Hoenig, J., and Hacker, M. 1954. "The metrazol-flicker threshold in neuropsyhiatric patients," *Electroenceph. Clin. Neurophysiol.,* 6:9.

Lion, J.R. 1969a. "Violent patients in the emergency room," *Amer. J. Psychiat.,* 125:1706.

_____. 1972. "The role of depression in the treatment of aggressive personality disorders," *Amer. J. Psychiat.,* 129:347.

_____. 1973. "Brain dysfunction among violent patients," Proc. of the NINDS Advisory Council on Neurological Basis of Abnormal Behavior.

_____. 1974a. *Personality disorders: Diagnosis and management.* Baltimore: Williams and Wilkins.

Lion, J.R., Bach-y-Rita, G., and Ervin, F. 1969b. "Enigmas of violence," (letter to the editor) *Science,* 164:1465.

Lion, J.R., Azcarate, C., Christopher, R., and Arana, J. 1974b. "A violence clinic." *Md. State Md. J.,* 23:45.

Lion, J.R., and Penna, M. 1974c. "The study of human aggression," in Whalen, R.E. (Ed.). *Neuropsychology of Aggression.* New York: Plenum Publishing.

Lion, J.R., and Monroe, R.R. 1975a. "Drugs in the treatment of human aggression," *J. Nerv. Ment. Dis.,* 160:75.

Lion, J.R., Hill, J., and Madden, D.J. 1975b. "Lithium carbonate and aggressions: A case report," *Dis. Nerv. Syst.,* 36:97.

Lion, J.R., Madden, D., and Christopher, R.L. 1976. "A violence clinic: Three years' experience," *Amer. J. Psychiat.,* 133:432.

Livingston, S., Pauli, L., and Berman, W. 1974. "Carbamazepine (Tegretol) in epilepsy," *Dis. Nerv. Syst.,* 35:103.

Lorimer, F.M. 1972. "Violent behavior and the electroencephalogram," *Clin. Electr.,* 3:193.

MacMurray, J. 1973. "Aggression, schizophrenic reactions and epilepsy: Some transcultural correlations," *Int. J. Soc. Psychiat.,* 19:25.

Maletsky, B.M. 1973. "The episodic dyscontrol syndrome," *Dis. Nerv. Syst.,* 34:178.

Maletsky, B.M., and Klotter, J. 1974. "Episodic dyscontrol: A controlled replication," *Dis. Nerv. Syst.,* 35:175.

Marinacci, A.A. 1963. "Special type of temporal lobe seizure following ingestion of alcohol," *Bull. Los Angeles Neurol. Soc.,* 28:241.

Mark, V.H., and Ervin, F.R. 1970. *Violence and the brain.* New York: Harper & Row.

Mark, V.H., Sweet, W., and Ervin, F.R. 1975. "Deep temporal lobe stimulation and destructive lesions in episodically violent temporal lobe epileptics," in Fields, W.S. and Sweet, W.D. (Eds.). *Neural bases of violence and aggression.* St. Louis: Warren H. Green.

McCabe, M.S., and Stromgren, E. 1975. "Reactive psychoses: A family study," *Arch. Gen. Psychiat.,* 32:447.

McCabe, M.S., and Cadoret, R.J. 1976. "Genetic investigations of atypical psychoses. I. Morbidity in parents and siblings," *Compr. Psychiat.,* 17:347.

Mignone, R.J., Donnelly, C.F., and Sadowsky, D. 1970. "Psychological and neurological comparisons of psychomotor and non-psychomotor epileptic patients," *Epilepsia,* 11:345.

Milstein, V., and Small, J. 1971. "Psychological correlates of 14 & 6 positive spikes, 6/sec. spike-wave, and small sharp spike transients," *Clin. Electr.,* 2:206.

Mitsuda, H. 1967. *Clinical genetics in psychiatry: Problems in nosological classification.* Tokyo: Igaku Shoin.

Mitsuda, H. and Mukuda, T. (Eds.). 1974. *Biological mechanisms of schizophrenia and schizophrenia-like psychoses.* Tokyo: Igaku Shoin.

Monroe, R.R. 1959. "Episodic behavior disorder-schizophrenia or epilepsy," *Arch. Gen. Psychiat.,* 1:205.

Monroe, R.R., Goulding, R., Kramer, M., and Wise, S. 1965a. "EEG activation of patients receiving phenothiazines and/or chlordiazepoxide," *J. Ment. Nerv. Dis.,* 141:100.

Monroe, R.R., and Wise, S. 1965b. "Combined phenothiazine, chordiazepoxide and primidone therapy for uncontrolled psychotic patients," *Amer. J. Psychiat.,* 122:694.

Monroe, R.R. 1970. *Episodic behavioral disorders.* Cambridge: Harvard University Press.

_____. 1974. "Episodic behavioral disorders," (Chapter II), in Arieti, S., and Brody, E.B. (Eds.). *American handbook of psychiatry.* New York: Basic Books.

Morgan, B.M., and Scott, D.F. 1970. "EEG activation in epilepsies other than petit mal," *Epilepsia,* 11:255.

Morrison, J.R., and Minkoff, K. 1975. "Explosive personality as a sequel to the hyperactive-child syndrome," *Compr. Psychiat.,* 16:343.

Musella, L., Wilder, B.J., and Schmidt, R.P. 1971. "Electroencephalographic activation with intravenous methohexital in psychomotor epilepsy," *Neurology,* 21:594.

Narabayashi, H. 1975. "Stereotaxic amygdalotomy," in Eleftheriou, B.E. (Ed.). *The neurobiology of the Amygdala.* New York: Plenum Publishing.

Narabayashi, H., et al. 1963. "Stereotaxic amygdalotomy for behavior disorders," *Arch. Neurol.,* 9:1.

Narabayashi, H., and Mizutani, T. 1970. "Epileptic seizures and the stereotaxic amygdalotomy," *Confin. Neurol.,* 32:289.

Nelson, G.K. 1974. "Neuropsychological research approaches in the epilepsies," *S. Afr. Med. J.,* 48:657.

Niedermeyer, E., et al. 1971. "The diagnostic significance of sleep EEG's in temporal lobe epilepsy. A comparison of scalp and depth tracings," *Electroenceph. Clin. Neurophysiol.,* 31:197.

Olson, S.F., and Hughes, J.R. 1970. "The clinical symptomatology associated with the 6 c/sec spike and wave complex," *Epilepsia,* 11:383.

Papatheophilou, R., James, S., and Orwin, A. 1975. "Electroencephalographic findings in treatment-seeking homosexuals compared with heterosexuals: A controlled study," *Brit. J. Psychiat.,* 127:63.

Pinel, J.P. J., Mucha, R.F., and Phillips, A.G. 1975. "Spontaneous seizure generated in rats by kindling: A preliminary report," *Physiol. Psychol.,* 3:127.

Pines, M. 1973. *The brain changers. Scientists and the new mind control.* New York: Harcourt Brace Jovanovich.

Pinto, A., Simopoulos, A.M., Uhlenhuth, E.H., and DeRosa, E.R. 1975. "Responses of chronic-schizophrenic females to a combination of diphenyl-hydantoin and neuroleptics: A double-blind study," *Compr. Psychiat.,* 16:529.

Planansky, K. and Johnston, R. 1977. "Homocidal aggression in schizophrenia man," *Acta Psychiat. Scand.,* 55:65.

Post, R.M., and Kopanda, R.T. 1976. "Cocaine, kindling and psychosis," *Amer. J. Psychiat.,* 133:627.

Ramamurthi, B., et al. 1970. "Stereotaxic ablation of the irritable focus in temporal lobe epilepsy," *Confin. Neurol.,* 32:316.

Reynolds, E.H. 1968. "Epilepsy and schizophrenia: Relationship and biochemistry," *The Lancet,* 2:398.

Richardson, D.E. 1972. "Stereotaxic cingulumotomy and profrontal lobotomy in mental disease," *Southern Med. J.,* 65:1221.

Rickels, K., and Downing, R. 1974. "Chlordiazepoxide and hostility in anxious outpatients," *Amer. J. Psychiat.,* 131:442.

Rim, C.S., Rodin, E.A., Kitano, H., Rennick, P.M., and Lewis, R. 1975. "Relative effectiveness of primidone versus carbamazepine in the treatment of psychomotor and grand mal epilepsy," *Neurology,* 4:394.

Rodin, E., Onuma, T., Wasson, S. Porzak, J., and Rodin, M. 1971. "Neurophysiological mechanisms involved in grand mal seizures induced by Metrazol and Megimide," *Electroenceph. Clin. Neuro-physiol.,* 30:1.

Rodin, E.A., Rim, C.S., Kitano, H., Lewis, R., and Rennick, P.M. 1976. "A comparison of the effectiveness of primidone versus carbamazepine in epileptic outpatients," *J. Nerv. Ment. Dis.,* 163:41.

Satterfield, J., et al. 1974. "Intelligence, academic achievement, and EEG abnormalities in hyperactive children," *Amer. J. Psychiat.,* 131:391.

Schvarcz, J.R., Driollet, R., Rios, E., and Betti, O. 1972. "Stereotactic hypothalamotomy for behavior disorders," *J. Neurol. Neurosurg. Psychiat.,* 35:356.

Shagass, C. 1976. "An electrophysiological view of schizophrenia," *Biol. Psychiat.,* 11:3.

Shah, S.A., and Roth, L.H. 1974. "Biological and psychophysiological factors in criminality," in Glaser, D. (Ed.). *Handbook of criminology.* Chicago: Rand McNally, 103-173.

Sheard, M. 1971. "Effects of lithium on human aggression," *Nature,* 230:113.

Shearer, M., and Finch, S. 1964. "Periodic organic psychosis associated with recurrent Herpes Simplex," *New Eng. J. Med.,* 271:494.

Sigal, M. 1976. "Psychiatric aspects of temporal lobe epilepsy," *J. Nerv. Ment. Dis.,* 163:348.

Simopoulos, A.M., et al. 1974. "Diphenylhydantoin effectiveness in treatment of chronic schizophrenics," *Arch. Gen. Psychiat.,* 30:106.

Simpson, G.M., Varga, E., and Haner, E.J. 1976. "Psychotic exacerbations produced by neuroleptics," *Dis. Nerv. Syst.,* 37:367.

Singh, M.M. 1976. "Dysphoric response to neuroleptic treatment in schizophrenia and its prognostic significance," *Dis. Nerv. Syst.,* 37:191.

Slater, E. 1965. "The schizophrenic-like psychoses of epilepsy," *Int. J. Psychiat.,* 1:6.

Small, I. 1977. Personal communication.

Small, J.G., Sharpley, P., Milstein, V., and Small, I. 1976. "Research diagnostic criteria and EEG findings in schizophrenia," *Electroenceph. Clin. Neurophysiol.,* 40:322.

Small, L. 1973. *Neuropsychodiagnosis in psychotherapy.* New York: Brunner-Mazel.

Smith, S., et al. 1973. "EEG and personality factors in baby batterers," *Brit. Med. J.,* 3:20.

Standage, K.F., and Fenton, G.W. 1975. "Psychiatric symptom profiles of patients with epilepsy: A controlled investigation," *Psychol. Med.,* 5:152.

Stevens, J.R. 1964. "Central and peripheral factors in epileptic discharge: II. Experimental studies in the cat." *Arch. Neurol.,* 11:463.

Stevens, J.R., and Milstein, V. 1970. "Severe psychiatric disorders of childhood (EEG and clinical correlates)," *Amer. J. Dis. Child.,* 120:182.

Stevens, J.R. 1973. "An anatomy of schizophrenia?" *Arch. Gen. Psychiat.,* 29:177.

Struve, F.A., Becka, D.R., and Klein, D.F. 1972a. "B-mitten patterns and process and reactive schizophrenia," *Arch. Gen. Psychiat.,* 26:189.

Struve, F.A., Klein, D.F., and Saraf, K.R. 1972b. "Electroencephalographic correlates of suicide ideation and attempts," *Arch. Gen. Psychiat.,* 27:363.

Struve, F.A., Saraf, K.R., Arko, R.S., Klein, D.F., and Becka, D.R. 1977. "Relationship between paroxysmal electroencephalographic dysrhythmia and suicide ideation and attempts in psychiatric patients," in Gershon, S., and Shagass, C. (Eds.). *Psychopathology and brain dysfunction.* New York: Raven Press.

Sweet, W.H., Ervin, F.R., and Mark, V.H. 1969. "The relationship of violent behavior to focal cerebral disease," in Garattini, S., and Sigg, E.B. (Eds.). *Aggressive behavior.* New York: John Wiley and Sons.

Trautman, E.C. 1961. "The suicidal fit (a psychobiologic study on Puerto Rican immigrants)," *Arch. Gen. Psychiat.,* 5:98.

Tunks, E.R., and Dermer, S.W. 1977. "Carbamazepine in the dyscontrol syndrome associated with limbic system dysfunction," *J. Nerv. Ment. Dis.,* 164:56.

Tupin, J.P. 1972. "Lithium use in nonmanic depressive conditions," *Compr. Psychiat.,* 13:209.

Tupin, J.P., Mahar, D., and Smith, D. 1973. "Two types of violent offenders with psychosocial descriptors," *Dis. Nerv. Syst.,* 34:356.

Uhlenhuth, E.H., et al. 1972. "Diphenylhydantoin and phenobarbital in the relief of psychoneurotic symptoms," *Psychopharm.,* 27:67.

Valenstein, E.S. 1973. *Brain Control: A critical examination of the brain stimulation and psychosurgery.* New York: John Wiley and Sons.

Vernet, K., and Madsen, A. 1970. "Stereotaxic amygdalotomy and basofrontal tractotomy in psychotics with aggressive behavior," *J. Neurol. Neurosurg. Psychiat.,* 33:858.

Waxman, S.G., and Geschwind, N. 1975. "The interictal behavior syndrome of temporal lobe epilepsy," *Arch. Gen. Psychiat.,* 32:1580.

Wells, C.E. 1975. "Transient ictal psychosis," *Arch. Gen. Psychiat.,* 32:1201.

Westermeyer, J. 1973. "On the epidemicity of amok violence," *Arch. Gen. Psychiat.,* 28:873.

Wilder, B. 1971a. "Electroencephalogram activation in medically intractable epileptic patients: Activation technique including surgical follow-up," *Arch. Neurol.,* 25:415.

Wilder, B.J., et al. 1971b. "Activation of spike and wave discharge in patients with generalized seizures," *Neurol.,* 21:517.

Williams, D. 1969. "Neural factors related to habitual aggression: Consideration of differences between those habitual aggressives and others who have committed crimes of violence," *Brain,* 92:503.

Yeudall, L.T. 1977. "Neuropsychological assessment of forensic disorders," *Can. J. Public Health,* 25:7-15.

3

Goals and Methods of the Study: A Two-dimensional Classification of Criminal Behavior

Russell R. Monroe,
George U. Balis,
John R. Lion, and
Matthew McDonald

The purpose of this study was to investigate whether a group of incarcerated recidivist aggressors could be described with more clinical relevance than heretofore available, utilizing a unique classification system. This system is based on Monroe's (1970) concept of the episodic behavioral disorders, particularly the subgroup, episodic dyscontrol (see Chapter 1). The objectives of this study were the following:

1. to test the validity of the proposed measures of dyscontrol behavior and of central nervous system instability. The two criterion variables tested were (1) the Monroe Dyscontrol Scale—a self-rating scale of impulsive behavior (see Chapter 6) and (2) the baseline and alpha chloralose-activated electroencephalogram—a measure of CNS stability (see Chapter 7);

2. accepting these measures as reliable to then investigate the characteristics of four groups of prisoners (see Chapter 8) to determine how well they fit the predicted characteristics based on Monroe's Classification (1970). This is summarized in Figure 3-1. The groups are tentatively labeled as follows: Group 1—high impulsivity, high CNS instability, "epileptoid" dynscontrol; group 2—high impulsivity, low CNS instability, "hysteroid" dyscontrol; group 3—low impulsivity, high CNS instability, "inadequate" psychopath; group 4—low impulsivity, low CNS instability, "pure" psychopath;

3. to test whether other groupings would be more parsimonious in explaining the clinical signs and symptoms of the episodic dyscontrol than the one hypothesized above (Chapter 9);

4. to test the clinical usefulness of this classification by measuring the therapeutic response to primidone (Mysoline), a drug known to raise the seizural threshold (Chapter 11);

5. to examine whether other procedures could replace our criterion variables or otherwise aid in distinguishing between epileptoid and hysteroid dyscontrol. For instance, we examined whether a neurologic scale could be developed that would aid in the discrimination (Chapter 10); or whether an

62

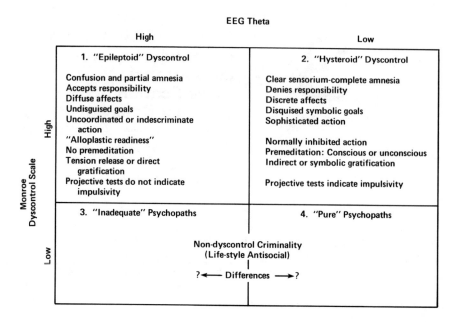

Figure 3-1. Predicted Characteristics in Episodic Disorders

MMPI scale would be sufficient for making this distinction (Chapter 8). We looked at the psychiatric history and current affect and behavior status as well as the value of previously established psychometric and projective tests for making this distinction. This study then consisted of hypotheses testing, as well as the empirical collection of new data.

The study was divided into four aspects: the preliminary data collection, Phase 1 and 2, periods of either drug or placebo therapy, and a follow-up evaluation (see Figure 3-2).

In selecting the rating instruments we wanted to encompass objective data such as serum drug levels (see Chapter 11); EEG data with both subjective and machine analyses (see Chapter 7); clinical neurologic data (see Chapter 10), particularly neurological signs of minimal brain dysfunction. Other clinical rating scales included psychiatric data (Current and Past Psychopathology Scales abbreviated as CAPPS) modified to include manifestations of episodic disorders; mood and affect scales; and the Lion symptom checklist. Self-ratings included the Monroe Dyscontrol Scale and MMPI. Infraction ratings and group therapy behavior ratings were provided by the staff of Patuxent (measuring instruments in Appendix A through F). The schedule of psychometric testing is illustrated in Figure 3-2 and the instruments described in Chapter 5 and Appendix B. This

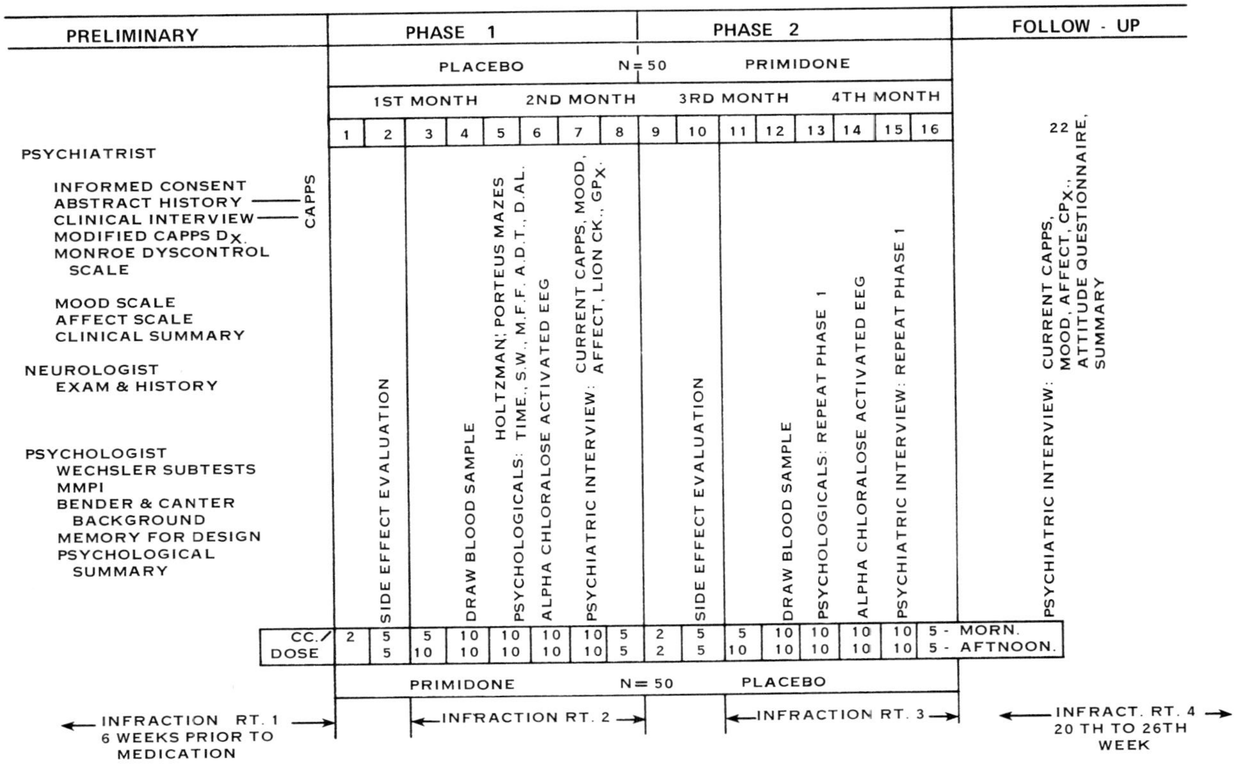

63

Figure 3-2. Research Flow Sheet

battery of measuring instruments resulted in over 700 individual variables collected on each of the 93 subjects. The number of variables was collapsed (roughly 200 variables) or expanded as necessary; the latter by item analyses of certain instruments, such as the MMPI.

The selection of instruments was partially determined by past studies so that comparisons could be made on the violent recidivists on previous Patuxent studies as well as with earlier research in similar (prison) or different (psychiatric ward) settings. Because of the novelty of the concept of episodic disorders, new tests were introduced (for example, Monroe Dyscontrol Scale) or old tests were given addenda that included the concept of the episodic disorders as a CAPPS Addenda (Appendix A). Some data utilized in our analysis were taken directly from the Patuxent Institution records and codified for computer analysis (for example, WAIS, infraction ratings); rarely, prison personnel were asked to score instruments provided by the research team such as the Group Therapist Rating Scale (see Appendix D). Some instruments were selected to collect baseline profiles on the subjects while other instruments were selected for their potential utility in detecting change during drug treatment. However, it was assumed that the repeated measure instruments could also be used for the baseline profile studies if one utilized the data collected in the placebo phase.

Preliminary Evaluation

A psychiatrist on the research staff, after obtaining informed consent, abstracted data from the subject's institutional record, translating this into numerical ratings on the CAPPS past history scale, rating specific symptoms or life events on an increasing severity scale of one to six with the option of question mark. This was followed by a sixty to ninety-minute interview with each subject for a current mental status examination (current CAPPS), as well as clarification of any questionable historical data. Again, this information was rated on a scale of one to six with the higher ratings representing more severe pathology. At the same time there was a specific elaboration of the symptoms of episodic dyscontrol, recording the frequency, duration, and severity of the dyscontrol acts, presence of premeditation, specificity of affect, type of affect represented during the impulsive act and coordination of act, as well as state of sensorium during the act and amnesia for the act. Furthermore, ratings were made as to the personal discomfort regarding dyscontrol behavior, the amount of responsibility the individual accepted for his actions, and the secondary gains that accrued from the dyscontrol act. Finally, prodromal symptoms, if present, were also rated for the dyscontrol behavior (see Appendix A CAPPS addenda).

The diagnosis on the CAPPS was modified to include a more detailed description of any epileptic phenomenon, the type of dyscontrol behavior (if present), and a global estimate with regard to whether or not the rater believed there was an epileptoid mechanism behind the aggressive behavior. The clinical psychiatric data also included a self-rating of dyscontrol behavior by the prisoner on eighteen statements rated on a four-point scale of "never," "rarely," "sometimes," or "often" which was developed by Plutchik (Monroe Dyscontrol Scale—see Chapter 6). Also included in the research records was a narrative social history which again was numerically scored to indicate the family structure of the prisoner, as well as a history of mental illness, antisocial behavior, alcoholism, or drug abuse, within this family structure.

Baseline psychological data included the WAIS which was collected by Institution personnel rather than the research staff. It included not only total IQ, verbal IQ, performance IQ, but also subtest scores. The baseline data also included the MMPI, the Bender Gestalt, (standard test and the interference procedure), the Memory for Design Test, as well as the infraction rating for the six weeks preceding the onset of the study (see Appendix E). Neurologic data were collected emphasizing not only the usual neurological history and examination but attempting, wherever possible, to collect detailed anamnestic data on birth trauma, head injury, seizures, school problems, explosiveness, repetitive dreams, and toxic psychosis. The examination emphasized motor coordination and hypersensitivity to external stimuli as well as handedness, birth marks, scars, and so on (see Chapter 10).

As already mentioned, tests given in Phase 1 and Phase 2, when the subject was on placebo, were also utilized in developing a baseline profile of the subjects.

Phase 1 and Phase 2

Phase 1 and Phase 2 (Figure 3-2) were exact replicas of each other, and the tests utilized were such as to reveal the effect of a drug regimen of primidone medication with blood samples and urine samples necessary for monitoring compliance (see Chapter 11). During Phase 1 and 2, half the subjects were randomly assigned to placebo-drug sequence; thus, the patients functioned as their own control. The study was double-blind. The battery of measuring instruments began with the fifth week on medication. According to blood serum analysis of primidone levels, in most instances subjects attained therapeutic levels in the second week and all had attained them by the third week. Thus, before the measures were taken, the subjects had been on primidone (Mysoline) for four weeks with effective blood levels for at least two to three weeks. During the fifth week of the study the subjects completed the Matching Familiar Figures test, the Porteus Mazes, slow writing task, time estimation, draw-a-line, and the Auditory Discrimination Task (ADT) test, as well as the Holtzman Inkblot which was divided (split-half) into two parts, one given to the subject in Phase 1 and the other in Phase 2. During the sixth week, an activated EEG was given to each subject. During the seventh week, psychiatrists on the research team completed a second current CAPPS (mental status) and as well as a symptom checklist (Lion checklist) indicating possible positive and negative effects from the medical regimen. The group therapist who saw the subject once a week also completed a questionnaire on the subject's behavior in the therapeutic setting. Mood and affect scales (Appendix C) were utilized in rating each subject during the mental status examination, not only during the preliminary period but also during Phase 1, 2, and during the follow-up period.

Follow-Up

In the follow-up period the psychiatrist completed another current CAPPS rating, as well as mood-affect questionnaires. The group therapist again rated the subject's behavior in therapy. Also obtained was a checklist (see Chapter 4) regarding the subject's perception of the experiment and reasons for participation. Specific methodological considerations will be discussed in the appropriate chapters which follow.

4

Problems and Issues in Prison Research
John R. Lion,
Russell R. Monroe,
and *Jeffrey S. Rubin*

In general, the problems of utilizing prisoners as research subjects revolve around their potential for giving informed consent. Recent guidelines proposed by HEW prohibit investigations on prison populations unless

(A) Study of the possible causes, effects, and processes of incarceration, provided that the study present minimal or no risk and no more than inconvenience to the subjects;

(B) Study of prisons as institutional structures or of prisoners as incarcerated persons, provided that the study presents minimal or no risk and no more than inconvenience to the subjects; or

(C) Research on practices, both innovative and accepted, which have the intent and reasonable probability of improving the health and well-being of the subject.

(D) Except as provided in paragraph (a) of this section, biomedical or behavioral research conducted or supported by DHEW shall not involve prisoners as subjects (Federal Register 1978).

This research project was a study of the causes of incarceration and whether the medication utilized might benefit the individual prisoner. Specifically, unlike research where new drugs are tested for toxicity or where inmates are given infectious agents to test the virulence of such agents or the efficacy of antibiotics or vaccines, our protocol was designed to isolate, understand, and possibly treat aggressive patients who wanted help with impulse control. Despite these aims, subjects were not assured of any help from the experimental findings; we told them that, at best, one quarter to one third of volunteers might be helped.

While the subjects were told that the drug under study, primidone (Mysoline), was available to any individual on a physician's prescription for the treatment of epilepsy, they were also informed that its use to treat impulsive disorders or individuals in a prison setting was considered experimental.

All members of the research team, except the EEG technician, were entirely disassociated from the Patuxent Institution itself, and hence had no authority roles vis-a-vis the prisoners. The research design was such that the institutional authorities knew who was participating in the study; however, they were not informed as to the criteria for selection of subjects; therefore, the prison administration had no way of knowing (unless the prisoner himself reported it) who had refused to participate in the study or whom we had rejected. There was

67

no rational way for the institutional personnel to retaliate against those who did or did not participate. If anything, there might have been unofficial pressure on inmates not to participate as it complicated the security system, but the administration usually cooperated and made special arrangements to facilitate the mechanics of the study.

Confidentiality of records was assured in that the material, collected under research code, was stored in the principal investigator's office at the University of Maryland. Information so obtained would only be supplied to the inmate himself or to someone he designated, such as his lawyer. If any communication was to be made with the institution, a letter would be prepared and reviewed by the subject for his approval. A copy of that communication would also be given to the subject himself. During the course of the study there was no pressure by the institution to receive any data.

Just as the research design was complicated, so was the procedure for obtaining informed consent. Most likely, the first few subjects who participated did not fully comprehend the study details despite our efforts to explain its mechanics and implications. However, inasmuch as only two subjects entered the study per week, the later subjects were aware of the study mechanics since there was communication between inmates who had progressed through the study.

We took advantage of the fact that subjects had already undergone extensive psychiatric, neurologic, electroencephalographic, and psychological evaluations prior to the court hearing to explain the part of the research program that was similar to their initial evaluation. We asked for permission to review the material already in their files and also pointed out that we would be requesting information regarding their participation in group therapy.

Use of alpha chloralose to activate the EEG is an experimental procedure. Alpha chloralose has been known for over seventy years and used as a sedative in Europe. However, it is not approved for use by the FDA in this country and the principal investigator required an IND exemption for clinical trials. The "experimental" nature of the drug was explained to prospective subjects. Further information regarding alpha chloralose was presented to the prisoner as follows. Prisoners knew that in a routine EEG it was necessary to get a sleep record and many had taken sedatives during previous EEGs. It was explained that alpha chloralose was a sedative used routinely in the principal investigator's laboratories, that subjectively they were likely to feel drowsy, go to sleep, or experience sensations similar to a "high" from alcohol. We explained that some subjects developed muscle twitches occasionally involving all four extremities, and that at times individuals were confused, disoriented, and poorly coordinated after the procedure. We pointed out that if they had such a reaction, they would be held in the hospital area until recovery. Additionally, they were told that they would be seen by a physician, and that such a reaction could be terminated by giving another medication. As the study progressed, several individuals had such reactions and reported this to other inmates. However, this had little bearing on inmate participation or discontinuation. One individual expressed hostility because termination of this reaction involved parenteral use of chlordiazepoxide (Librium). He was assured that if such a reaction occurred a second time, he would simply be allowed to sleep it off.

The most difficult information to present to the inmates was the detailed description of the medication primidone (Mysoline) and its possible side effects. Again, inmates had some familiarity with these problems from previous participation in other drug studies involving phenytoin (Dilantin). We explained the use of primidone for the treatment of epilepsy and the possibilities of its effectiveness for certain individuals who got into trouble because of a hyperexcitability or hyperirritability of the central nervous system. We pointed out that subjects might experience some mildly unpleasant side effects such as nausea, dizziness, or sleepiness and that rarely medical complications could be serious enough so that the drug would have to be discontinued. Again, we stressed that if a subject felt ill or feared such complications, a research physician was on call at all times and we would be sure that the subject received adequate medical attention. No individual had a serious reaction to the drug; in 3 subjects medication was discontinued temporarily because of unexplained and unrelated symptoms such as fever, generalized aches, rash, and so on.

Patuxent Institution required yearly physical examinations, although many times inmates refused to cooperate. Before a subject entered the study he had to undergo a physical examination. The research team reviewed hospital and medical records and if there were any complicating physical illnesses found on examination or previous history, the inmate was rejected as a candidate.

We assured the individual that participation in this study would neither speed nor delay his release from the institution and also that if he were released while under a medical regimen based on this study, the research team would assume responsibility for continued outpatient treatment.

In obtaining informed consent, three persons were always present; the subject, the research physician, and an auditor witness. The auditor witness followed a checklist of the various points that had to be covered in obtaining informed consent. The permission form was then signed by the subject, the requesting physician, and the auditor witness. Occasionally several prisoners, up to 4 in a group, were briefed and presented the consent forms simultaneously.

No inmate, including those who dropped out of the study for whatever reasons, complained to the investigators that they had been duped or that the program was misrepresented. While the study was underway there was a prison riot with the taking of hostages. One of the complaints directed toward the institution concerned experimentation on prisoners, particularly our study, as it was the only study in progress at that time. However, no participant in the study complained or participated in the riot. Rather, study participants were resentful of this complaint because they felt it interfered with their civil right to volunteer.

Prisoners were paid for their participation. It was felt to be justified and not a form of unnecessary coercion. Most of the inmates in the institution had jobs with monetary remuneration. Although they could not possess money in their own pockets, it would be credited to their accounts and utilized to purchase personal luxuries and supplies. Pay for study participation was in addition to that received for usual prison job assignments. Originally, subjects were paid fifty cents per day for the period of participation, with a twenty-dollar bonus at completion. As there were objections to this bonus as representing unnecessary or unfair coercion, the payment had to be modified in the middle of the project. However, we felt we could not in any way significantly change the ultimate remuneration received. The modification included payment of fifty cents per day for each day on medication (or placebo) as well as ten dollars for the predrug-period work-up and ten dollars for the follow-up period. Total payment amounted to sixty dollars. We did not feel that the payment unduly influenced the prisoners into entering or continuing their participation in the study.

Two hundred and twenty-two patients were asked to participate in this study. Only overt psychoses (1 subject) and complicating drug regimens or physical illness (2 subjects) were contraindications for admission to the study group. One hundred sixty-two signed informed consent although 69 (43 percent) discontinued during the course of the study (discussed later).

At the completion of the study, we gave a questionnaire (Table 4-1) to 88 of a total of 93 inmate participants who completed the project and interviewed them individually to discuss their attitudes toward research. Five prisoners were not given the questionnaire because this instrument was designed after they had finished participation in the project. Either we could not interview them due to unavailability (work release) or we felt that their comments would not be valid because several months had elapsed. We did not feel justified in studying the sample of inmates who refused involvement in the research project. To have done so would have been viewed by both inmates and staff as coercive and we were fearful of jeopardizing the research project by such a maneuver. The same policy was followed for inmates who dropped out of the study, although their reasons are summarized in Table 4-2. With these reservations, then, our sample was "unselected."

Table 4-1, "Follow-up Interview Questionnaire," was utilized to collect the prisoners' explicit reasons for participating in this study. They were asked to select one answer for each of the three subgroups which elicited reasons for (1) agreeing to participate in the project, (2) remaining in the study, and (3) what they objected to most regarding the study. This was followed by four true-false questions that were of particular interest to us. Perhaps the bottom line was most significant in that 92 percent said that they would be willing to participate in a subsequent study, although we did not test their sincerity by initiating a second project. The fact that one-fifth to one-sixth still did not understand the project at the end of their participation and a similar number had

Table 4-1
Follow-up Interview Questionnaire

1. *I agreed to participate in this research study because:*
   (88 respondents)
   A. I am bored and want a change in the routine (5%)
   B. I want the money (23%)
   C. I want to find out what, if anything, is wrong with me (35%)
   D. I want to help out with research that may help others (24%)
   E. I hope that the medication will make me feel better (10%)
   F. I want to take the special medication associated with the brain wave (3%)

2. *I remained in this study because:*
   (86 respondents)
   A. I need the money (29%)
   B. The medication helps me (16%)
   C. I never quit anything once I begin (27%)
   D. Someone is pressuring me to stay (1%)
   E. I enjoy the attitudes of the investigators (27%)

3. *The one thing I object to most in the study is:*
   (76 respondents)
   A. Interviews with the investigators (6%)
   B. Psychological testing (12%)
   C. Brain wave (16%)
   D. Neurological examination (0%)
   E. Blood tests (18%)
   F. Coming up to the hospital twice a day (28%)
   G. The effects of the medication (20%)

True-false statements (88 respondents)
1. I feel that my participation will help me get out of Patuxent faster (True – 18%; False – 82%)
2. On occasions, I deliberately have not taken my medication (True – 17%; False – 83%)
3. I do not understand the purpose of this research project (True – 15%; False – 85%)
4. I would be willing to participate in another study (True – 92%; False – 8%)

ulterior motives, that is getting out of the institution, and showed noncompliance with regard to medication, probably reflects the exploitative, rebellious, and uneducated character of some of our research population. Perhaps the fact that these fractions are so small is the significant finding.

Item 1 reflecting the reasons subjects entered the project indicates that 45 percent (C + E) were seeking help. This finding has been reported by others (Monroe 1970, Ervin 1973), namely that impulsive subjects often do want help. Twenty-four percent expressed altruistic motives, while an equal number

Table 4-2
Volunteer "Drop Outs"

Reason	No. of Subjects
Physical illness	1
Legal risk	1
Released or due to be released	9
No record available	1
Did not reliably take drug	1
Did not reliably come for interviews	3
Determined to be psychotic	3
Study deadline prevented completion	2
Escaped	1
Died	1
Alleged drug side effects	17
Miscellaneous personal reasons	29
Total	69

admitted to a desire for money as a primary reason for cooperating. Only 8 percent (A + F) admitted to ulterior or spurious motivation.

Item 2 indicates that money remained a significant motivation for continuing in the study. It did seem to the investigative team that they had good rapport with the prisoners and this seems to be reflected in response E. The relatively high number of responses to selection C, "I never quit anything once I begin," is difficult to explain because it certainly does not reflect their social behavior prior to incarceration. However, we do find that the rigid controls of the institution reduce impulsivity even in those where we presume there is a significant neurophysiologic mechanism behind the impulsivity. Thus, these external controls may modify attitudes, at least during the confinement.

Section 3 indicates the diversity of objections to the experimental procedure. Inasmuch as the neurologist was the one female on the research team, perhaps it is significant that none objected to the neurological examination. The objections to a twice-daily trip to the hospital was justified because this was a complicated procedure requiring passes at numerous checkpoints, as well as locked doors. It would sometimes take one-half to three-quarters of an hour for each trip to the dispensary where the medication was given.

A total of 69 (Table 4-2) out of a pool of 162 volunteers dropped out or were dropped by us during some phase of the study. One patient had multiple physical complaints and one died of cancer. One patient was litigious and was already filing suit against another researcher who had carried out a drug study at the facility several years earlier. Three patients were felt by us to be psychotic subsequent to signing the consent form but prior to the taking of medication and were dropped from the study. A total of 17 patients alleged various drug side effects. We could not establish whether the side effects were related to the drug or not in the majority of the cases; in some instances, gastrointestinal disturbances, a common side effect with this type of drug, were present. In other instances, inmates were subsequently found to have the "flu" or "colds." In no instance was any side effect of sufficient degree to warrant medical attention beyond simple discontinuance of the medication. A total of 29 patients left the study for reasons having to do with personal inconvenience, "change of mind," or fear of medication. In the majority of these cases, inmates refused to give any reason at all beyond notifying us of their refusal to continue in the project.

Our research project then involved a high number of inmates who dropped out, but a larger number who remained in the study and stated that they had financial, inquisitive, and altruistic motives for participation. Objections to the research were varied and had primarily to do with inconvenience. Despite such behavior, the vast majority of participants expressed sentiments in favor of becoming involved in a future research project.

The subject of prisoner participation in research has been reviewed by Ayd (1972) who has described the financial motives as well as the issue of inmate prestige and status derived from research involvement. While we did not specifically query inmates on this latter issue, our subjective impression would not support this notion. Ayd has also discussed the fact that participation in research yields the inmate greater access to the physician and better health care; in the Patuxent facility, there is daily contact with a member of the medical staff and free access to health needs so that, at least in our case, such a reason for participation is not valid. McDonald (1967) has commented on an "esprit de corps" that develops among prisoners involved in research. Again, while we did note some group cohesiveness and personal involvement of inmates with research staff, we do not feel that the research group had the solidarity described by McDonald as representative of volunteers in medical research.

We do, however, concur with Ayd's description of what he terms the "spiritual" motives for research participation. By this he means the positive and long-lasting value of having done something "good" for medical research or society, an experience that often stands out in the minds of individuals who otherwise have an intensely diminished sense of self-esteem. Our own feelings in this regard is that research involvement, even if it does not lead to any direct enhancement of self-esteem, does offer some measure of dignity deriving from a contact with professional persons which is otherwise often lacking in their lives.

At the present time, there is much scientific sentiment directed against research in general (McDonald 1967). Bach-y-Rita (1974) has recently questioned the validity of any prison research and raised the issue of whether or not consent in research can ever really be informed in a coercive setting. There is no doubt that numerous overt and covert forces exist which exert duress on a prisoner to participate in research. However, it has recently been pointed out that the state of our knowledge (APA 1974) of the clinical parameters of violent individuals must progress, and we submit that such gains require study of those persons who find their ways into the prison system. To this end, we perceive prison research as essential. If carried out in a manner conducive to self-respect and privacy, it permits participation in projects that raise personal and scientific consciousness.

References

Ayd, F.J. 1972. "Motivations and rewards for volunteering to be an experimental subject," *Clin. Pharmacol. Ther.*, 13:771-778.

Bach-y-Rita, G. 1974. "The prisoner as an experimental subject," *JAMA*, 229:45-46.

Clinical aspects of the violent individual. 1974. American Task Force Report #48, American Psychiatric Association, Washington, D.C.

Lion, J.R., and Monroe, R.R. 1974. "Future hazards for clinical research," (editorial) *J. Nerv. Ment. Dis.*, 158:397-398.

McDonald, J.C. 1967. "Why prisoners volunteer to be experimental subjects," *JAMA*, 202:511-512.

"Protection of human subjects: Proposed regulations on research involving prisoners." 1978. *Federal Register*, 43:3, January 5.

Demographic and Clinical Characteristics of Subjects
John R. Lion,
Russell R. Monroe,
and *Jeffrey S. Rubin*

Patuxent Institution is a special treatment unit combining psychiatric care with maximum security. The inmates, after having been sentenced for a crime, are sent by court order to the institution for diagnostic evaluation and then returned to the court where the decision is made as to commitment as a "defective delinquent" with indeterminate sentences (see Preface). It is assumed, on the basis of their past record, that without such special intervention these recidivist aggressors would immediately transgress upon being released from a conventional prison. After being housed on a maximum security level during diagnostic procedures, inmates work their way toward a second, third, and finally a fourth level, attaining increasing privileges and freedom on each level. The main treatment modality is group therapy, although some may receive individual psychotherapy and occasionally pharmacologic regimens. The therapeutic regimen is continued during their work release and parole status.

The typical prisoner at Patuxent Institution is an individual with a history of repeated violent criminal behavior. Ostensibly, there is little to differentiate these individuals from those found at any maximum security prison in terms of the nature of their acts and their general demeanor within the institution. Table 5-1 summarizes the crimes that resulted in their current incarceration. The mean of previous incarcerations for this group was at least 4.2 (19 inmates had eight or more). Many of these individuals (88 percent) had been either in training schools, prisons, or state hospitals prior to arriving at Patuxent. In fact, 40 percent had spent more than five years in such facilities. The average period of incarceration at the Patuxent Institution had been five and a half years, although the average length of sentence is far longer. Finally, it should be noted that over 80 percent of this population had committed seven or more antisocial acts and 90 percent of these acts resulted in at least work incapacity, incarceration, or permanent damage to self or others.

The demographic data on the study population were abstracted from both institutional files and from in-depth interviews with the inmates. Although portions of the clinical data originated from the institutional records of the prisoners, all information was verified and rated by the research psychiatrists during initial interviews. All psychometric data were collected during the study period by the research psychologist except for the Wechsler Adult Intelligence Scale which was abstracted from records.

Table 5-1
Criminal Offenses

Offense	No. of Subjects
Assault to murder	7
Rape	10
Attempted rape	2
Assault to rape	1
Carnal knowledge	1
Assault to carnally know	2
Indecent exposure	1
Perverted practice	8
Assault on child	1
Assault and battery	4
Assault	3
Narcotics laws	1
Abduction	1
Robbery	5
Robbery with a deadly weapon	20
Assault to rob	3
Explosives violation	1
Arson	4
Burglary	7
Breaking and entering	3
Housebreaking	2
Storehouse breaking	2
Rogue and vagabond	1
Grand larceny	1
Auto larceny	1
Ambiguous	1
Total	93

Source: Table 1 from Russell R. Monroe, et. al., "Neurologic Findings in Recidivist Aggressors," in *Psychopathology and Brain Dysfunction* edited by C. Shagass, S. Gershon, and A.J. Friedhoff © 1977 by Raven Press, New York, p. 242. Reprinted by permission.

Column 1 of Table 5-2 summarizes the demographic data of our subjects, illustrating that this population was relatively young (under thirty-five years of age), single, with a majority having no more than a grammar school education, and mostly unskilled employees. Of the 93 subjects, 62 percent were white, 37 percent black, and 1 percent Indian.

In reviewing the family backgrounds of the subjects, we noted that the head of the household was usually identified as the natural father or mother of the inmate, although the availability of the parents was low and they were rarely

Table 5-2
Comparison of Demographic Data

	Patuxent Population N = 93 %	Endicott Population N = 800 %
Age		
19-24	34.4	40.1
25-34	45.2	29.9
35-44	16.3	14.1
45-54	4.4	8.0
Sex		
Male	100.0	41.1
Marital Status		
Single	68.8	45.8
Married	12.9	34.6
Separated	12.9	4.2
Divorced	5.4	5.6
Race		
White	62.4	80.5
Black	36.6	10.2
Other	1.1	1.1
Education		
College grad.	1.1	17.5
High school grad.	3.2	22.1
10-11 yrs.	12.9	10.9
7-9 yrs.	45.2	8.2
Less than 7 yrs.	36.6	1.7
Uncoded	1.1	7.9
Occupation		
Minor executive	2.2	10.0
Clerk, technician	3.3	16.4
Skilled manual	6.5	3.7
Semiskilled employee	21.7	3.1
Unskilled employee	55.4	4.5
Not working	7.6	— ⎫
Uncoded	3.3	— ⎬ 39.6
Missing	1.1	— ⎭
Diagnosis		
Organic brain syndrome	1.1	0.4
Schizophrenia	1.1	36.5
Neurosis	3.3	17.1
Personality disorders	92.6	22.1

Source: Portion from Jean Endicott and Robert Spitzer, "Current and Past Psycho-pathology Scales (CAPPS): Rationale, Reliability, and Validity," Table 2 *Archives of General Psychiatry*, 27:680 © 1972 by American Medical Association. Reprinted by permission.

functioning as rearing figures. Most often, a female relative or nonrelative was the person who reared the inmate. Alcoholism among rearing fathers was high, as was mental illness. There was a history of criminal activity in 46 percent of the rearing fathers. Generally, the occupation of the head of household was lower administrative, clerical, skilled, or semiskilled worker. The majority had education below that of high school level. The families from which the inmates came were large, containing four or more siblings and/or a larger number of half- or step-siblings. Family histories revealed a propensity toward criminal behavior in the siblings. Interestingly, parental education was somewhat higher than that of their children, that is, our subjects.

In general, the physical health of this group was good. Psychiatric diagnosis is summarized in Table 5-3 with most of the subjects having a diagnosis of personality disorders, sexual deviation, alcoholism, or drug dependency. Overt psychotics with criminal behavior were sent to another institution.

Table 5-3
Diagnoses of Subject Population

Diagnosis	No. of Subjects*
Mental retardation	3
Epilepsy	1
Psychoses	1
Neuroses	3
Personality disorders	
True personality disorders	
Paranoid personality	1
Schizoid personality	10
Explosive personality	10
Antisocial personality	44
Passive-aggressive personality	21
Sex deviations	
Homosexuality	3
Pedophilia	9
Exhibitionism	1
Other sex deviation	4
Alcoholism	
Episodic excessive drinking	13
Habitual excessive drinking	5
Alcohol addiction	1
Narcotic drug dependence	15

Source: Table 2 from Russell R. Monroe, et al., "Neurologic Findings in Recidivist Aggressors," in *Psychopathology and Brain Dysfunction* edited by C. Shagass, S. Gershon, and A.J. Friedhoff © 1977 by Raven Press, New York, p. 243. Reprinted by permission.
*Some subjects had multiple diagnoses.

The assessment of psychiatric adjustment and social behavior was evaluated by the research psychiatrists using the Current and Past Psychopathology Scales (CAPPS—see Appendix A). The CAPPS consists of items related to present illness as well as to past psychiatric history, rated on an increasing severity scale of one to six. During the analysis phase of this project, we made use of the individual items of the CAPPS to present a clinical picture of the population. These items are presented in Tables 5-4, 5-5, 5-6, and 5-7, organized in four major areas: neurotic symptoms, psychotic symptoms, antisocial behavior, and social ineptness. In these tables, the six-point scale was dichotomized by the "absent to mild" and "moderate to severe" categories. Where the item was rated in both the psychiatric history and the mental status, the table reflects the duplication under the headings of Past CAPPS and Present CAPPS. One notices that there are very few neurotic symptoms except for anxiety, hypochondriasis, depression and suicidal thoughts, stubbornness, and inhibited anger (Table 5-4). In Table 5-5 the only possible psychotic symptom of any note is suspiciousness. Table 5-6 lists antisocial behavioral patterns, indicating that in most instances,

Table 5-4
Neurotic Symptoms

Symptom	Past CAPPS		Present CAPPS	
	Absent to Mild %	Moderate to Severe %	Absent to Mild %	Moderate to Severe %
Anxiety	84	16	84	15
Agitation			93	7
Mood swings	99			
Elation	99		97	3
Phobias	96	2	100	
Obsessive-compulsive traits	96	1	99	1
Hypochondriasis	89	5	88	12
Psychophysiologic reaction	94	5	93	7
Conversion reaction	96	1	100	
Fatigue	96	2		
Anorexia, weight loss	100			
Lack of enthusiasm	93	4	98	2
Guilt	91	3	96	4
Insomnia	97	3		
Depression	85	10	96	4
Suicidal thoughts	85	11	98	2
Sullenness, pouts	91	3		
Stubbornness	75	18		
Inhibited anger	90	10		

Table 5-5
Psychotic Symptoms

Symptom	Past CAPPS		Present CAPPS	
	Absent to Mild %	Moderate to Severe %	Absent to Mild %	Moderate to Severe %
Memory, orientation impaired	98		100	
Speech incoherent	97	2	100	
Appearance disheveled	95			
Silliness			98	1
Abnormal posturing			99	
Retardation movement, speech	96	2	94	5
Inappropriate affect			98	1
Amnesia, fugue, dissociative state	93	5		
Depersonalization	92	2		
Religiosity	99			
Grandiosity	97	3	94	6
Ideas of reference	96	4	100	
Suspiciousness	82	16	95	5
Illusions	94	2		
Delusions	95	5	99	1
Hallucinations	95	1	100	

half or more of the subjects were rated moderate to severe in these categories. This was also true for the symptoms and behavior of social ineptness as listed in Table 5-7.

We supplemented the CAPPS with an addenda that characterized dyscontrol behavior and found the following. Sixty-nine percent of the subjects stated that often to always their aggressive acts were premeditated while 31 percent claimed that the acts never or only occasionally were premeditated. The emotions expressed during the antisocial acts were moderate to severe aggression in 55 percent of the individuals while fear and panic were the predominant emotions in only 8 percent of the subjects. Sexual feelings were the prominent affect in 23 percent. The motor behavior during the act was uncoordinated and thrashing in nature in 14 percent of the subjects. Over 69 percent of the subjects claimed some confusion during antisocial acts. Only 17 percent of the population assumed full responsibility for their behavior and only 21 percent showed significant discomfort regarding their antisocial acts.

Regarding prodromal feelings of our subjects for the acts, the CAPPS addenda yielded valuable information. Twenty-six percent of the subjects claimed moderate to severe irritability or frustrations prior to the dyscontrol

Table 5-6
Antisocial Behavior

Behavior	Past CAPPS		Present CAPPS	
	Absent to Mild %	Moderate to Severe %	Absent to Mild %	Moderate to Severe %
Anger, temper	43	55		
Violence, assaultiveness	45	55		
Hostility, belligerence			91	9
Antisocial acts	17	83		
Antisocial attitude	30	70	74	14
Sexual deviation	81	19	86	9
Impulsivity	40	58		
Overreactiveness	59	41		

acts, and another 17 percent claimed moderate to severe motor restlessness. Twenty-three percent reported moderate to severe anger immediately prior to the acts, with 16 percent admitting to intense sexual feelings.

The individual items of the CAPPS have been grouped by Endicott and Spitzer (1972) into clinically recognizable syndromes on both the current and past history. These scales are presented in Table 5-8. For the purposes of our study, we eliminated from analysis those individual items not applicable to our study sample. The basis for excluding an item was determined by the criteria of 85 or more of the 93 subjects receiving a rating of one on the six-point scale and none of the remainder scoring beyond three on that item. The items not included in the analysis are indicated by an asterisk on Table 5-8. This deletion in the scale items was done after the profiles were formulated (Figures 5-1 and 5-2). The items deleted relate to affective, schizophrenic, or organic brain syndrome symptoms.

Utilizing these data to compare our research sample with a normal and psychiatric population upon whom Endicott and Spitzer established profiles, we can compare psychiatric data for our subjects to Spitzer's "normals" by looking at the profiles of Figure 5-1 (see page 86). The first point to note is that the present CAPPS shows very little pathology in the Patuxent population and is quite comparable to the pathology shown on mental status examinations of a nonpatient population. This suggests that in the controlled environment of the prison setting, deviant behavior is relatively infrequent; the external controls exerted within the prison result in reasonably controlled behavior in a group that otherwise (when on the street) is quite deviant.

The deviancy of the Patuxent population shows up as greater in the past CAPPS and more so on intellectual performance than in any other area. This is not a reflection of marked deviation in IQ since in our population the mean

Table 5-7
Social Ineptness

| | Past CAPPS | |
Behavior	Absent to Mild %	Moderate to Severe %
Unduly concerned with work	98	
Brooding	84	8
Adaptation to stress	33	66
Poor judgment	22	78
Self-defeating attitude	25	75
Lack responsibility	41	58
Capacity for pleasure	37	62
Superficial/excessive involvement activities	81	15
Poor adult friendship patterns	25	66
Unduly sensitive to people	75	22
Emotionally unresponsive	75	18
Dependency on others	85	12
Passive-aggressive	70	26

WAIS full scale was 88.5, mean verbal 90.3, and mean performance 90.7, but rather an overall evaluation of school performance and the efforts of the individual to improve his social status.

As might be expected, the next most deviant scale is impulse control, a category that includes antisocial behavior, impulsiveness, poor judgment, and lack of responsibility. In comparison with the norms, our subjects also were rated poorly on social-sexual relations, dependency, anger-excitability, and sexual disturbance, giving a very typical picture of what would appear to be a homogenous, antisocial group. This must be kept in mind when one evaluates intergroup differences later in our study.

Figure 5-2 compares the psychiatric profiles of the Patuxent study group with a psychiatric inpatient population. One notices that in terms of current functioning our population is more normal than inpatients and, in fact, in terms of past history does not deviate dramatically from the psychiatric inpatient group except in terms of impulsiveness and intellectual performance.

The remainder of this chapter describes the psychological test data collected on all 93 subjects. The data presented here include means and standard deviations as well as normative data, when available.

MMPI

The MMPI was administered on audio tape with the research psychologist present to answer questions and make sure the subject was answering the right question. The 566 items were completed in two one hour and fifteen-minute sessions. The standard scores of the Patuxent sample are represented in Figure 5-3, a theoretical picture of the study population in terms of MMPI inference. The personality "type" described below is a clinical picture of a group of individuals which has been transposed to a single prototype that reflects the group as a whole.

Turning first to the validity scales, one notes that the L score does not reflect a deliberate attempt to deny having socially unacceptable impulses, feelings, thoughts, and behavior; yet at the other extreme it does not indicate that the respondent is completely frank and candid. The F score results indicate admittance to some unusual and strange experiences, and the F elevation is found with individuals diagnosed as severe character or behavioral disorders or more intact psychotics. These individuals acknowledge some disturbances in the way they see the world about them and how they function in this world. The elevation on this scale reflects problems with impulse control, individual nonconformity, and conflicts with family and society, along with moderate feelings of alienation. There is also the suggestion of some peculiar or idiosyncratic thinking. The K scores indicate, however, an orientation not to appear emotionally or psychologically weak, inept, or vulnerable, with an attempt to deny serious self-dissatisfaction. The level of sophistication reflected is that of an individual with no more than high school education and coming from a socio-economic status of middle to lower class. The validity scales do not indicate gross or significant distortion and indicate that the clinical scales are likely to be an accurate self-description of these individuals.

Prominent in the clinical profile is the fact that these individuals are likely to be rather immature, impulsive, and rebellious men who are narcissistic and self-centered. They tend to act more on immediate need than on mature reflection. Their frustration tolerance is low and they are generally restless, adventurous, and high risk-takers. They tend to "leap before they look" and their social and practical judgment seems impaired by needs for immediate gratification. Noteworthy is their repeated difficulties with authority figures. They harbor resentment and hostility for authority figures whom they generally oppose and view in a derisive and disparaging manner. They have poor parental relations and are generally labeled delinquent by the family even as youngsters. They lack feelings of empathy and trust in others. They are flippant in manner and quick to antagonize. Characteristically they avoid accepting responsibility for their repeated difficulties with the law, and consistently offer rationalizations or project the blame for their problems onto others. They show a general callous disregard for the feelings or rights of others and are blatantly manipulative. Even mild anxiety or tension is difficult for them to tolerate and they frequently have problems involving drugs and alcohol. They tend to act out their discomfort and generally show dyscontrol problems. They are at times superficially personable and friendly, but are extremely unreliable and also unpredictable. Resenting any limits placed on them, they respond with temper outbursts when crossed.

Table 5-8
Current and Past Psychiatric Rating Scales

Current Scales

C1– *Reality testing–social disturbance*
    Social isolation
    Suspicion-persecution
    Hallucinations*
    Belligerence-negativism
    Delusions*
    Denial of illness

C2– *Depression-anxiety*
    Anxiety
    Depression
    Suicide-self-mutilation
    Daily routine-leisure time
    Agitation-excitement

C3 *Impulse control*
    Alcohol abuse
    Narcotics-drugs
    Antisocial attitudes or acts
    Sex deviation

C4– *Somatic concern-functioning*
    Somatic concerns
    Conversion reaction*
    Psychophysiologic reactions

C5– *Disorganization*
    Dissociation*
    Retardation-lack of emotion
    Speech disorganization*
    Disorientation-memory*

C6– *Obsessive-guilt-phobic*
    Phobia
    Guilt
    Obsessions-compulsions

C7– *Elation-grandiosity*
    Elated mood
    Grandiosity
    Inappropriate affect, appearance, behavior*

Past Scales

P1– *Depression-anxiety*
    Tired, lack of energy*
    Appetite or weight loss*
    Insomnia
    Brooding
    Depression
    Guilt
    Suicidal thoughts, gestures, attempts
    Anxiety
    Loss of interest, enjoyment
    Agitation, restlessness
    Painful relations

P2– *Impulse control*
    Antisocial child
    Nonacademic school difficulties

P2– *Impulse control* (cont.)
    No occupational goals and plans
    Narcotics-drugs
    Alcohol abuse
    Illegal acts
    Antisocial traits
    Impulsive
    Poor judgment
    Self-defeating behavior
    Lack of responsibility

P3– *Social sexual relations*
    Adolescent friendship pattern
    Adolescent sexual adjustment
    Adult heterosexual adjustment
    Adult friendship pattern
    Emotionally unresponsive
    Pleasure capacity

Table 5-8 (cont.)

P4— *Reality testing*
Suspicious
Religious metaphysical preoccupation
Grandiosity
Ideas of reference
Delusions*
Depersonalization*
Illusions*
Hallucinations*

P5— *Dependency*
Ineffectual adaptation to stress
Sensitive
Fluctuation in interpersonal
feelings
Dependency
Clinging
Passive-aggressive
Blames others

P6— *Somatic concern-functioning*
Physical health
Hypochondriasis
Psychophysiological reactions

P7— *Obsessive-compulsive*
Obsessions-compulsions*
Compulsive*
Unduly concerned with work*

P8— *Anger-excitability*
Emotional over-action
Histrionic
Sullen
Angry
Violent

P9— *Manic*
Elated mood, over-talkativeness
overactivity*
Alternating elation, sadness*
Superficial over-involvement

P10— *Sexual Disturbance*
Sexual perversion
Homosexual acts
Preoccupied with sex

P11— *Memory-orientation*
Memory-orientation*

P12— *Disorganized*
Speech disorganization*
Disheveled*
Eccentric*

P13— *Organicity*
CNS impairment
Epileptic attacks*

P14— *Neurotic childhood*
Neurotic childhood

P15— *Phobia*
Phobia

P16— *Retardation-stubborn*
Speech or motor retardation
Stubborn
Inhibited

P17— *Hysterical symptoms*
Amnesia, fugue, dissociation
Conversion reaction*

P18— *Intellectual performance*
Highest grade in school
Overall academic performance
Efforts to improve status
Estimated IQ

Source: Table 3 from Jean Endicott and Robert Spitzer "Current and Past Psycho-pathology Scales (CAPPS): Rationale, Reliability, and Validity," *Archives of General Psychiatry*, 27:681 © 1972 by American Medical Association. Reprinted by permission.
*Items eliminated after profiles obtained (see text).

86

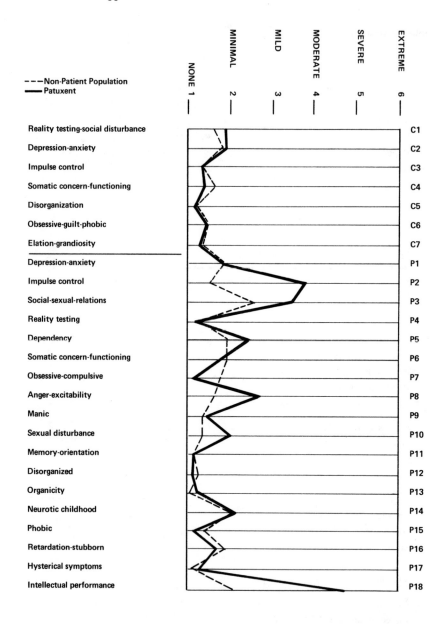

Source: Portion from Jean Endicott and Robert Spitzer, "Current and Past Psychopathology Scales (CAPPS): Rationale, Reliability, and Validity" *Archives of General Psychiatry*, 27:685. © 1972 by American Medical Association. Reprinted by permission.

Figure 5-1. Comparison of Endicott-Spitzer in a Nonpatient Population ($N = 87$) with Patuxent Study Population ($N = 93$)

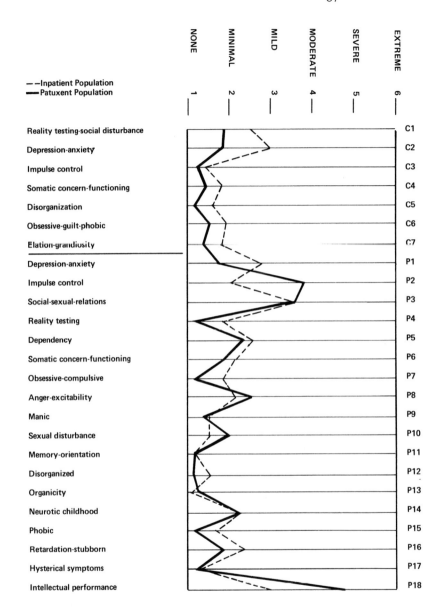

Source: Portion from Jean Endicott and Robert Spitzer, "Current and Past Psychopathology Scales (CAPPS): Rationale, Reliability, and Validity" *Archives of General Psychiatry*, 27:685. © 1972 by American Medical Association. Reprinted by permission.

Figure 5-2. Comparison of Endicott-Spitzer Inpatient Population (*N* =341) with Patuxent Study Population (*N* = 93)

88

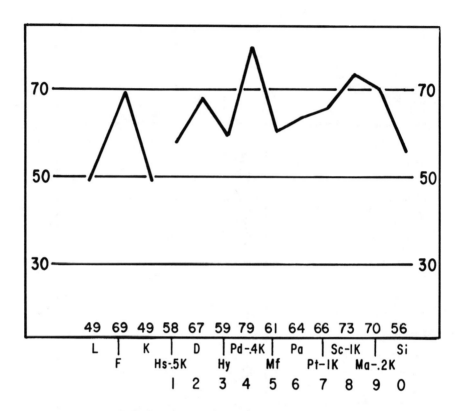

Figure 5-3. Mean MMPI Standard Scale Scores for Patuxent Population

There is a deficiency in ego and superego control, and these men don't seem to learn even from aversive experiences. They repeatedly tend to act with insufficient deliberation and poor judgment and they seem to be governed by the "pleasure principle." For them, to have an impulse is to act it out immediately, for these individuals generally have a rapid personal tempo and are usually not depressed with the exception of being slowed down or prevented from gratifying narcissistic needs, such as by being institutionalized. They seem to have exaggerated needs for affection and want, if not demanding attention, but at the same time are incapable of establishing the kind of emotional contact and commitment necessary for a true friendship or mature relationship. They generally avoid close interpersonal ties and keep others at a distance.

Although impaired in their practical judgment and social learning, their thinking appears intact. As a whole their school achievement has been below average.

One hundred percent of the time marital discord is reported for men with this particular pattern. One out of 10 men with this profile has been born illegitimately. One out of every three is responsible for the birth of illegitimate children himself, while close to one-fourth are responsible for illegal abortions.

Patients with this particular profile are typically reported as making "no response" to treatment. A high percentage of them also terminate treatment against their therapist's advice. The diagnosis associated with this group is antisocial personality.[a]

Memory for Designs

Errors for this test are classified as follows: 0-4 = normal, 5-11 = borderline, and 12 and over = brain damaged. The mean total error score for the population was 3.3 with a standard deviation of 5.4. A normal population of 43 subjects presented in the test manual indicates a mean error score of 2.1, (S.D. not available). Our correlational data indicate a positive correlation with CAPPS data on history of epileptic attacks, amnesia, fugues, dissociative states, prodromal irritability and poor coordination during the act, and EEG-activated theta. There is a negative correlation with CAPPS personal discomfort regarding the act, estimated nonepileptoid mechanism, and history of narcotics-drug abuse. Most of these are characteristics of dyscontrol behavior, but do not differentiate between "epileptoid" and "hysteroid" dyscontrol.

Canter Background Interference Procedure for the Bender Gestalt Test

The test manual indicates a formula for assessing organic brain damage using the "class score" as an overall estimate of brain damage. Sixty-nine subjects were classified as normal, 5 were borderline, and 19 were classed as brain damaged.

Although the great majority of our subjects are not classified as brain damaged, the actual shape of the distribution for class scores was somewhat bimodal with 25 percent of our subjects falling into the brain-damaged category and 74 percent falling into the normal category.

There were significant positive correlations of the Canter-Bender class score with the Monroe Dyscontrol Scale and the Group Therapist Questionnaire on physical hostility, and significant negative correlations with current antisocial attitudes or acts. These significant correlations lend themselves to the following interpretation: class score, which may be viewed as a measure of CNS integrity, positively correlates with dyscontrol both on a self-rating (Monroe Dyscontrol Scale) and behavioral assessment (Group Therapist Hostility Item) level, but

[a]This description of the group was provided by Lawrence Donner, Ph.D., Associate Professor of Psychiatry (Psychology), University of Maryland School of Medicine.

does not help separate out the true organic from the more subtle epileptoid subject.

Auditory Discrimination Task

The mean score on the quiet subtest for our subjects was 1.4 (S.D. 1.0) and on the noise subtest the mean score was 7.0 (S.D. 2.2). This compares with a normal adult mean of 0.4 (S.D. 5.7) on quiet subtest and 5.9 (S.D. 2.1) on a noise subtest.

On the whole our subjects do significantly poorer on both the quiet and noise subtest than do the normal adult population.

Slow Writing Task

This test has no normative data, so comparisons of performance will be made within our subject population. The mean time score was 42.5 seconds (S.D. 34.6). Significant positive correlations were found with a history of narcotics-drug abuse, current antisocial attitudes or acts, spike slow on EEG, and impulsiveness on the affect scale. A negative correlation was found with the Monroe Dyscontrol Scale.

Time Estimation Task

Although there exist no normative data on this test, we found a mean score in seconds of 45.0 (S.D. 17.8). Positive correlations with other data indicate that this estimation correlates with head injury, history of narcotics-drugs, and alcohol abuse, current antisocial attitudes or acts, spike slow on the EEG, and emotional lability on the affect scale. Negative correlations were found with a history of fluctuation of feelings.

Draw-a-Line

This test has no literature or normative data, being introduced in this study. It was considered to be similar to the time estimation task in that it is an estimate of a line one inch long. The mean for our population was 0.8 inches (S.D. 0.5).

Porteus Maze

A high test quotient reflects higher overall intelligence while a low quality score reflects better performance. The means of these two scores were 126.5 (S.D. 10.6) on test quotient and 11.8 (S.D. 10.1) on quality score.

Positive correlations with Porteus Quality Score exist with history of CNS disorders, epileptic attacks, amnesia-fugue-dissociative state, and guilt. Negative correlations exist with ratio: primary/secondary dyscontrol, history of narcotics-drugs, emotional lability and impulsiveness on the affect scale. Correlations between the Porteus Test Quotient and other data appear in analyses presented in Chapters 8 and 9.

Matching Familiar Figures

The mean reaction time for our subjects was 12.1 (S.D. 5.2) and the mean total errors were 4.2 (S.D. 2.2).

No normative data are available for this test. Positive correlations for the MFF reaction time were found with head injury, prodromal irritability, current suicide-self-mutilation, and 6 and 14 positive spike data on activated EEG.

Wechsler Adult Intelligence Scale (WAIS)

The WAIS was abstracted from the subject's institutional record. The mean IQs for our population were 90.3 (S.D. 14.6) for verbal, 90.7 (S.D. 26.8) for performance, and 88.5 (S.D. 26.6) for full scale.

Holtzman Inkblot Technique

Although the Holtzman Inkblot Technique was administered in an unorthodox fashion—that is, one half of the blots were administered in each of the two treatment regimens—for present purposes the scores obtained from these two administrations have been combined to make them roughly comparable to the scores that would have been obtained had the rules for administration been followed. The Patuxent subjects seemed to demonstrate an overly cautious approach to the testing situation. It was as if, if they were unsure, they did not act. There is an extraordinarily high preoccupation with sexual ideation which is not uncommon for a prison population. Furthermore, the high abstraction scores combined with relatively low scores on form definitiveness and form appropriateness, and popular responses suggest some real limits in the area of reality testing but not of psychotic proportions. Rather one could anticipate poor planning and coping in realistic life situations.

References

Canter, A. 1968. "The BIP-Bender Test for the detection of organic brain disorder: Modified scoring method and replication." *J. of Cons. Clin. Psycho.*, 32:522-526.

Davis, A. 1969. "Ego functions in disturbed and normal children: Aspiration, inhibition, time estimation, and delayed gratification." *J. of Cons. Clin. Psycho.*, 33:61-70.

Davis, K.R., and Sines, J.O. 1974. "An antisocial behavior pattern associated with a specific MMPI profile." *J. of Cons. Clin. Psycho.*, 36:2 229-234.

Endicott, J., and Spitzer, R.L. 1972. "Current and past psychopathology scales (CAPPS): Rationale, reliability, and validity." *Arch. Gen. Psychiat.*, 27:678-687.

Goldman, R., Fristoe, M., and Woodcock, R. 1970. *Test of auditory discrimination.* Minnesota: American Guidance Service.

Graham, F.K., and Kendall, B.S. 1946. *Memory for design test.* St. Louis: Washington University Press.

Holtzman, W.H., Thorpe, J.S., Swartz, J.D., and Herron, W.E. 1961. *Inkblot perception and personality.* Austin: University of Texas Press.

Kagan, J. 1965. "Impulsive and reflective children: Significant of conceptual tempo," in Krumboltz, J. (Ed.). *Learning and the educational process.* Chicago: Rand-McNally.

Kagan, J., Pearson, L., and Welsh, L. 1966. "Conceptual impulsivity and inductive reasoning." *Child Dev.*, 37:583 594.

Porteus, S.D. 1965. *Porteus Maze Test: Fifty years' application.* Palo Alto: Pacific Books.

Wechsler, D. 1958. *The measurement and appraisal of adult intelligence.* (4th edition). Baltimore: Williams and Wilkins.

6

Criterion of Dyscontrol: A Self-rating Scale

Russell R. Monroe

Plutchik (1976), on the basis of Monroe's monograph (1970), selected eighteen statements that patients often made regarding their episodic dyscontrol that seemed to represent "epileptoid" impulsive acts (Table 6-1). In actuality, Monroe considers that only three of these statements (items 3, 4, and 8) are characteristic of epileptoid impulsiveness, while item 13 reflects "hysteroid" impulsiveness. The other fourteen statements are common to both epileptoid and hysteroid impulsiveness. That the epileptoid mechanism is reflected by activated nonspecific theta waves (see Chapter 7) seems to be confirmed by a study of impulsive psychiatric patients referred to Monroe's EEG laboratory. However, this unpublished study in progress shows no correlation between activated generalized nonspecific theta and the Monroe Scale.

Plutchik's studies on 11 groups did show higher ratings on the Monroe Dyscontrol Scale among temporal lobe and nontemporal lobe epileptics than in other groups including violent self-referrals and male and female prisoners, as well as several control groups including psychiatric outpatients, college students, neurology patients, and pain patients (Figure 6-1). The scores on these various subgroups were somewhat different for the Feelings About Violence Scale (FAV) as indicated in Figure 6-2 showing that the dyscontrol scale measures something different than pure violence despite the presence of five items (7, 11, 12, 17, 18) on the Monroe Dyscontrol Scale that reflect overt violence (Table 6-1). Thus, episodic dyscontrol is by no means the same as violent behavior, although the two are often associated.

Plutchik then analyzed those data with separate intercorrelational matrices for each of 7 groups. These variables are listed in Table 6-2 with the correlations and the number of groups in which these correlations occur with the Monroe Dyscontrol Scale. This analysis shows a correlation with the violence scale and also a correlation with the MMPI schizophrenia scale, as well as a number of other factors indicating medical, sexual, and social deviance.

In our own population, a product-moment correlation was performed on the Monroe Dyscontrol Scale with two hundred and fifty variables consisting of both global and specific ratings, the neurologic examination, mental status material (Current CAPPS), characteristics of the dyscontrol behavior (CAPPS Addenda), and psychiatric history (Past CAPPS). The correlations seemed to confirm that the dyscontrol scale reflected an epileptoid impulsive action because a positive relation existed with primary dyscontrol, that is, primitive aggressive acts; with the global estimation of an epileptoid mechanism by the

93

Table 6-1
Monroe Dyscontrol Scale

1.	I have acted on a whim or impulse.
2.	I have had sudden changes in my moods.
3.	I have had the experience of feeling confused (even) in a familiar place.
4.	I do not feel totally responsible for what I do.
5.	I have lost control of myself even though I did not want to.
6.	I have been surprised by my actions.
7.*	I have lost control of myself and hurt other people.
8.	My speech has been slurred.
9.	I have had "blackouts."
10.	I have become wild and uncontrollable after one or two drinks.
11.*	I have become so angry that I smashed things.
12.*	I have frightened other people with my temper.
13.	I have "come to" without knowing where I was or how I got there.
14.	I have had indescribable frightening feelings.
15.	I have been so tense I would like to scream.
16.	I have had the impulse to kill myself.
17.*	I have been angry enough to kill somebody.
18.*	I have physically attacked and hurt another person.

Self-rating: never (0), rarely (1), sometimes (2), often (3)

Source: Appendix A from Russell R. Monroe, et al., "Neurologic Findings in Recidivist Aggressors," in *Psychopathology and Brain Dysfunction* edited by C. Shagass, S. Gershon, and A.J. Friedhoff © 1977 by Raven Press, New York. Reprinted by permission.
*Overt Violence Subscale.

psychiatrist; and with suspicion of possible epilepsy by the neurologist (Table 6-3, column 1).

Also, a number of symptoms such as somatic concerns and psychophysiologic reactions, as well as prodromal restlessness, hypochondriasis, and insomnia all suggest a possible preictal or ictal autonomic instability. It should be noted that individuals rating high on the Monroe Dyscontrol Scale also rated high in anxiety, depression, belligerence-negativism, agitation-excitement, and amnesia-fugue-dissociative states. Additionally, the impulsive behavior not only was considered more severe and aggressive but also was associated with prodromal restlessness, depression, and anger. There was a correlation with poor academic achievement and a lack of premeditation with regard to the acts themselves.

There was no correlation between the Monroe Dyscontrol Scale and activation ratings; however, there was a correlation between the Monroe Dyscontrol Scale and machine-analyzed alpha chloralose-activated theta frequency counts during the five-minute periods, pre-, during, and post-hyperventilation (see Chapter 7).

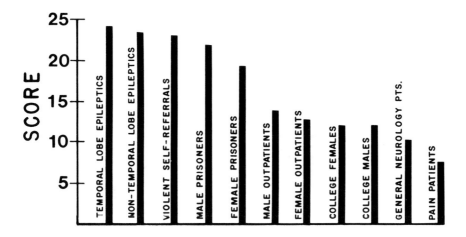

Source: Figure 3 from Robert Plutchik, Carlos Climent, and Frank Ervin, "Research Strategies for the Study of Human Violence," in *Issues in Brain/Behavior Control* edited by W. Lynn Smith and Arthur Kling © 1976 by Spectrum Publications, Inc., New York, p. 84. Reprinted by permission.

Figure 6-1. Mean Scores Obtained by Eleven Different Groups on the Monroe Dyscontrol Scale

Five of the eighteen items in the Monroe Dyscontrol Scale that reflect the admission of overt violent acts are

7. I have lost control of myself and hurt other people.
11. I have become so angry that I smashed things.
12. I have frightened other people with my temper.
17. I have been angry enough to kill somebody.
18. I have physically attacked and hurt another person.

These five items proved to be a relatively powerful subtest in that there were forty-nine significant correlations at the .05 level from two hundred and fifty psychiatric and psychometric variables (see Table 6-3, column 2 and Table 6-4).

A percentage of the significant correlations might be explained on the basis that the Monroe Dyscontrol Scale was used in part as a data source, being administered to the subject at the same time he was interviewed regarding his current and past psychiatric history and at the time he was evaluated on the Mood and Affect Scales. Thus, the Monroe Dyscontrol Scale report may have entered into the belligerence-negativism and agitation-excitement items on the

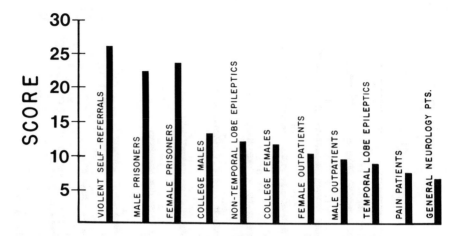

Source: Figure 2 from Robert Plutchik, Carlos Climent, and Frank Ervin, "Research Strategies for the Study of Human Violence," in *Issues in Brain/Behavior Control* edited by W. Lynn Smith and Arthur Kling © Spectrum Publications, Inc., New York, p. 83. Reprinted by permission.

Figure 6-2. Mean Scores Obtained by Eleven Different Groups on FAV Self-reported Violence Scale

current CAPPS; impulsiveness on the Affect Scale; lack of inhibition on the past CAPPS; impulsiveness on the Affect Scale; lack of inhibition on the past CAPPS; and on three items from the CAPPS addenda—severity of dyscontrol acts, aggressiveness during the acts, and prodromal anger. Therefore, seven of the forty-nine significant correlations could represent circular reasoning.

Clinically significant correlations between the Monroe Overt Violence Subscale (Table 6-4) and other data include antisocial behavior during childhood and adulthood, as well as prison infraction ratings made by the custodial staff. The group therapist ratings show a correlation between the Monroe Overt Violence Subscale and verbal hostility to group members and therapist as well as a wide range of emotional responses, a higher level of motor activity, and more impulsive speech or action during therapeutic sessions. On the Mood Scale there was a correlation between the Monroe Dyscontrol Scale and the vigor-activity rating.

Table 6-4 shows the unique correlations between the Monroe Violence Subscale and other psychometric tests including the MMPI Episodic Scale (Table 6-5).

Correlations between the Monroe Violence Subscale and data collected by

Table 6-2

Variables Significantly Correlated with the Monroe Dyscontrol Scale in Two or More of Seven Groups

Variable	Number of Groups	Mean Correlation
Schizophrenia scale (subset of MMPI items)	7	.42
FAV Violence Scale	7	.61
Total number of problems (health, job, social, etc.)	5	.58
Number of emotional problems	5	.56
Number of behavior problems (truancy, drugs, etc.)	5	.53
Number of health problems	4	.46
Number of sexual problems	4	.62
Number of social problems	4	.57
History of family violence	4	.56
Psychopathic Deviate Scale (subset of MMPI items)	4	.52
Lie Scale (MMPI)	3	− .40
FAS Sex Drive Scale	3	.53
Social Deviance Index	3	.46
M-D Depression Scale	2	.58
History of family disease	2	.53

Source: Table 3 from Robert Plutchik, Carlos Climent, and Frank Ervin, "Research Strategies for the Study of Human Violence," in *Issues in Brain/Behavior Control* edited by W. Lynn Smith and Arthur Kling © 1976 by Spectrum Publications, Inc., New York, p. 91. Reprinted by permission.

the neurologist included history of head injury, suspicion of epilepsy, "short fuse," and CNS toxicity. Correlations were negative with motor retardation and lack of emotion. Several correlations that were not as easily explained included the tendency to blame others and grandiosity both in the past and present. The correlation with depression reinforces the clinical impression that aggression may be a cover-up for depression, and the correlation with adolescent sexual adjustment may reflect adolescent sexual aggressiveness. A surprising correlation with the Monroe Overt Violence Subscale is the correlation with a history of insomnia, which might be associated with excessive motor activity. Time estimation was elevated and draw-a-line was shortened in this group. The interpretation of this remains obscure.

Monroe selected items (on the basis of face validity) from the MMPI as possibly reflecting episodic dyscontrol (Table 6-5). There proved to be a high correlation between those items and the Monroe Dyscontrol Scale, as well as

Table 6-3

Product-Moment Correlations with the Monroe Dyscontrol Scale and the Monroe Overt Violence Subscale

Variable Description	Dyscontrol Scale Coefficient $p \leqslant .05$	Overt Violence Subscale Coefficient $p \leqslant .05$
Global Ratings		
Primary dyscontrol/secondary dyscontrol	.18	
Predict epileptoid mechanism*	.34	.33
Neurological Exam		
Epilepsy suspect*	.34	.33
Photophobia	.18	
Impaired sensation	−.17	
Mental Status		
Somatic concerns*	.21	
Psychophysiological reactions*	.21	
Anxiety*	.22	
Depression*	.26	.20
Belligerence-negativism*	.27	.35
Agitation−excitement*	.32	.29
Dyscontrol Behavior		
Severity	.19	.20
Lack of premeditation	.27	
Specificity of affect	.24	
Aggressive affect*	.35	.36
Prodromal restlessness*	.18	
Prodromal depression*	.21	
Prodromal anger*	.18	.28
Psychiatric History		
Poor academic achievement	.20	
Amnesia, fugue, dissociative state	.22	
Hypochondriasis	.18	
Insomnia*	.22	.24
Response to Group Therapy		
Verbal hostility to therapist*	.21	.30
EEG Activation		
Theta frequency counts*	.23	

Table 6-3 (cont.)

Variable Description	Dyscontrol Scale Coefficient $p \leqslant .05$	Overt Violence Subscale Coefficient $p \leqslant .05$
Psychometrics		
MMPI Standard Scale Scores		
L*	−.31	−.27
F*	.35	.20
K*	−.38	−.27
Hs*	.30	.23
D*	.30	
Hy*	.27	.21
Mf*	.21	
Pa*	.30	.18
Pt*	.34	
Sc*	.38	.19
Ma*	.27	.33
Si*	.30	.20
Bender-BIP		
No. of positives*	.19	
BIP difference score*	.22	
Class*	.25	
Holtzman: Abstract*	−.22	−.18
WAIS Arithmetic Subtest	−.20	
Draw-a-line*	−.35	−.20

*Common with the MMPI Episodic Scale.

similarly high correlations with other data (Table 6-6). This then offers an opportunity of reanalyzing previously collected MMPI data for the dyscontrol syndrome.

Eighty-eight of our 93 subjects showed the 4-3 MMPI profile (Davis 1974) purportedly reflecting violent antisocial behavior (see Chapter 5). The WAIS Violence Scale (Kunce 1976) did correlate with this MMPI dyscontrol scale, but did not show intergroup differences in our study, nor did it show other significant correlations with our clinical or psychometric data. In fact, the similarities ratio within our population was 9.58 whereas Kunce, et al. reported ratios of 6.73 for violent behavior and 9.87 for nonviolent behavior.

On the basis of the data presented in this chapter, we believe that the Monroe Dyscontrol Scale is an adequate measure of the dyscontrol syndrome. It appears to be weighted in favor of the epileptoid pole of the epileptoid-hysteroid extremes.

Table 6-4
Product-Moment Correlations with the Monroe Overt Violence Subscale Not Found on the Total Monroe Dyscontrol Scale

Variable Description	Overt Violence Subscale Coefficient $p \leqslant .05$
Neurologic Exam	
Head injury	.22
Short fuse	.25
CNS toxicity	.23
Mental Status	
Grandiosity*	.27
Antisocial attitudes or acts	.18
Retardation-lack of emotion	−.28
Dyscontrol Behavior	
No. of previous antisocial acts	.20
Psychiatric History	
Inhibited	−.19
Blames others	.19
Grandiosity	.20
Antisocial traits in childhood*	.24
No. of previous institutionalizations	.23
Adolescent sexual adjustment	.21
Antisocial	.21
Mood and Affect	
Vigor-activity	.18
Impulsiveness*	.32
Psychometrics	
Holtzman barrier responses	−.18
Time estimation	.22
Response to Group Therapy	
Range of emotional responses	.30
Speech or action is impulsive	.26
Verbal hostility to group	.28
Verbal hostility to therapist	.30
Motor activity	.20
Other Scales or Ratings	
Infraction rating (baseline)*	.25
Acting out on hand test	.23
Modified acting out on hand test	.21
MMPI episodic scale	.39
WAIS violence scale	−.19

*Common with the MMPI Episodic Scale.

Table 6-5
MMPI Episodic Scale

True

22. At times I have fits of laughing and crying that I cannot control. (epilepsy)*

23. I am troubled by attacks of nausea and vomiting.

33. I have had very peculiar and strange experiences. (impulsivity, delinquency)

39. At times I feel like smashing things. (neurotic undercontrol, impulsivity)

47. Once a week or oftener I feel suddenly hot all over without apparent cause. (epilepsy)

62. Parts of my body often have feelings like burning, tingling, crawling, or like going to sleep. (impulsivity)

72. I am troubled by discomfort in the pit of my stomach every few days or oftener.

75. I get angry sometimes.

97. At times I have a strong urge to do something harmful or shocking. (impulsivity)

102. My hardest battles are with myself.

134. At times my thoughts have raced ahead faster than I could speak them. (CN control)

156. I have had periods in which I carried on activities without knowing later what I had been doing. (epilepsy)

168. There is something wrong with my mind.

182. I'm afraid of losing my mind.

194. I have had attacks in which I could not control my movements or speech but in which I knew what was going on around me.

227. I have been told that I walk during sleep.

234. I get mad easily and then get over it soon.

238. I have periods of such great restlessness that I cannot sit long in a chair. (epilepsy, CN control, neurotic undercontrol)

251. I have had blank spells in which my activities were interrupted and I did not know what was going on around me. (hostility control–reverse)

288. I am troubled by attacks of nausea and vomiting. (epilepsy)

323. I have had very peculiar and strange experiences.

334. Peculiar odors come to me at times.

345. I often feel as if things were not real.

349. I have strange and peculiar thoughts. (impulsivity)

381. I am often said to be a hot head. (impulsivity, neurotic undercontrol)

543. Several times a week I feel as if something dreadful is about to happen.

545. Sometimes I have the same dream over and over. (impulsivity)

False

103. I have little or no trouble with my muscles twitching or jumping. (epilepsy)

154. I have never had a fit or convulsion.

174. I have never had a fainting spell. (epilepsy, CN control)

175. I seldom or never have dizzy spells.

187. My hands have not become clumsy or awkward. (epilepsy)

330. I have never been paralyzed or had any unusual weakness of any of my muscles.

Source: Items from the Minnesota Multiphasic Personality Inventory reproduced by permission. Copyright 1943, renewed 1970 by the University of Minnesota. Published by the Psychological Corporation, New York, N.Y. All rights reserved. Reprinted by permission.

*( ) indicates usage of this item on other scale.

Table 6-6
Product-Moment Correlations with the MMPI Episodic Scale

Variable Description	Correlation Coefficient $p \leqslant .05$
Global Ratings	
Predict epileptoid mechanism*†	.25
Neurological Exam	
Epilepsy suspect*†	.24
Stigmata	.20
Mental Status	
Somatic concerns*	.24
Psychophysiological reactions*	.23
Anxiety*	.19
Depression*†	.32
Suspicion-persecution	.24
Grandiosity†	.22
Belligerence-negativism*†	.34
Agitation-excitement*†	.23
Dyscontrol Behavior	
Aggressive affect during act*†	.32
Poor coordination during act	.19
Lack of personal discomfort regarding act	.20
Prodromal irritability	.32
Prodromal motor restlessness*	.29
Prodromal depression*	.37
Prodromal anger*†	.24
Prodromal thinking disturbance	.21
Prodromal sexual	.26
Prodromal autonomic	.26
Psychiatric History	
Clinging behavior	.22
Poor intellectual capacity	.28
Antisocial traits in childhood†	.21
Insomnia*†	.36
Alcohol abuse	−.20
Depression	.20
Obsession-compulsions	−.20
Response to Group Therapy	
Range of emotional responses	.21
Verbal hostility to therapist*†	.19
Thinking modified	.20

Table 6-6 (cont.)

Variable Description	Correlation Coefficient $p \leqslant .05$
EEG Activation	
Theta counts (−3dB)*	.22
Mood and Affect	
Anger-hostility	.22
Fatigue-inertia	.19
Impulsiveness†	.21
Monroe Dyscontrol Scale	
Total Scale	.51
Violence subscale	.39
Infraction Rating†	.22
Psychometrics	
MMPI	
L*†	−.47
F*†	.70
K*†	−.68
Hs*†	.46
D*	.30
Hy*†	.26
Mf*	.24
Pa*†	.57
Pt*	.56
Sc*†	.68
Ma*†	.52
Si*†	.46
Memory for Designs	.24
Bender-BIP	
Total deviation on BPI	.22
No. of positives*	.18
BIP difference score*	.20
Class*	.22
Holtzman Abstract*†	−.19
Slow Writing Task	−.20
Draw-a-Line*†	−.27

*Common with Monroe Dyscontrol Scale correlations.
†Common with Monroe Overt Violence Subscale correlations.

104

References

Davis, K.R., and Sines, J.O. 1974. "An antisocial behavior pattern associated with a specific MMPI profile." *J. Cons. Clin. Psychol.,* 36:2, 229-234.

Kunce, J.T., Bryan, J.J., and Eckelman, C.C. 1976. Violent behavior and differential WAIS characteristics." *J. Cons. Clin. Psychol.,* 44:42-45.

Monroe, R.R. 1970. *Episodic behavioral disorders.* Cambridge: Harvard University Press.

Plutchik, R., Climent, C., and Ervin, F. 1976. "Research strategies for the study of human violence," in Smith, W.L., and Kling, A. (Eds.). *Brain/Behavioral Control.* New York: Spectrum.

7

Criterion of Brain Instability: EEG Activation

Russell R. Monroe,
George U. Balis, and
Duncan McCulloch

In Chapter 1, the continuum of "faulty equipment versus faulty learning" was discussed as it relates to episodic dyscontrol. We hypothesize that certain aggressive behavior is associated with EEG abnormalities that reflect central nervous system instability, particularly low seizural threshold in the limbic system. Therefore, the EEG data are crucial to the analysis of these data. Furthermore, EEG data are relatively "hard," at least compared to many other measures used in this study. We have made an effort to make these data as reliable as possible through the use of many techniques both in recording the EEG and in interpreting the tracings. At least they are objective data in that the records are available and subject to review. Since there is always a subjective element in interpreting the EEG recording, we have attempted a machine analysis of the "nonspecific" patterns, that is, the paroxysmal high amplitude theta activity that is associated with the activation procedure. There has proven to be a high correlation between the machine analysis and that of our two raters, as we discuss later.

A single routine EEG is not a reliable measure of electroencephalographic abnormalities even in individuals with an unquestionable history of epilepsy. Furthermore, seizural activity can occur in subcortical structures without any reflection on the cortex (Monroe 1970). To minimize such false negatives we use physiological activation of sleep and hyperventilation as well as drug activation with alpha chloralose.

Alpha Chloralose Activation

Alpha chloralose was selected as an activating agent because of its unique activating potential as described elsewhere (Monroe 1970). Most drugs utilized as activators are either sedatives that induce sleep or stimulants such as Metrazol. Alpha chloralose has both sedative and stimulant qualities; hence it is a potent activator (Balis 1964). It has been demonstrated to induce abnormalities in 15 percent of normal individuals, that is, those who had no history of epilepsy, neurologic disease, head trauma, or behavioral abnormalities. On the other hand, alpha chloralose-activated abnormalities have been seen in over 90 percent of epileptics, many of whom had normal baseline recordings. Similarly, abnormalities were activated by alpha chloralose in those individuals with other evidence of focal central nervous system disease even though baseline records were normal (Monroe 1970). The alpha chloralose activation response also occurs in patients with neurologic lesions but without epilepsy, as well as in patients whose resting baseline EEGs have shown borderline or definitive abnormalities. It is higher in that portion of the normal population that has a history of past neurologic disease, head trauma, or a hereditary history of epilepsy. Studies in psychiatric patients have shown that it occurs in 80-90 percent of patients who have demonstrated episodic psychopathological and dyscontrol behavior. This pattern and its relationship to behavioral disorders has been reviewed by Monroe (1970). Alpha chloralose has other advantages as an activating agent. It induces sleep without producing the obscuring drug effects of fast spindle activity accompanying barbiturate sedation. Furthermore, it does not induce subjective discomfort as does Metrazol. In over one thousand studies reported previously (Monroe 1970) only 2 subjects refused repeat studies because they found the procedure uncomfortable. In the Patuxent study no individual refused a second activation procedure. Subjectively, the individual reports a feeling of pleasant drowsiness, giddiness, or euphoria much as if he had had one too many drinks.

The procedure does have some disadvantages. First, the drug is relatively insoluble in water and most other vehicles; thus parenteral administration is difficult. For this reason it is given orally. Oral administration produces an unpredictable response time. The maximum response generally occurs between forty-five to seventy-five minutes after the drug has been ingested; however, rarely, a delayed response can occur two to three hours after oral administration. Side effects of alpha chloralose may include mild clonic jerking movements of the fingers or hand. Rarely this extends to all four extremities and can be accompanied by unconsciousness. Under this condition, the behavior of the patient appears similar to the clonic phase of a typical grand mal seizure, but is not preceded by a tonic phase nor does it include tongue biting or incontinence. If the clonic reaction occurs, medication is not necessarily required as the reaction wanes within several hours. However, if an immediate termination is desired, parenteral administration of either phenobarbital or chlordiazepoxide will accomplish this. Occasionally, during the height of the chloralose reaction, sensorium may become clouded and the individual may show psychotic or dyscontrol behavior similar to that which he has spontaneously shown in the past. In these circumstances, such dyscontrol action may be easily managed through minimal restraint.

EEG Activation Procedures

Each subject had two recording sessions within the sixteen-week period (see Figure 3-2). EEG recordings were performed on the sixth and fourteenth week of the project; thus for the first EEG half the subjects were on the active drug, primidone, and the other half on placebo. At the time of EEG recordings, subjects on active drug were receiving the maximum dosage of 1,000 mg. per day. Subjects were monitored by urine analysis for illicit drugs, as well as serum levels for determining whether primidone had reached therapeutic range (Chapter 11).

During each session, a baseline record was obtained including periods of wakefulness, five-minute hyperventilation, and spontaneous sleep, whenever possible. This baseline recording lasted at least thirty minutes, utilizing ten montages with the international system of electrode placement (twenty-one electrodes). Recordings were both bipolar and monopolar to the ipsilateral ear. Recordings were made on an eight-channel Offner Model T portable machine. If abnormalities or borderline recordings were obtained during baseline, the recording period was extended.

Following completion of the baseline EEG the subject was given alpha chloralose suspended in a solution of lukewarm water at the approximate dose of 3 mg. per pound of body weight. Recordings were resumed forty-five minutes after medication was given. Recording was at a minimum of twenty pages per montage. At the end of this recording period, approximately one and one-half hours after drug administration, the individual again hyperventilated. During the five minutes prior to hyperventilation, the individual was asked to count to himself and tap a key, which would indicate that he was awake during the hyperventilation phase. This alertness check was done both during and after the hyperventilation. Thus, there was an effort, not always successful, to maintain a waking record during this fifteen-minute period.

Analysis of activation data included the five-minute periods prior to, during, and after hyperventilation. The monopolar montage was identical to that used during the baseline hyperventilation period.

For the machine analysis of the data, the pre-, during, and posthyperventilation EEG was recorded on a four-channel Hewlett-Packard #3960 FM tape record reproducing system with three channels of EEG data taping so that further analysis of the data could be made. Notes regarding the subject's behavior were both written on the EEG record and verbally recorded on the one AM channel on the tape recorder. Behavioral observations were routinely recorded during the period immediately following the EEG procedure.

If the subject had significant behavioral effects from the drug itself, he remained under observation on the hospital ward immediately adjacent to the EEG laboratories. If the behavioral changes were outstanding, the patient was evaluated by a project physician. In only one instance was it necessary to counteract the alpha chloralose effects by giving IM chlordiazepoxide.

Electroencephalographic Analysis

The narrative report by the encephalographer, Curtis Marshall, M.D., was tabulated for computer analysis as follows. Those patients with a normal recording involving absolutely no abnormalities were classified together with those patients producing a borderline recording manifested by disorganized or unstable frequencies with minor amplitude assymetries. Baseline abnormalities consisted of (1) generalized frequencies in the delta-theta range, the type that were augmented or developed spontaneously after alpha chloralose activation, (2) random spikes or sharp waves, (3) focal spike or sharp waves, (4) spike slow waves, (5) 6 and 14 per second positive spikes, and (6) focal slow waves.

Baseline and activation abnormalities were classified as two distinct types following the example of Ajmone-Marsan (1970). The first type we designated as a "specific" abnormality. This included focal theta or delta activity, transients such as spikes or sharp waves (either focal or random), spike slow wave activity, and 14 and 6 positive spikes. The second abnormality was labeled "nonspecific." This was a generalized paroxysmal high amplitude activity in the two to seven per second range with a frontal predominance. Such activity is typical in six-year old children they pass through a drowsy state but tends to disappear by late adolescence. If seen after that age, it is usually considered as presumptive evidence of seizural disorder (Monroe 1974).

Ratings of the nonspecific generalized activation after alpha chloralose administration were done by two independent raters (Monroe and Balis) analyzing the five-minute periods prior to, during, and after hyperventilation. The extent of activation was graded on a zero to four scale by each rater as follows:

0—no significant slow waves as defined below;

1—occasional bursts of frequencies less than 8 cycles per second and greater than 50 millivolts occurring only during hyperventilation or in the ten seconds immediately following hyperventilation;

2—similar findings except that the bursts occurred during hyperventilation and continued longer than ten seconds posthyperventilation;

3—the same condition except that the bursts occurred during prehyperventilation as well as during hyperventilation and posthyperventilation;

4—continuous or almost continuous high amplitude bursts of frequencies less than 8 cycles per second in all three epochs.

Of the 184 records (2 per patient) rated by the two observers there was exact agreement between raters in 70 percent of the records. Of the remaining records, there was disagreement of only one point in 25 percent, and a disagreement greater than one scale point in 5 percent. In the latter instance, agreement within one point was accomplished by joint review of the record. This high level of agreement reflects the dramatic quality of the activation response to the extent that it is easily discerned from the background EEG pattern no matter how varied that might be. The agreement between this scoring system and that of the machine analysis will be discussed later. As both raters analyzed all records, for statistical analysis the abnormal ratings were expanded to a possible score of eight by adding the ratings of the two observers. Thus, in each instance where the rating is an even number there was complete agreement between raters, whereas an odd number indicates that the raters disagreed by one scale point.

Baseline EEG Abnormalities

Each individual had two separate baseline and activation recordings. These data are presented in Table 7-1 and Table 7-2. In the awake record of the first EEG (Table 7-1) only 13 of the total sample showed abnormality. With sleep, 4 more demonstrated abnormalities, and during hyperventilation, twenty new abnormalities appeared. In the second EEG recording (Table 7-2) results are roughly similar.

The increase in abnormalities with the usual physiologic activators emphasizes the importance of using such a procedure in any complete EEG study. Also, analysis of our data reveals the importance of repeated EEG studies since 16 individuals with normal first baseline recordings showed abnormalities on the second EEG. Thus after both procedures only 39 subjects or 42 percent of the population had normal or borderline records on both baseline EEGs.

Generalized theta and delta activity were the most common baseline abnormalities and patients showing these patterns develop a nonspecific pattern with alpha chloralose activation (column 4 Tables 7-1, 7-2).

Of the subjects who showed some baseline theta or delta activity on either recording number one or number two, all showed an increase in such activity with activation. The next most common abnormality was nontemporal spike or sharp waves (random or focal) and this was considerably augmented by drug activation. This type of abnormality emphasizes that in looking at unselected groups of aggressive individuals one rarely finds temporal lobe abnormalities. Only 1 subject showed focal spiking in the temporal lobe in the baseline recording and 2 others showed theta activity. Two other subjects developed temporal lobe theta activity after alpha chloralose and another temporal spike (Tables 7-1, 7-2).

Table 7-3 summarizes the effect of chloralose activation in eliciting further abnormalities (not present in baseline recordings), both in terms of nonspecific generalized paroxysmal theta waves (in this table only those who rated greater than or equal to five are listed) and specific abnormalities. Eighteen showed abnormalities as defined on both the first and second recording. There seemed to be some sequence effect on the generalized activation in that 13 activated only on the first recording and 7 activated only on the second. There was an exact

Table 7-1
First EEG Cumulative

Type of Abnormality	Baseline Awake	Sleep	Hyperventilation	Activation
Nonspecific				
Theta	9	10	16	
Theta-Delta	1	1	7	40[a] (Nonspecific Augmentation)
Delta	0	1	5	
Total	10	12	28	
Specific Abnormality				
Left temporal spike	0	0	0	0
Right temporal spike	0	0	0	1
Anterior spike	0	0	0	7
Left frontal spike	0	0	0	0
Random spike	1	1	4	9
14 and 6	0	2	2	4
Anterior temporal slow	1	1	1	2
Bilateral temporal slow	0	0	0	2
Spike-slow	0	0	1	1
Left anterior slow	0	0	0	1
Anterior slow	1	1	1	1
Post slow	0	0	0	1
L amp elevation	0	0	0	2
R amp elevation	0	0	0	4
Total	3	5	9	35
Total nonspecific and specific	13	17	37 (40%)	75 (82%)

[a]Number who showed even minimal activation (one or greater); 23 additional subjects showed one or greater activation, but also had a specific abnormality.

reversal of these figures as far as the specific activation is concerned, that is, 7 activated on the first EEG while 13 activated on the second. In both instances, there were thirty-eight positive generalized or specific activation patterns on one or the other EEG. This suggests that repeated EEGs may elicit abnormalities not seen in one activation procedure alone.

From the experimental design it is obvious that one of the two EEGs was performed while the subject was receiving therapeutic doses of primidone. This apparently had some influence on baseline abnormalities as 6 individuals showed abnormalities on placebo regimen, and not on the drug regimen, while 17 subjects developed abnormalities on the drug regimen but not on placebo. Thus, it seems that primidone augmented basline abnormalities.

Table 7-2
Second EEG Cumulative

		Baseline			
	Type of Abnormality	Awake	Sleep	Hyperventilation	Activation
Nonspecific	Theta	13	15	23	39.[a] (Nonspecific Augmentation)
	Theta-Delta	1	1	12	
	Delta	0	0	0	
	Total	14	16	35	
Specific Abnormality	Left temporal spike	1	1	1	1
	Right temporal spike	0	0	0	0
	Random spike	0	2	5	10
	Left frontal spike	0	0	0	3
	Anterior spike	0	1	1	10
	14 and 16	0	2	2	4
	Anterior temporal slow	1	1	1	1
	Bilateral temporal slow	0	0	0	0
	Spike slow	0	0	0	7
	Left anterior slow	0	0	0	0
	Anterior slow	0	0	0	2
	Post slow	0	0	0	1
	L amp elevation	0	0	0	2
	R amp elevation	0	0	0	0
	Total	2	7	10	41
	Total nonspecific and specific	16	23	45 (49%)	80 (88%)

[a]Number who showed even minimal activation (one or greater); 24 other subjects showed one or greater, but had a specific abnormality.

Table 7-4 shows the effects of primidone on the activated EEG. It is apparent on the nonspecific measures that primidone enhances the appearance of abnormalities, that is, 18 subjects showed positive activation on primidone but not on placebo; only 2 showed a positive activation on placebo, not primidone. This suggests that in some ways primidone is acting synergistically or facilitating the alpha chloralose activation response.

Table 7-4 also summarizes the effects of primidone on specific abnormalities. Note that primidone seems to suppress 6 and 14 and spike or sharp waves while increasing spike slow waves. There did not seem to be any effect on focal slowing.

Table 7-3
Alpha Chloralose-activated EEG Abnormalities

	1st Not 2d	2d– Not 1st	Both
Nonspecific activation (paroxysmal $\Delta\Theta \geqslant 5$)	13	7	18
Specific	7	13	18

Comparisons of Specific and Nonspecific EEG
Patterns and Behavior

For the purpose of gaining an empirical understanding of the contributions of specific and nonspecific EEG activation to clinical behavior, five groups were defined as follows:

Group No. I–*"Pure"* activation group, with a nonspecific activation rating greater than or equal to five on the highest EEG activation rating, but specific abnormalities absent on both EEGs ($N = 13$);

Group No. II–*"Mixed"* activation group, with a nonspecific activation rating greater than or equal to five on the highest EEG activation plus a specific abnormality on either EEG ($N = 25$);

Group No. III–*"Pure Specific"* group, sum of nonspecific activation on both EEGs less than or equal to three plus any specific abnormality on either EEG ($N = 13$);

Group No. IV–*"Normal EEG"* group, sum of nonspecific activation on both EEGs less than or equal to three and no specific abnormalities on either EEG ($N = 27$);

Group No. V–*"Intermediate"* group, sum of nonspecific activation on both EEGs greater than three and less than five on the highest EEG activation with or without specific abnormalities ($N = 14$); as an intermediate group this was discarded in the subsequent behavioral analysis.

Comparing specific abnormalities in groups II, III, and V we made the following observations. In group II, twenty-nine abnormalities were recorded in 25 subjects while in group III, fourteen abnormalities were recorded in 13 subjects. The most common specific abnormality was random sharp waves and this occurred at a similar level in both groups, approximately 42 percent. Group III showed more focal theta-delta than group II, 29 percent versus 14 percent respectively. Two patients showed focal sharp waves or spikes in both groups representing a percentage of 10 percent for group II and 21 percent for group III. In group V, the specific abnormalities occurred in only 5 of 14 subjects.

Table 7-4
Effect of Primidone on Activated EEG

	Primidone– Not Placebo	Placebo– Not Primidone	Both
Nonspecific (paroxysmal $\Theta \geqslant 5$)	18	2	18
6 and 14	1	4	0
Spike slow wave	4	1	1
Spike or sharp wave	6	13	11
Focal slow	6	4	1
Total specific	17	22	13

Paired group differences (I, II, or III versus IV) and intergroup differences utilizing the least significant difference test (LSD) in the Oneway Anova analysis is summarized in Figures 7-1 and 7-2 for the psychiatric, neurologic, and psychologic data.

The first point to make is that these groups were remarkably similar in terms of the number of impulsive acts, the severity of these acts, and the range of offenses committed. Nevertheless, we did find some significant differences between groups at the .05 and the .01 levels. In the most tentative way, we are proposing that this reflects that those with nonspecific abnormalities alone (group I) are more likely to be overactive, hostile, sexually deviant individuals with more emotional liability than subjects with completely normal EEGs. Interestingly, this group is less likely to have amnesia for the act than those with normal EEGs. The mixed group, that is those that showed both nonspecific generalized abnormality and specific abnormalities (group II) seemed to be the most severely disturbed group and were characterized by symptoms more typical of the inadequate psychopath, such as aimless, unstable behavior with little effort at self-improvement, poor performance in school, and much self-defeating behavior in social interrelationships. These individuals had varied prodromal affects prior to committing the antisocial act.

The third group, those without nonspecific activation but manifesting varied specific abnormalities (group III), were more characteristically aggressive during the act.

The psychological data (Figure 7-2) suggest that individuals in group IV (without EEG abnormalities) are more socially aware and show a greater capacity to modulate their responses when required to do so. They seem to have a greater capacity to plan and be more deliberate in responding to ambiguous stimuli. The data suggest that the normal EEG group might make a better adjustment to prison life, or for that matter any other environment in which they find themselves, than the other groups.

What is surprising, however, is that even within a highly homogeneous group of subjects one can find behavioral differences utilizing broad electroencephalo-

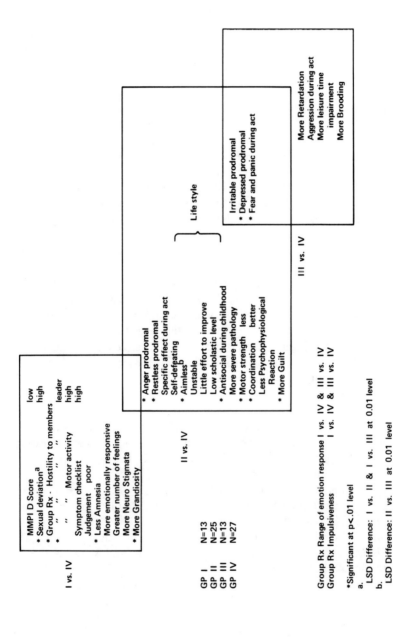

Figure 7-1. Neuropsychiatric Variables: Differences between EEG Groups ($p \leq .05$)

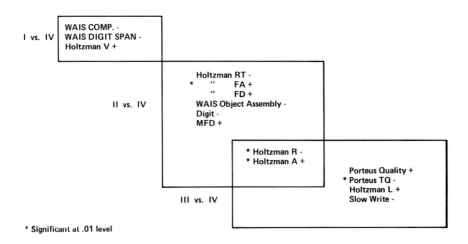

Figure 7-2. Psychological Variables: Differences between EEG Groups ($p \leqslant .05$)

graphic characteristics as the criterion variable. Furthermore, even though these EEG abnormalities suggest some form of central nervous system instability, only if the EEG abnormalities summate as in group II does a significant abnormality of motor strength appear. As we will note later (Chapter 8) gross coordination is significantly better in those with activated nonspecific abnormalities.

Product-Moment Analysis of Delta and Theta Activity

One question that is repeatedly raised by the electroencephalographer and neurologist is, how significant in neurologic or behavioral terms is the activated nonspecific generalized theta activity? The clinical scoring of such activity was described earlier. Instrumentation was also utilized in an effort to establish a precise method of quantifying EEG activity in the theta range (3-7 Hz.) which was scored in terms of equivalent pulse counts per fixed five-minute interval when it exceeded one of two preselected levels. The set-up was as follows.

A portable FM tape recorder, Hewlett-Packard #3960A, was utilized on location at Patuxent to field record three channels of EEG data at 15/16 ips. The data of particular interest was an incremental theta wave form which appears paroxysmally in the left-prefrontal to left ear electrode configuration after administering the drug, alpha chloralose. Accordingly, tape recording and playback levels were fixed with reference to a DC calibration voltage. An active band-pass filter, Multimetrics #AF-520A, was utilized in the maximally flat position to attenuate frequencies outside the —3dB points, at 3 and 7 Hz., by

24dB/octave. Since the data was played back at 3 3/4 ips, the equivalent pass-band translated to 12-28 Hz. under four-fold time compression.

Filtered data was the input to the amplifier section of the Ballentine #340A VTVM, which had a low frequency time constant below 5 Hz. Positive going output wave-forms that exceeded a fixed input triggering threshold then generated pulses at the output of a pulse generator, Hewlett-Packard #8005A. Since pulse width was adjusted to 33 milliseconds, counting rates in excess of 30 Hz., or 7.5 Hz. real time, cannot occur. Thus, the faster changing EEG wave-forms within the theta pass-band were counted only once. A monitor oscilloscope was used for the time-shared display of the output pulse with the filtered or unfiltered EEG.

Activity was scored by utilizing output pulses to trigger a five-digit decade counter, Baird-Atomic #123 G-M Scaler (originally part of an α-particle X-ray counter). The readout thus indicated theta activity above a preselected amplitude threshold, since the gain at the VTVM amplifier may be altered in 3dB steps.

The correlations seemed clinically relevant in the predicted direction of episodic dyscontrol with the analysis of either the machine or the clinically scored EEG activity (see Tables 7-5 and 7-6). The correlations with machine-scored theta (Table 7-5) were significant for the global estimation of epileptoid mechanism as well as the neurologist's evaluation of possible epilepsy. Furthermore, there was correlation with history of central nervous system toxicity and a negative correlation with coordination obtained in the neurologic examination (see Chapter 10).

The psychiatric history correlations with theta activity were emotional overreactivity, anger, violence, impulsiveness, self-defeating behavior, overall severity of symptoms, outpatient treatment, total time of institutionalization, the number of previous institutionalizations, the number of contacts with law enforcement agencies, and the history of antisocial activity, both in childhood and adulthood, as well as lack of responsibility; all suggesting a severe dyscontrol syndrome. There was also a significant correlation with aggression during the dyscontrol acts as well as an anger prodromal phase, and impulsiveness and lack of fatigue-inertia on the Mood Scale. These factors are also characteristic of the dyscontrol syndrome as defined. Contrary to our prediction, there was a positive correlation between theta activity and secondary gains in dyscontrol behavior.

These correlations seem to be supported by independent observers (group therapists) where the theta activity data correlated with their ratings on the wide range of emotional responses, impulsive speech or action, physical hostility during group sessions, and increased motor activity.

There was a correlation between theta activity and the self-rating measures such as the Monroe Dyscontrol Scale, the Monroe Overt Violence Subscale, as well as with the MMPI Episodicity Scale (see Chapter 6).

On the psychological tests, theta activity correlated with the Bender

Table 7-5

Product-Moment Correlations with −3dB Machine-scored Theta Activity

Variable Description	Coefficient p ⩽ .05
Global	
Predict epileptoid	.19
Neurological Examination	
Epilepsy suspect	.22
CNS toxicity	.26
Coordination	−.20
Psychiatric History	
Overreact emotionally	.22
Anger	.19
Violent	.22
Impulsivity	.18
Self-defeating	.20
Lack of responsibility	.19
Grandiosity	.18
Overall severity	.21
Antisocial traits in childhood	.26
Outpatient treatment	.26
Total time of institutionalization	.20
No. of previous institutionalizations	.29
Insomnia	.22
Narcotics-drugs	.19
Illegal acts	.19
Antisocial	.28
Suicide-self-mutilation	.20
Mental Status	
Leisure time impairment	−.17
Dyscontrol Behavior	
Aggressive affect during act	.17
Secondary gains of behavior	.20
Prodromal anger	.21
Mood and Affect	
Lack of fatigue-inertia	.22
Impulsiveness	.19
Response to Group Therapy	
Range of emotional responses	.19
Speech or action is impulsive	.24

Table 7-5 (cont.)

Variable Description	Coefficient $p \leqslant .05$
Physical hostility	.19
Motor activity	.24
Thinking modified	.19
Monroe Dyscontrol Scales	
Total scale	.23
Violence subscale	.27
MMPI Episodic Scale	.22
EEG Activation Data	
Clinical rating	.62
Sharp waves	.21
Behavior disturbances	.17
Psychometrics	
MMPI	
D	.18
Hy	.21
Pa	.24
Pt	.33
Sc	.22
Si	.24
Bender-BIP	
Total deviation on BIP	.19
WAIS	
Digit span	−.19
Vocabulary	−.30

Deviation BIP suggesting distractibility, and showed a negative correlation with digit span and vocabulary on the WAIS. Based on the correlations between the theta activity and MMPI scales, there appears to be an MMPI profile with the following high scales: D, Hy, Pa, Pt, Sc, and Si.

Electroencephalographically, there was a correlation between theta activity and sharp waves and also a correlation with behavioral disturbances during the chloralose procedure. Finally, there was a highly significant correlation between machine-scored theta and the delta-theta activation ratings made by the experimenters ($r = .62$).

Because previous studies utilized clinical ratings of delta-theta, we used

Table 7-6
Product-Moment Correlations with Clinical Rating of Delta-Theta Waves

Variable Description	Coefficient $p \leqslant .05$
Neurologic	
Head injury	.21
Motor strength	.19
Coordination	−.21
Psychiatric History	
Antisocial traits in childhood	.21
Outpatient treatment	.25
Aimless	.24
Narcotics-drugs	.22
Stubborn	.24
Lack of responsibility	.19
Poor intellectual capacity	.18
Mental Status	
Somatic concerns	−.20
Psychophysiological reactions	−.20
Guilt	.19
Social isolation	−.18
Dyscontrol Behavior	
Specificity of affect	.21
Fear-panic affect during act	.21
Prodromal motor restlessness	.26
Prodromal anger	.29
Mood	
Lack of fatigue-inertia	.26
Response to Group Therapy	
Physical hostility	.22
EEG Activation Data	
EEG other sharp	.29
EEG spike slow	.18
Psychometrics	
Memory for designs	.17
WAIS digit span	−.22
Holtzman abstract	−.18

clinical ratings as one of the criterion variables in our subsequent analyses of the data (Chapters 8 and 9). However, a comparison of Tables 7-5 and 7-6 shows that while correlations with the clinical scoring of delta-theta also seem clinically relevant with regard to the concept of the dyscontrol syndrome, there were fewer correlations and somewhat less clinically relevant correlations than with the machine-scored theta. A reanalyses of our data utilizing this machine-scored theta in establishing a three- or four-group subclassification may be even more effective, and will be done in the future.

The data in this chapter support the clinical validity of utilizing clinically scored activated delta-theta as one of our criterion variables. Although the machine-analyzed data seemed somewhat more clinically relevant than the rater-scored delta-theta, further refinement of the former technique is necessary; therefore, in our criterion variable quantitating EEG activation, we relied on the rater-scored EEG. As the specific EEG abnormalities were so varied and the Ns for any given abnormality so small, they were not considered in the subsequent analyses, although there is evidence that individuals with combined "specific" and "nonspecific" abnormalities may be more deviant than those with one or the other alone.

References

Ajmone-Marsan, C., and Zivin, L.S. 1970. "Factors related to the occurrence of typical paroxysmal abnormalities in the EEG records of epileptic patients," *Epilepsia,* 11:361-381.

Balis, G.U., and Monroe, R.R. 1964. "The pharmacology of chloralose: A review," *Psychopharmacologia,* 6:1-30.

Monroe, R.R. 1974. "Maturational lag in central nervous system development as a partial explanation of episodic violent behavior," *Determinants and origins of aggressive behavior,* 337-344.

Monroe, R.R. 1970. *Episodic behavioral disorders.* Cambridge: Harvard University Press.

8 Intergroup Differences in the Two-dimensional Classification

Russell R. Monroe,
George U. Balis,
J. David Barcik,
Matthew McDonald,
Jeffrey S. Rubin, and
John R. Lion

Three statements made by Monroe (1970) are pertinent at this point. First, there is a group of individuals showing dyscontrol behavior that fall near the "hysteroid" or "motivated" pole of the "faulty learning-faulty equipment" continuum rather than the epileptoid pole on the other extreme. This group manifests dyscontrol behavior that is not significantly related to CNS instability, the latter reflecting an "epileptoid" mechanism and/or a "maturational lag" (Monroe 1974). Second, there are some individuals with a "dyscontrol way of life" who must be differentiated from those with the episodic disorders, that is, individuals whose lifestyle is characterized by impulsive, spur-of-the-moment decisions and actions. These individuals, however, do not see their impulsivity as deviant behavior, but as a natural part of their personality. Third, both the "nonspecific" EEG pattern and the "specific" focal EEG abnormalities—the latter usually evidence for some focal CNS damage—do not necessarily result in dyscontrol behavior.

Based on these considerations, Figure 3-1 (see Chapter 3) illustrates the four possible groups that would occur in any sampling of a prison population. The population is split two ways along two parameters, the first being "nonspecific" EEG abnormalities. In this parameter, activated theta waves were rated as five or greater for high EEG abnormalities and less than five for low EEG abnormalities (see Chapter 7, Analyses of Electroencephalographic Data, for definition). The other parameter, dyscontrol symptoms as measured by the Monroe Dyscontrol Scale, was represented by a high dyscontrol group receiving a score of twenty or greater, and a low dyscontrol group receiving a score of less than twenty (see Chapter 6, Monroe Dyscontrol Scale). Included also in Figure 3-1 are those behavioral patterns that characterize the "epileptoid" and "hysteroid" dyscontrol groups on the basis of the clinical and empirical data reported by Monroe (1970) (see Chapter 1, Definitions, Descriptions, and Measurement).

The labels for these groups are the following: group 1—"epileptoid" dyscontrol; group 2—"hysteroid" dyscontrol; group 3—"inadequate" psychopath; and group 4—"pure" psychopath. Figure 8-1 is a scattergram showing the

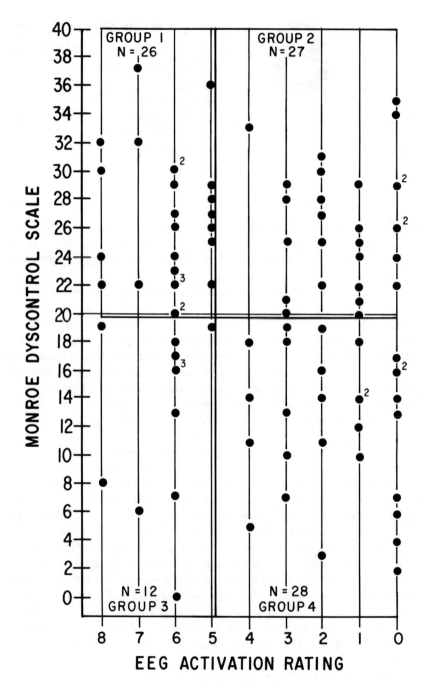

Figure 8-1. Scattergram of The Four-group Schema

actual number and position of our subjects within the four-group system on a scale of zero to thirty-seven for the Monroe Dyscontrol Scale and zero to eight for EEG activation ratings.

Based upon a series of Oneway Anovas there were no statistically significant differences between groups regarding type of offense, nor were there any differences between the severity of antisocial behavior or the frequency of antisocial acts as rated on the psychiatric history (CAPPS). Other measures of violence such as the WAIS Violence Scale (Kunce 1976) and the 4-3 MMPI profile (Davis 1974) showed no intergroup differences. However, despite this superficial homogeneity as far as the criminal justice system is concerned, we did find intergroup differences. We will demonstrate these differences and discuss their clinical importance in the remainder of the chapter.

Figure 8-2 shows the MMPI standard scale profiles illustrating the parallelism of groups 1 and 2 and groups 3 and 4 respectively. These data were subjected to a Oneway Anova analysis using the least significant difference criterion to find any intergroup differences. There were no significant differences between groups 1 and 2 and none between groups 3 and 4, leading us to conclude that the MMPI profile does not differentiate between those who show activation of theta waves and those who do not. In Chapter 7 we mentioned that machine-scored theta does correlate with MMPI scores, but the data reported in this chapter used the clinical activation ratings as a criterion variable. There were two significant differences between groups 2 and 3 and groups 2 and 4 at the .05 level but six significant differences between groups 1 and 4 and seven differences between groups 1 and 3. Comparison of MMPIs of groups 1 and 2 with groups 3 and 4 in Figure 8-2 reflects the finding that on the psychotic tetrad (clinical scales: Pa, Pt, Sc, and Ma) groups 1 and 2 are clearly and consistently higher than groups 3 and 4 in absolute elevation. Furthermore, groups 1 and 2 have respectively five and four of their validity and clinical scales falling at or in the "interpretable range" (two standard deviations above the mean) whereas groups 3 and 4 have only one scale (Pd) in this range.

Furthermore, groups 3 and 4 show a more characterological picture (Pd spike) whereas groups 1 and 2 suggest more severe pathology by virtue of the absolute elevation of F scores (≥ 70) and of the psychotic slope particularly evident in the profile of group 1.

Group 1 ("epileptoid" dyscontrol) is the most distinctly different profile among the four groups. The validity scales reflect a candid admittance to having and engaging in socially unacceptable feelings, impulses, and behaviors. These individuals also acknowledge rather unconventional ideas and experiences. They do not show any attempt to deny these experiences as one might expect from the population in general and are the least defensive of the four groups in revealing themselves. The validity pattern suggests veracity of the individuals' self-reports. Note should be taken also that there is some acknowledgement of low morale, but this may be related to the fact that these men are incarcerated.

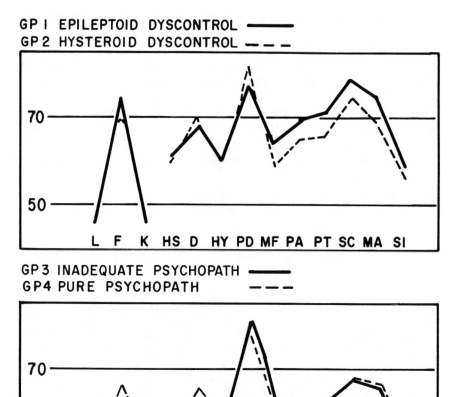

GP I EPILEPTOID DYSCONTROL ——————
GP 2 HYSTEROID DYSCONTROL —— —— ——

GP 3 INADEQUATE PSYCHOPATH ——————
GP 4 PURE PSYCHOPATH ————— —— ——

Figure 8-2. Mean MMPI Profile Scales for the Four-group Schema

The clinical picture is one of individuals with severe problems in impulse control who can be considered extremely dangerous as a group. These individuals lack basic sensitivity to, compassion for, and ability to empathize with others. They are, as a result, low in social compliance and social attachment. Of the four groups these individuals are the most likely to suffer some form of thought disturbance and although not overtly psychotic, their thinking is quite peculiar, strange, and autistic. As a group these individuals are the most erratic and unpredictable in behavior of the four groups. They are quick to explode into verbal rage and/or physical violence with the least provocation. Group 1 generally shows the highest level of irritability, restlessness, tension, and negativism, being the most agitated of the groups. In interpersonal interaction these individuals are likely to be aggressive, moody, and provocative, leaving others feeling quite uneasy and intimidated. As a group they are also the least trusting and most suspicious of the motivation of others. They tend to move too fast to use good judgment. Furthermore, they are self-aggrandizing. Hallucinations are occasionally evident in individuals with this profile and projection is one of their major defense mechanisms. Individuals with this MMPI profile are capable of bizarre and heinous crimes of violence.

It should be noted that the mean scale scores of group 2 ("hysteroid" dyscontrol) are consistently lower on the psychotic tetrad scales (Pa, Pt, Sc, and Ma) than group 1, and slightly higher on the neurotic and characterological scales of D, Hy, and Pd than group 1, as we would have predicted; however, none of these differences are significant.

With the exception of one clinical scale (Pd) the mean scale scores of groups 3 and 4 seem the least indicative of psychiatric pathology based on the MMPI. The individuals in these two groups are also the most defensive of the four groups and least willing to admit to any psychiatric shortcomings, problems or worries. They are more rigid and less comfortable about their impulse problems. Generally, they would be considered as immature, irresponsible, childish, demanding, impulsive and egocentric, emotionally unstable, and restless. Their low frustration tolerance leads them to become tense, moody, and depressed. Suicide attempts, assaultiveness, aggressive outbursts toward women, and heavy drinking along with emotional instability are evident in the histories of these men. They show a rather poor work adjustment and their financial status is generally poor. They would be diagnosed as having a personality trait disturbance; passive-aggressive personality, aggressive type; or antisocial personality.[a]

The Spitzer-Endicott profile scales of the current and past psychiatric data (CAPPS—see Chapter 5, Table 5-8) show significant differences between high and low EEG activation within this four-group classification based on a series of Oneway Anovas using the LSD criterion. Our results indicate (Table 8-1) that the EEG activation rating does indeed reflect behavioral correlates as measured on the CAPPS, although these correlates are not reflected in the MMPI.

For instance, high theta activation that differentiates group 3 ("inadequate" psychopath) from group 4 ("pure" psychopath) is characterized by poor impulse control (P2) and more dependency (P5) even though their Monroe Dyscontrol Scale scores are both low. It is important to note here that the CAPPS impulse control score is quite different from the Monroe Dyscontrol Scale (see Tables 5-8 and 6-1 for comparison). Another measure of difference between high theta

[a]MMPI data interpreted by Lawrence Donner, Ph.D., Associate Professor of Psychiatry (Psychology), University of Maryland School of Medicine.

Table 8-1
Group Differences Across the CAPPS Scales
(p ≤ .05)

	Group					
Scale	*1 vs 2*	*1 vs 3*	*1 vs 4*	*2 vs 3*	*2 vs 4*	*3 vs 4*
C4—Somatic concern				+		
P1—Depression-anxiety		−				
P2—Impulse control				−		+
P3—Social-sexual relations		−		−		
P5—Dependency		−				+
P13—Organicity	+					
P18—Intellectual capacity			+			

activation and low theta activation in comparing group 3 ("inadequate") with group 2 ("hysteroid") dyscontrol is that group 3 shows poor impulse control as defined on the CAPPS, as well as poor social-sexual relations when compared to group 2, while, as would be predicted because of the neurotic overlay, group 2 shows more somatic concern. A review of the CAPPS items that make up these differentiating categories (Table 5-8) which delineate group 3 from both groups 2 and 4 reveal that the label "inadequate" psychopath or inadequate personality (DSM II) is an appropriate designation for group 3. The "inadequate" label is further supported by the differentiation between group 3 and group 1 (both high on EEG activation, but differing on the Monroe Dyscontrol Scale) in that group 3 shows more depression-anxiety as well as more dependency and poorer social-sexual relations.

Further support for the idea that the psychiatric history does identify significant differences between high theta activation and low theta activation is shown in the fact that group 1 (high theta activation) displays more organicity than group 2 (low theta activation) and more impaired intellectual capacity with respect to group 4 (also low theta activation).

These data as well as those reported below indicate that the psychiatric history is crucial in identifying a group of prisoners, who, while demonstrating few dyscontrol symptoms, nevertheless have high EEG theta activation (group 3). On the other hand, the data reported below and again in Chapter 9 indicate that specific differentiation of group 1 (high theta activation and also high dyscontrol scores) from all others is only accomplished by the neurologic scale score (see Chapter 10). Therefore, to characterize this four-group classification, the conventional psychiatric profiles require supplementation by EEG and neurologic data. A detailed analysis of the four groups in this two-dimensional classification based on two hundred and fifty items from our variable pool was performed using a series of Oneway Anovas with the least significant difference

(LSD) criterion employed for mean group differences. Figures 8-3 through 8-6 examine the intergroup differences in terms of the original concepts of episodic dyscontrol (see Chapter 1). Whereas Monroe postulated a continuum of dyscontrol behavior of "epileptoid" origin on one extreme and "hysteroid" on the other, he also postulated an impulsive lifestyle, which in this population would be reflected in the "pure" psychopath group. Items indicated by an asterisk (Figures 8-3, 8-4, and 8-6) are those that were predicted by Monroe in his 1970 study. That study, however, made no predictions as to group 3 ("inadequate" psychopath) which had high EEG theta activity without dyscontrol symptomatology.

The findings not predicted on previous clinical studies are that the "epileptoid" group showed more perversion and more emotional responsiveness than the "hysteroid" group, and were more stubborn, had lower scholastic achievement, and more insomnia than the "pure" psychopaths (Figure 8-3).

The surprising finding for the "hysteroid" dyscontrol group (Figure 8-4) is that they were more aggressive and more prone to alcohol abuse than the "pure" psychopaths. There is confirmation of Monroe's observation that psychodynamic considerations are more important than either neurologic or characterologic mechanisms in determining amnesia for dyscontrol acts (1970), at least to the extent that the "hysteroid" group were more likely to show amnesia for their dyscontrol behavior.

The only surprising finding in the "pure" psychopathic group was that they had completed a higher school grade than the "epileptoid" group and did better in the WAIS similarities subtest (Figure 8-6).

The "inadequate" group, which was not characterized in Monroe's 1970 monograph, differed from all others in poor adaptation to stress and lack of responsibility (Figure 8-5). These two items (425 and 435 in Appendix A) are described respectively as "characteristically has tended to be ineffectual when confronted with stress or had difficulty adapting himself to changes in his life or circumstances" and "in his dealing with family, friends, or associates he has felt no obligation to carry out actions necessitated by his relationships to these people or to avoid actions harmful to them." These individuals differed from at least two other groups in terms of more painful interpersonal relations, alcohol abuse, poor judgment, and aimless behavior. Also, they were globally rated as being more severely disturbed and, quite appropriately, were more likely to have had outpatient therapy. This group was also more likely to have specific EEG abnormalities, particularly random sharp waves, and the analyses of EEG data alone revealed that those with the combined abnormalities seemed to be "sicker" than either those with no activation or those with only the nonspecific generalized activation pattern (see Chapter 7).

It was disappointing that the psychometric tests contributed so little to group differentiation although Monroe mentioned in his 1970 monograph that this lack of psychometric differentiation may reflect the transitory nature of the

GP 1 "Epileptoid" Dyscontrol

*High neurologic scale (gps 2,3, &4)
*More neurologic stigmata
*More neurologic hyperacusis (gps 2&3)
 Less passive-aggressive
 More emotional responsiveness
 More perversion
*More guilt
*More CNS impairment
*Less amnesia for act
*More prodromal motor restlessness
*More prodromal autonomic symptoms
*Higher infraction rating

vs.

"Hysteroid"
GP2 Dyscontrol

GP 1 "Epileptoid" Dyscontrol

 High neurologic scale (gps 3,2, &4)
 More epilepsy suspect (gps 3&4)
 More repetitive dreams
 More neurologic hyperacusis (gps 3&2)
 More photophobia
 Better adaptation to stress
 More friends
 Less sensitive
 Less painful relations
 Less fluctuation of feelings
 More responsibility
 Less alcohol abuse
 Less brooding
 Less agitation
 More belligerence-negativism
 More agitation-excitement
 Younger

vs.

"Inadequate"
GP3 Psychopath

GP 1 "Epileptoid" Dyscontrol

*Higher estimated epileptoid mechanism
   (psychiatrist)
*High neurologic scale (gps 4,3, &2)
*More epilepsy suspect (gps 4&3)
*More photophobia
 More stubborn
 Lower completed school grade
 More insomnia
*More aggressive affect during act
*More fear-panic affect during act
*More prodromal anger
*Speach or action is more impulsive
     in group therapy
*More verbal hostility to group therapist

vs.

"Pure"
GP4 Psychopath

*Predicted in Monroe's previous study (1970).
 Underlined item differentiates from all other groups.

Figure 8-3. Group Differences in "Epileptoid" Dyscontrol

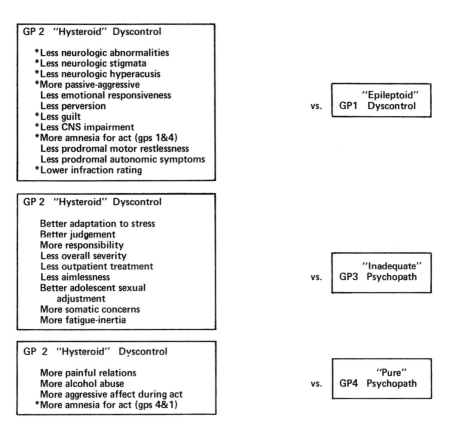

Figure 8-4. Group Differences in "Hysteroid" Dyscontrol

CNS dysfunction in the dyscontrol syndrome. As dyscontrol behavior with an epileptoid mechanism is thought to represent an episodic phenomena—and formal testing is difficult during the episodes—it would not be surprising that psychometric tests show little deficit in the interval between dyscontrol acts. Psychometrics might show more deficit in the episodic reactions where it is presumed the limbic seizural activity is prolonged.

In summary, one can see that much of the clinical data that would be predicted to characterize the four groups, as presented in Monroe's monograph (1970), was substantially confirmed even though his 1970 data were predominantly psychodynamic evaluations whereas the present data is more phenomenologic. The present study did attempt to gather the same types of dynamic data surrounding dyscontrol behavior. In fact, a global rating of an epileptoid

GP 3 "Inadequate" Psychopath

    Less epilepsy suspect
    Less repetitive dreams
    Less hyperacusis
    Less photophobia
    Less neurologic abnormalities
    Poorer adult friendship patterns
    More sensitive
    More painful relations (gps 1&4)
    More fluctuation of feelings
    More alcohol abuse (gps 1&4)
    More brooding
    More agitation
    Less belligerence-negativism
    Less agitation-excitement
    Poorer adaptation to stress (gps 1,2, &4)
    Greater lack of responsibility (gps 1,2, &4)
    Older

vs.   GP1   "Epileptoid" Dyscontrol

GP3 "Inadequate" Psychopath

    Poorer judgement (gps 2&4)
    More overall severity (gps 2&4)
    More outpatient treatment (gps 2&4)
    More aimless behavior (gps 2&4)
    Poorer adolescent sexual adjustment
    Less somatic concern
    Less fatigue-inertia
    More emotional responsiveness
    Poorer adaptation to stress (gps 2,1, &4)
    Greater lack of responsibility (gps 2,1, &4)

vs.   GP2   "Hysteroid" Dyscontrol

GP3 "Inadequate" Psychopath

    More stubborn
    Poorer judgement (gps 4&2)
    More emotionally distant
    More painful relations (gps 4&1)
    More grandiosity
    More overall severity (gps 4&2)
    More outpatient treatment (gps 4&2)
    More aimless (gps 4&2)
    More alcohol abuse (gps 4&1)
    More fear-panic affect during act
    More prodromal anger
    Poorer adaptation to stress (gps 4,2, &1)
    Greater lack of responsibility (gps 4, 2, & 1)

vs.   GP4   "Pure" Psychopath

Underlined item differentiates from all other groups.

Figure 8-5. Group Differences in "Inadequate" Psychopath

GP 4 "Pure" Psychopath

*Lower estimated epileptoid mechanism
  (psychiatrist)
*Less neurologic abnormalities
*Less epilepsy suspect
*Less photophobia
 Less stubborn   (gps 1&3)
 Higher completed school grade
 Less insomnia
*Less aggressive affect during act (gps 1&2)
*Less fear-panic affect during act (gps 1&3)
*Less prodromal anger (gps 1&3)
*Speech or action is less impulsive
  in group therapy
*Less verbal hostility to group therapist

vs. GP1   "Epileptoid"
           Dyscontrol

GP 4 "Pure" Psychopath

 Less painful relations (gps 2&3)
 Less alcohol abuse (gps 2&3)
*Less amnesia for act
*Less aggressive affect during act (gps 2&1)

vs. GP2   "Hysteroid"
           Dyscontrol

GP 4 "Pure" Psychopath

 Less stubborn (gps 3&1)
 Better adaptation to stress
 Better judgement
 Less emotionally distant
 Less painful relations   (gps 3&2)
 More responsibility
 Less grandiosity
 Less overall severity
 Less outpatient treatment
 Less aimlessness
 Less alcohol abuse (gps 3&2)
 Less fear-panic affect during act (gps 3&1)
 Less prodromal anger (gps 3&1)

vs. GP3   "Inadequate"
           Psychopath

*Predicted in Monroe's original study (1970).

Figure 8-6. Group Differences in "Pure" Psychopath

mechanism based on Monroe's original concepts did prove useful in discriminating group 1 from group 4, and somewhat so in discriminating group 1 from 2; however, more subtle evaluations of dyscontrol behavior were difficult since three psychiatrists acted as independent raters.

These data strongly suggest, as Monroe originally postulated, that if a person for whatever reason is destined to become "psychopathic," the pathology is more severe if there is superimposed an underlying CNS involvement (group 1 and group 3 versus group 4) and even somewhat more severe if there is a superimposed neurotic process (group 2 versus group 4). It also seems clear that group 2, as predicted, does represent a more neurotic process, that is, of an overcontrolled individual denying both guilt and memory for his aggressive antisocial behavior.

Finally, the one measure that differentiated our target group "epileptoid" dyscontrol from all others is the neurologic scale (see Chapter 10). The findings reported in this chapter suggest that a discrimination of these groups is important but requires a combination of EEG, neurologic, psychiatric, and self-reporting measures.

References

Davis, K.R., and Sines, J.O. 1974. "An antisocial behavior pattern associated with a specific MMPI profile." *J. of Cons. Clin. Psycho.*, 36:2, 229-234.

Kunce, J.T., Bryan, J.J., and Eckelman, C.C. 1976. "Violent behavior and differential WAIS characteristics." *J. of Cons. Clin. Psycho.*, 44:42-45.

Monroe, R.R. 1970. *Episodic behavioral disorders.* Cambridge: Harvard University Press.

————. 1974. "Episodic behavioral disorders." (Chapter II), in Arieti, S., and Brody, E.B. (Eds.). *American handbook of psychiatry.* New York: Basic Books.

Predicting Group Membership in the Two-dimensional Classification

Jeffrey S. Rubin and *J. David Barcik*

The classification of dyscontrol behavior as presented in Chapters 3 and 8 involves the presence or absence of dyscontrol behavior and CNS instability. Thus, both brain mechanisms and learned behavior are critical mechanisms in determining the form of aggressive recidivism. These two dimensions have been measured by the clinical evaluation of activated theta activity and by the Monroe Dyscontrol Scale respectively. While these two variables are involved in dyscontrol, they are not significantly correlated statistically ($r = 0.14$, $N = 93$) which provides a basis for classifying dyscontrol behavior into the four groups previously mentioned: group 1—"epileptoid" dyscontrol, high theta activation, high Monroe Dyscontrol Scale; group 2—"hysteroid" dyscontrol, low theta activation, high Monroe Dyscontrol Scale; group 3—"inadequate" psychopath, high theta activation, low Monroe Dyscontrol Scale; and group 4—"pure" psychopath, low theta activation, low Monroe Dyscontrol Scale.

Ninety-five variables including the composite item CAPPS scales were chosen for analysis on the basis of clinical judgment and statistical analyses described in previous chapters. The neurological variables were not included in the analysis but are evaluated in Chapter 10. These variables were then used in multiple regression analysis to develop two sets of predictor variables for the activated EEG theta ratings and Monroe Dyscontrol Scale scores. Table 9-1 summarizes those variables in order of greatest amount of variance accounted for by the predictor variable for the EEG theta activation and the Monroe Dyscontrol Scale scores respectively. Five variables were common to both lists so that the total nonoverlapping variable list for both activated EEG theta and the Monroe Dyscontrol Scale contained thirty-five variables.

These thirty-five variables were then used as the variable set upon which discriminant analysis was performed. This would provide an additional means for the classification of new cases into the four-group schema. The solution method was direct and the adequacy of the derived discriminant functions was checked by determining the number of known cases correctly classified. Ns for the groups were as follows: "epileptoid" dyscontrol, 26; "hysteroid" dyscontrol, 27; "inadequate" psychopath, 12; and "pure" psychopath, 28.

The results of the discriminant analysis are summarized in Table 9-2 which demonstrates that discriminating power rests primarily with function 1 and the relative percentage of the total variance accounted for by this function is

Table 9-1

Predictor Variable Set for EEG Theta and Monroe Dyscontrol Scale Scores

EEG Theta Activation Rating	*Dyscontrol Scale*
1. Past CAPPS Scale: intellectual performance*	1. MMPI: L Scale
2. WAIS: Similarities	2. Psychiatrist: Estimated nonepileptoid mechanism
3. Prodromal anger	3. WAIS: Arithmetic
4. Past CAPPS Scale: Manic*	4. Prodromal anger
5. Affect Scale: Level of tension	5. Current CAPPS Scale: Somatic concern-functioning*
6. Mood Scale: Anger-hostility	6. Affect Scale: Emotional responsiveness
7. WAIS: Verbal	7. Mood Scale: Anger-hostility
8. Thinking disturbance during act	8. Affect Scale: Level of tension
9. Poor coordination during act	9. Current CAPPS Scale: Poor impulse control*
10. Mood Scale: Fatigue-inertia	10. Past CAPPS Scale: Poor intellectual performance*
11. MMPI: L Scale	11. Past CAPPS Scale: Poor social-sexual relations*
12. Past CAPPS Scale: Disorganized*	12. Personal discomfort regarding act
13. WAIS: Full Scale	13. Current CAPPS Scale: Elation-grandiosity*
14. Past CAPPS Scale: Hysterical symptoms*	14. MMPI: F Scale
15. MMPI: Sc Scale	15. Past CAPPS Scale: Poor impulse control*
16. MMPI: Si Scale	16. MMPI: Pt Scale
17. WAIS: Block Design	17. Denies responsibility for act
18. Mood Scale: Lack of friendliness	18. Perceptual distortions during act
19. Mood Scale: Tension-anxiety	19. Bender: Class
20. WAIS: Comprehension	20. Sexual feelings during act

*Composite item Current and Past Psychopathology Scales; see Table 5-8 for scale definitions.

approximately 49. The separation of group 3, "inadequate" psychopath, from the other groups is the primary result of function 1 while the secondary separation, function 2, occurs in separating group 1, "epileptoid" dyscontrol, from group 3. Group 2, "hysteroid" dyscontrol, and group 4, "pure" psychopath, were not successfully separated.

Employing all three functions, the cases were classified as to group membership using the correction procedure for unequal group N. From Table 9-3, the result of this classification procedure yields 76.34 percent of the cases correctly classified. The predicted group membership and number of mistakes are summarized in that table. The largest number of mistakes involved classifying

Table 9-2
Discriminant Analysis with a Four-group Schema

Discriminant Function	Eigenvalue	Relative Percentage	Cannonical Correlation
1	1.24398	48.65	0.745
2	0.85959	33.61	0.680
3	0.45366	17.74	0.559

	Wilks' Lambda	Chi-Square	DF	Sig.
1	0.1649	130.695	105	0.043
2	0.3699	72.097	68	0.348
3	0.6879	27.121	33	0.754

group 2, "hysteroid" dyscontrol, cases as group 4, "pure" psychopath, cases and vice versa. It should be noted that discrimination between group 2 and group 4 individuals interprets as a distinction between high and low dyscontrol behavioral scores, not between activated theta ratings, as both groups have a low theta rating. This is not surprising as in Chapter 8 we had found only four variables discriminating between these two groups in a Oneway Anova. Furthermore, the difference, if any, between 2 and 4 would be determined by psychodynamic factors. Such data were not systematically collected in this study.

The variables that represent the three functions are summarized in Table 9-4. Both variables representing function 1 were important in predicting activated theta as represented in Table 9-1. Again, the greatest difficulty in classification involved the low activated theta groups (2 and 4), while the high activated theta groups (1 and 3) were more successfully distinguished.

Groups 2 and 4 represent "hysteroid" and "psychopathic" processes respectively and do not necessarily involve any CNS impairment, unlike group 1, "epileptoid" dyscontrol, and group 3, "inadequate" psychopath. The differenti-

Table 9-3
Predicted Group Membership with a Four-group Schema

Actual Group	N	Group 1	Group 2	Group 3	Group 4	
1	26	22	1	1	2	(4 mistakes)
2	27	3	19	0	5	(8 mistakes)
3	12	1	1	10	0	(2 mistakes)
4	28	2	6	0	20	(8 mistakes)

Note: The largest number of mistakes involved classifying group 2 (Hysteroid) cases as group 4 (Pure) cases and vice versa.

Table 9-4
Variables Representing Each Function in a Four-group Schema

Function	Variable
1	Mood Scale: Fatigue-inertia
	Affect Scale: Level of tension
2	CAPPS: Poor social-sexual relations
	CAPPS: Poor intellectual performance
	WAIS: Similarities
	WAIS: Block design
3	CAPPS: Poor social-sexual relations
	Mood Scale: Tension-anxiety

ating factor for both CNS impairment conditions is dyscontrol behavior, as measured by the Monroe Dyscontrol Scale. On this basis, a three group-schema was developed wherein the CNS-impaired groups (high activated theta) remained separated as a function of impulsivity (dyscontrol scale) while the two "functional" (low theta groups) were combined into a single group. This schema provided the basis for placing emphasis on CNS instability factors in impulsivity. The revised three-group schema including the Ns can be stated as follows: "epileptoid," $N = 26$; groups $2 + 4$, "functional," $N = 55$; and "inadequate," $N = 12$. Using the thirty-five variables the discriminant analysis was repeated within this framework and the adequacy of the derived discriminant functions was again checked by determining the number of known cases correctly classified.

The results of the discriminant analysis are summarized in Table 9-5 which demonstrates that discriminating power rests primarily in function 1, although there is some discriminating power available in function 2. The relative percentage of the total variance accounted for by functions 1 and 2 are 59 percent and 40 percent respectively. The separation of group 3 ("inadequate")

Table 9-5
Discriminant Analysis with a Three-group Schema

Discriminant Function	Eigenvalue	Relative Percentage	Cannonical Correlation
1	1.24398	59.15	0.745
2	0.85919	40.85	0.680

	Wilks' Lambda	Chi-Square	DF	Sig.
1	0.2397	104.273	70	0.004
2	0.5379	45.270	34	0.094

Table 9-6
Predicted Group Membership with a Three-group Schema

Actual Group	N	Group 1	Group 2 + 4	Group 3	Mistakes
GP 1 Epileptoid	26	22	3	1	4
GP 2 + 4 Functional	55	4	51	0	4
GP 3 Inadequate	12	1	1	10	2

from group 2 + 4 ("functional") was the primary result of function 1, while the secondary separation (function 2) occurs in separating group 1 ("epileptoid") from group 3 ("inadequate").

Using both functions, the three groups were classified as to group membership using the procedure for unequal group size. The result of this classification procedure was that 89 percent of the cases were correctly classified. The predicted group membership and number of mistakes are summarized in Table 9-6. The largest number of mistakes involved classifying group 1 cases as group 2 + 4 cases and visa versa.

The variables that represent the two functions are summarized in Table 9-7. Both variables that represent function 1 are the same as in the four-group schema and function 2 is the same as the combination of functions 2 and 3 in the four-group schema except for the variable of sexual affect during act. The three-group schema is essentially the same as the four-group schema, while the percentage of correct classifications is increased from 76 to 89.

Given the three-group schema, it becomes important to know how the groups differ on the variables used in the prediction of group membership. Therefore, oneway fixed-effects analyses of variance were completed using these three groups on each of the thirty-five variables independently. Group differences were tested using post priori contrasts by the least significant difference test. Where group differences were statistically significant ($p \leqslant .05$), the groups involved and the direction of difference were noted. The results of these analyses are summarized in Table 9-8.

Table 9-7
Variables Representing Each Function in a Three-group System

Function 1	Function 2
Mood Scale: Fatigue-inertia	CAPPS: Poor social-sexual relations
Affect Scale: Level of tension	CAPPS: Poor intellectual performance
	WAIS: Similarities
	WAIS: Block design
	CAPPS ADD: Sexual affect during act

Table 9-8

Oneway Fixed Effects Analysis of Variance Using a Three-group Schema with the Predictor Variable Set

Group 1-Group 3 Differences (p ≤ .05)	Group 1-Group 2 + 4 Differences (p ≤ .05)	Group 3-Group 2 + 4 Differences (p ≤ .05)
MMPI: L (1 < 3)	CAPPS: Poor intellectual Performance (1 > 2 + 4)	Prodromal Anger (3 > 2 + 4)
MMPI: Sc (1 > 3)	Prodromal anger (1 > 2 + 4)	Mood Scale: Fatigue-inertia (3 < 2 + 4)
CAPPS: Poor social-sexual relations (1 < 3)	Mood Scale: Fatigue-inertia (1 < 2 + 4)	CAPPS: Somatic concern (3 < 2 + 4)
MMPI: F (1 > 3)	MMPI: Sc (1 > 2 + 4)	Affect Scale: Emotional responsiveness (3 > 2 + 4)
MMPI: Pt (1 > 3)	Est. Nonepil. mechanism, (1 < 2 + 4)	CAPPS: Poor social-sexual relations (3 > 2 + 4)
	MMPI: F (1 > 2 + 4)	CAPPS: Poor impulse control (3 > 2 + 4)
	MMPI: Pt (1 > 2 + 4)	

While the thirty-five variables useful in predicting activated EEG theta or high dyscontrol scale scores are important in establishing group differences, the remaining sixty variables from the original ninety-five-variable pool may also provide information in the demonstration of group differences. Therefore, oneway fixed-effects analyses of variance were completed using the three-group schema with these variables on each of the sixty variables independently. Group differences were tested using post priori contrasts by the least significant difference test. Where group differences were statistically significant ($p \le .05$), the groups involved and the direction of difference are noted in Table 9-9. Group differences may be reviewed as follows.

Group 1 ("Epileptoid") Versus Group 2 + 4 ("Functional")

Group 1 performs or has been poorer in intellectual performance than group 2 + 4. Intellectual performance consists of the highest grade in school, overall academic performance, efforts to improve status, and estimated IQ, with highest number meaning the poorest intellectual performance.

Prodromal anger to dyscontrol acts in group 1 is higher than in group 2 + 4. Group 2 + 4 shows higher fatigue rating than group 1. Group 2 + 4 has less evidence for an epileptoid mechanism than group 1.

Note that less prodromal anger and more fatigue seemed to be characteristic of group 2 + 4 because they not only differentiate 2 + 4 from 1, but also 2 + 4 from 3.

139

Table 9-9

Oneway Fixed Effects Analysis of Variance Using a Three-group Schema with Variables Not Used in the Predictor Variable Set

Group 1-Group 3 Differences (p ≤ .05)	Group 1-Group 2 + 4 Differences (p ≤ .05)	Group 3-Group 2 + 4 Differences (p ≤ .05)
MMPI: K (1 < 3)	MMPI: Ma (1 > 2 + 4)	Fear-panic during act (3 > 2 + 4)
MMPI: Hs (1 > 3)	Prodromal motor restlessness (1 > 2 + 4)	CAPPS: Dependency (3 > 2 + 4)
MMPI: Ma (1 > 3)	Prodromal autonomic symptoms (1 > 2 + 4)	
CAPPS: Depression (1 < 3)	Affect Scale: Speed of Reaction (1 > 2 + 4)	
CAPPS: Dependency (1 < 3)	CAPPS: Organicity (1 > 2 + 4)	

On the other hand, the MMPI Sc Scale, MMPI F Scale and the MMPI Pt Scale differentiate not only 1 from 2 + 4 but also 1 from 3. Thus, in group 1 these scales—Sc, F, and Pt—are higher than the other two groups. Both the high Sc and Pt scores suggest social isolation, as well as generalized symptoms of anxiety and impaired reality testing.

Group 1 seems to be higher in a number of related factors, that is, prodromal motor restlessness, prodromal autonomic symptoms, and increased speed of emotional reaction, and the elevated Ma scale suggests high energy, restlessness and hyperactivity. All these seem to be related. Also, group 1 shows greater "organicity" (CNS impairment and possible epileptoid mechanism).

Group 1 ("Epileptoid") Versus Group 3 ("Inadequate")

For the MMPI data, group 3 shows a higher MMPI L score. In this instance it may reflect concealment, with the subject trying to appear socially acceptable. Group 3 reflects more pathology in social-sexual relations, meaning impaired adolescent friendship patterns, adolescent sexual adjustment, adult heterosexual adjustment, and adult friendship patterns, as well as emotional unresponsiveness and poor pleasure capacity.

Group 3 shows more depression-anxiety, which includes lack of energy, appetite or weight loss, insomnia, brooding, depression, guilt, suicidal thoughts, anxiety, loss of interest, agitation, and painful relations, than group 1. The MMPI K scale is high (defensive) in group 3 and the MMPI Hs scale reflects high somatic concern and irritability in group 1.

Group 3 ("Inadequate") Versus Group 2 + 4 ("Functional")

As already mentioned, group 2 + 4 when compared to group 1 shows less anger and more fatigue-inertia. Group 2 + 4 also shows more somatic concern [which includes conversion reaction and psychophysiologic reactions] than group 3.

Impulse control composite scale as defined on the CAPPS is elevated in group 3 when compared with group 2 + 4. This scale includes antisocial childhood, nonacademic school difficulties, lack of occupational goals or plans, narcotic-drug abuse, alcohol abuse, illegal acts, antisocial traits, impulsiveness, poor judgment, self-defeating behavior, and lack of responsibility. It is likely that the label "impulse control" is inappropriate. Inadequate social adjustment seems more appropriate—hence our label "inadequate" for group 3. Group 3 also shows greater disturbance in social-sexual relations and also more emotional responsiveness on the Affect Scale than group 2 + 4. Group 3 is more likely to show the fear-panic affect during acts than group 2 + 4 and also rates higher on the CAPPS dependency scale which includes ineffectual adaptation to stress, sensitiveness, fluctuation in interpersonal feelings, dependency, passive-aggressive behavior, and blame of others.

It is not surprising that there were no significant differences between the original groups 2 and 4 in that it was in groups 2 and 4 where most of the mistakes were made in utilizing predictors of group membership. In Chapter 8, utilizing a larger data pool (two hundred items) there were few differences (see Chapter 8, Figure 8-4); the most clinically significant ones being the higher incidence of amnesia and aggression in group 2 as compared to group 4. This is supported by clinical impressions, namely the difficulty in differentiating, for instance, malingering (as in the psychopath) from conversion (as in the hysteric). Psychodynamic rather than phenomenologic differentiation is necessary and even from a psychodynamic point of view this distinction is not always easy. For instance, one has to differentiate between the lack of conscience mechanism in the psychopath from the "easy" conscience mechanism of the hysteric. Also, many clinicians feel that the self-dramatization of hypersexuality seen in female hysterics is psychodynamically equivalent to the self-dramatization of tough masculinity seen in many males who demonstrate psychopathic behavior.

10 Neurologic Abnormalities in Prison Subjects

Russell R. Monroe and
Barbara Hulfish

As the research population was not expected to show dramatic neurologic disorders, the neurologic history and examination were directed toward those factors that could be related to minimal brain dysfunction in adults. All subjects were examined by Barbara Hulfish, M.D., on the prison hospital ward under far from optimal conditions. Examinations were done in accordance with the usual principles of clinical examination in neurology (Vazuka 1962) and the data rated on an ordinal scale from zero, equating normal or no findings, to six, reflecting extreme abnormalities.

Table 10-1 lists the twenty-two factors so rated with descriptive statistics for each item. The neurologic evaluation of intellectual functioning was so confounded by social-economic deprivation that we relied on a more formal psychometric battery for these data.

In the analysis of our total data pool, using either EEG activation patterns or the Monroe Dyscontrol Scale as the criterion variable, a number of neurologic findings correlated well with these measures. This suggested that a scale of neurologic signs and symptoms could be developed that would correlate highly with the psychiatric-psychometric or electroencephalographic characteristics of our population. Eleven such variables were selected (with asterisk in Table 10-1). The neurologic scale variables were part of the neurologic data collected and organized as either historical data or part of the examination.

Historical data consisted of evidence of birth trauma, head injury, possible epilepsy, and other central nervous system "insult." School problems, "short fuse," and repetitive dreams were not significantly correlated with the criteria.

In evaluating birth data, consideration was given to the age of the parent at the time of the patient's birth, the number of children the mother had borne, birth difficulties including prolonged labor, forceps delivery, bleeding or other complications of pregnancy, multiple births, prematurity, resuscitation problems, or combinations of these factors. Head injury was rated as minimal to maximal, that is, from trauma to facial soft tissues to repeated closed head injuries with periods of unconsciousness.

Epilepsy suspect referred to a range of symptoms from dizziness, light-headedness, headaches, blurred vision, deja vu or jamais vu, forgetfulness, size, space, shape, or time distortion, absentmindedness, dropping objects, episodic enuresis, frequent falls, to a definite history of tonic-clonic convulsions.

Other central nervous system "insult" noted various infections with delir-

 142

Table 10-1
Neurologic Data

	Mean	Variance	Std. Deviation
History			
Birth data*	2.4	2.9	1.7
Head injury*	3.5	2.3	1.5
Epilepsy suspect*	4.4	1.2	1.1
School problems	4.3	1.3	1.2
"Short fuse"	3.4	3.7	1.9
Repetitive dreams	0.9	3.1	1.8
CNS "insult"*	3.4	1.7	1.3
Examination			
Scars and birthmarks	3.5	1.8	1.4
Congenital stigmata*	2.3	0.9	1.0
Hyperacusis*	1.6	3.0	1.7
Photophobia*	1.3	2.0	1.4
Hypersensitivity to touch	1.0	1.5	1.2
Cranial nerves II	2.0	1.1	1.0
Cranial nerves III, IV, and VI	1.4	0.6	0.8
Cranial nerves other	1.5	1.3	1.2
Motor observation I	1.0	0.1	0.3
Motor observation II	1.1	0.1	0.3
Motor strength*	2.9	3.2	1.8
Reflexes	2.1	1.8	1.4
Coordination* (−)	1.7	1.3	1.1
Sensation* (−)	2.5	2.2	1.5
Apraxia*	2.7	3.7	1.9

*Items selected for neurologic scale.

ium, or drug abuse to a point of unconsciousness with evidence of frontal lobe symptoms such as poor judgment and recent memory impairment.

The neurologic examination included congenital stigmata, hyperacusis, photophobia, apraxia, motor strength, coordination, and sensation.

Congenital stigmata included small head, small ears, pectus excavatum, extra toes or fingers, large birth marks, amblyopic eyes, strabismus, and odd behavior or hyperactivity during the examination.

Hyperacusis was rated on the basis of distractibility, intolerance of high pitches, or cacaphony with an evaluation of the patient's distractibility by extraneous noises during the neurologic examination itself.

Photophobia was rated on the basis of intolerance to bright fluorescent lights, as well as the aversive responses to such lights during the examination itself including a history of wearing dark glasses, excessive pupilary reaction to a bright light, and spontaneous remarks on questioning regarding the intolerance to bright or flashing lights.

Apraxia evaluated fine motor dexterity varying from assembling a four-part stapler (for the more intelligent subjects) to simply replacing batteries in a flashlight (for the less intelligent subjects).

Motor strength (in the absence of orthopedic reasons) was evaluated in terms of the extremities, with particular emphasis on whether there was a difference between the strength in opposite extremities, tested by the two arms held overhead against resistance; external rotation against resistance; flexion and extension of the elbows and wrists; as well as grasp. In the lower extremities, there was a test for flexion and extension of the knees, and dorsiflexion of the feet and toes with the patient being asked to hop first on one foot and then on the other.

Coordination was tested in terms of finger to thumb coordination, looking for mirror movements, dysdiadochokinesia, rapid alternating tongue movement, and foot tapping. Sensation was tested for pain (pin prick), vibration, proprioception, but not for light touch or temperature. Scars, handedness, cranial nerve dysfunction, speech, and reflexes were not statistically significant.

A neurologic scale was developed as the algebraic sum of eleven neurologic variables:

+ birth data

+ head injury

+ epilepsy suspect

+ other CNS "insult"

+ neurologic stigmata

+ hyperacusis

+ photophobia

+ apraxia

+ motor strength

− coordination

− sensation (as coordination and sensation seem consistently less disturbed in our high EEG activation group)

The descriptive statistics of the neurologic scale for the 93 subjects were a range in actual scores from +6 to +36 with a possible range of −3 to +52. The mean was 19.6 and the standard deviation 6.6.

Multiple regression analyses suggest that these eleven neurologic variables might be reduced to seven, but future analysis of the data will be necessary before the reduced scale is proven more useful than that reported.

Significant product-moment correlations with the two hundred and fifty-variable pool are listed in Tables 10-2 and 10-3. There proved to be a surprising consistency on the correlational analysis between these disparate instruments and different observers who were totally naive regarding the data collected by their peers. With exceptions noted later, the correlations showed a consistency with the clinically evolved concept of the "epileptoid" dyscontrol act.

Correlations of the neurologic scale at the .05 level and beyond were found with the psychiatric history for anger, violent behavior, overreactive emotional behavior, as well as fluctuation of feelings, poor judgment, poor efforts to improve, self-defeating action, lack of responsibility, grandiosity, illusions, hypochondriasis, fugue state, and specific health concerns. This was also true for neurotic or antisocial traits in childhood and poor peer relationships during adolescence. It may appear incongruous, but it was predicted on the basis of the early findings that these particular subjects were more likely to have received specific medical or psychiatric treatment for their problems (Monroe 1970).

The mental status examination revealed correlations with belligerent-negativistic behavior, and psychophysiologic and conversion symptoms. Again, as was predicted, there was a correlation between dyscontrol behavior in those with evidence of CNS impairment and absence of premeditation, but contrary to the original predictions Monroe 1970) we found that such dyscontrol behavior was more likely to be accompanied by specific rather than diffuse affects (usually anger). Correlations with prodromal feelings of anger or physiologic instability were also found.

It is important to note that the psychiatrist's estimate of an epileptoid mechanism based on behavioral symptoms (see Table 10-2) correlated with the neurologic scale at the .001 level. Correlations on the Mood and Affect Scales were consistent with the psychiatric history in that these individuals were more likely to show current emotional liability or impulsivity with a high level of tension and little evidence for fatigue or inertia.

Not surprisingly, there was a correlation at the .001 level between the neurologic scale and dyscontrol behavior as measured by the Monroe Dyscontrol Scale (inasmuch as the Monroe Dyscontrol Scale was one of the criterion variables in formulating the neurologic scale), but this seemed to be supported by institutional ratings of the custodial staff where there was also a correlation with institutional rule infractions.

Ratings by the institutional group therapists, who were totally naive regarding the research hypothesis, showed a correlation with a wide range of emotional responses and verbal hostility toward the therapist. Also, the neurologic scale correlated highly with active participation in therapy.

On the psychometric tests, the BIP-Bender indicating evidence for distractibility and this as well as the Holtzman inkblot pattern suggesting concrete thinking with a poor form response and a low capacity for abstraction—all

Table 10-2

Product-Moment Correlations with the Neurological Scale (Items from the Modified Current and Past Psychopathology Scales)

Data Source	Variable Description	Coefficient $p \leqslant .05$
Past History (psychiatrist)	Neurotic traits in childhood	.18
	Antisocial traits in childhood	.31*
	Adolescent friendship patterns	.21
	Outpatient treatment	.23
	Received treatment for psychopathology	.25*
	Poor efforts to improve	.17
	Somatic concerns	.17
	Amnesia, fugue, dissociative state	.22
	Hypochondriasis	.17
	Overreact emotionally	.27*
	Anger	.31*
	Violent	.28*
	Impulsivity	.39*
	Poor judgment	.27*
	Self-defeating	.20
	Fluctuation of feeling	.21
	Lack of responsibility	.22
	Grandiosity	.24*
	Overall severity	.19
Current Behavior (psychiatrist)	Conversion reaction	.22
	Psychophysiological reactions	.18
	Grandiosity	.27*
	Belligerence-negativism	.26*
Dyscontrol Characteristics (psychiatrist)	Lack of premeditated acts	.18
	Specificity of affect during act	.18
	Prodromal anger	.20
	Prodromal autonomic symptoms	.17
Global Estimate (psychiatrist)	Epileptoid mechanism	.40*

Source: Table 4 from Russell R. Monroe, et al., "Neurologic Findings in Recidivist Aggressors," in *Psychopathology and Brain Dysfunction* edited by C. Shagass, S. Gershon, and A.J. Friedhoff © 1977 by Raven Press, New York, p. 247. Reprinted by permission.
*$p \leqslant .01$.

suggesting the possibility of minimal organic damage correlated with the neurologic scale. Psychological variables that were not significant, thus not reported in Table 10-3, were the Wechsler Adult Intelligence Test, the Minnesota Multiphasic Personality Inventory, the Memory for Design Test, the Porteus

Table 10-3
Product-Moment Correlations with the Neurological Scale Items from the Psychological Tests and Clinical Scales)

Data Source	Variable Description	Coefficient $p \leqslant .05$
Mood Scale (psychiatrist)	Lack of fatigue-inertia	.17
Affect Scale (psychiatrist)	Level of tension	.19
	Emotional lability	.25*
	Impulsiveness	.27*
Monroe Scale (self-rating)	Dyscontrol score	.31*
Infraction Rating (custodial staff)	Prison infraction rating	.21
EEG (clinical)	Chloralose-induced paroxysmal theta	.33*
Bender BIP (psychologist)	Distractibility	.18
	Degree of organicity	.19
Holtzman (psychologist)	Form definitiveness (FD)	.18
	Animal (A)	.17
	Anatomy (At)	.21
	Abstract (Ab)	−.18
Draw-a-Line (psychologist)	Distance estimation	−.29
Group Behavior Questionnaire (staff therapist)	Active participation	.25*
	Wide range of emotions	.34*
	Verbal hostility to therapist	.23

Source: Table 5 from Russell R. Monroe, et al., "Neurologic Findings in Recidivist Aggressors," in *Psychopathology and Brain Dysfunction* edited by C. Shagass, S. Gershon, and A.J. Friedhoff © 1977 by Raven Press, New York, p. 248. Reprinted by permission.
*$p \leqslant .01$

Mazes, Matching Familiar Figures, Time Estimation Test, and Slow Writing Test.

Davis (1975) noted that schizophrenics who also had cerebral dysrhythmias similar to those found in the above studies, were more likely to have had birth trauma, head injuries, and high fever with delirium during childhood, as well as to have demonstrated clumsiness, tantrums, phobias, and so on. Morrison (1975) reported that individuals with childhood symptoms of hyperactivity as well as brain insult or epilepsy showed explosive dyscontrol behavior during adulthood.

Considering these reports and the data presented here on the correlations between the neurologic scale and aggressive dyscontrol behavior as well as the data previously reported on EEG abnormalities (Chapter 7), it seems likely that central nervous system dysfunction plays a part in certain forms of aggressive antisocial action.

The importance of these observations is highlighted by Wolfgang (1975) in a study regarding adolescent delinquency in an inner city ghetto area. His findings that up to 35 percent of the adolescents will have a police record before they reach adulthood is astounding, but even more so is the fact that 52 percent of the offenses leading to the police record were committed by only 6.3 percent of this cohort. This suggests that there are a small group of recidivist offenders who are responsible for most of these antisocial acts. Our study population is probably this recidivist aggressor group. On the average, our subjects had six or more convictions prior to the time of our study. Thus, if a significant group of offenders could be identified as having a neuropsychiatric disorder and if such a disorder is treatable, as we believe it is, then the medical model for the control of criminal behavior becomes important.

The most surprising and enigmatic finding is that despite other neurologic pathology these dyscontrol recidivists with activated EEG abnormalities are more likely to be normal on sensory and gross motor coordination examinations than are the rest of the Patuxent population.

Admittedly our findings leave many questions unanswered and demand further investigation. First, is our neurologic scale something that can be communicated to other neurologists and would there be a high interrater reliability in utilizing this scale? Such interrater reliability was tested as far as the psychiatric ratings but not for the neurologic evaluations. Second, how does the neurologic scale correlate with recidivism in an unselected group of convicted criminals; that is, is the population of the Patuxent Institution a unique group? Third, we will need prospective studies of young delinquents to see how accurately this neurologic scale will predict recidivism.

References

Davis, R.K., Neil, J.F., and Himmelhoch, J.M. 1975. "Cerebral Dysrhythmias in schizophrenics receiving phenothiasines: Clinical correlates." *Clin. Electroenceph.,* 6:103-115.

Monroe, R.R. 1970. *Episodic behavioral disorders.* Cambridge: Harvard University Press.

Morrison, J.R., and Minkoff, K. 1975. "Explosive personality as a sequel to the hyperactive child syndrome." *Comp. Psychiat.,* 16:343-348.

Wolfgang, M.E. 1975. "Delinquency and violence from the viewpoint of criminology." In: *Neural bases of violence and aggression,* edited by W.S. Field and W.A. Sweet. St. Louis: Warren H. Green.

Vazuka, F.A. 1962. Film: *Essentials of the neurological examination.* Smith, Kline and French Laboratories, Philadelphia, Pennsylvania.

11

Response to Anticonvulsant (Primidone) Medication

Russell R. Monroe,
David A. Paskewitz,
George U. Balis,
John R. Lion, and
Jeffrey S. Rubin

Previous studies on hospitalized psychotic patients (Monroe 1965) had shown that primidone (Mysoline) either alone or in combination with other drugs that elevate seizural threshold, controlled impulsive aggressive behavior. An attempt was made therefore to repeat these findings in nonpsychotic individuals who were also prone to violent behavior. Primidone was selected over other anticonvulsants such as phenytoin (Dilantin) on the basis of this earlier study even though less systematic clinical observations had also demonstrated that phenytoin was equally effective in individuals showing episodic dyscontrol.

Booker (1970) studied serum primidone levels in 105 chronic seizure patients comparing these levels with previous studies on phenytoin and phenobarbital. He found that the serum half-life of primidone following a single oral dose varied from 10 to 12 hours, a finding similar to that of Gallagher (1970) who reported a half-life range of 3.3 to 19 hours and a mean of 8.0 plus or minus 1.1 hours. Also Gallagher found that peak plasma concentrations of primidone occurred on the average of 2.7 hours following a single dose with a range from 0.5 to 7 hours. In subjects receiving 1,000 mg. per day of primidone over a two-month period Gallagher found that the peak level was delayed, occurring 4 to 5 hours after the oral dose, and the half-life was elevated, with a range of 9 to 25 hours. Both Booker and Gallagher noted that after a delay of 24 to 96 hours following initiation of primidone treatment, phenobarbital, as a metabolite, appeared in the blood serum, ultimately attaining a blood serum level two to three times that of primidone itself. This was explained by Booker on the basis of the more prolonged half-life of phenobarbital (three to four days) compared to the relatively short half-life of primidone. Booker suggested that in view of this relatively short half-life of primidone as compared to other anticonvulsants, including both phenobarbital and phenytoin (half-life of 22 hours), it was of particular importance to administer primidone in divided doses throughout the day. In subjects whose primidone serum levels were monitored several times throughout the day, Booker found a mean fasting level in the morning of 6.2 mcg. per milliliter, rising throughout the day to a high of 10.6 in late afternoon. In one subject whose serum level was monitored during the night

149

the evening level maintained itself, but by early morning, just prior to the first dose, it reached a level below therapeutic range. In Booker's study the mean value of primidone in the group whose seizures were controlled was 7.6; however, this was not significantly different from a group where the seizures were uncontrolled, and he concluded that beyond a serum level of 10.0 the control of seizures was not facilitated. Simple side effects such as drowsiness and nystagmus occurred at a mean serum level of 8.7 while the more complicating side effects such as ataxia and sleepiness occurred when the mean serum value reached 15.0.

Booker also found that the pharmacologically "naive" volunteer subjects who took an initial dose of 500 mg. of primidone suffered marked side effects within one hour, complaining of lightheadedness and giddiness; after four hours they were still drowsy. During the remainder of the day they were unable to concentrate and some slurring of the speech was apparent. Horizontal nystagmus was noted in some subjects at the time that the serum level was maximal. These volunteers continued to complain of difficulty in concentrating on the following day. Booker points out the value of determining serum drug levels, particularly when monitoring outpatient treatment with anticonvulsant medication. Such measures are sufficient to reveal whether patients are taking their medication on a regular basis.

Prison is somewhat like the outpatient situation because subjects are not on a hospital ward, hence not under close supervision. Thus, prisoners may refuse to take medication and also on occasion will go to great lengths to hide medication, take illicit drugs, or swap placebos and active drugs. Tupin (1972) observed this behavior while studying the effect of lithium on impulsive behavior among prisoners. Those who disliked the lithium effect would save up active medication to sell to those who liked it. Also, prisoners recognized placebo medications and often switched to fool experimenters. This switching caused serious difficulty in the experimental protocol as one could not be sure who was taking what. The only solution to this problem is to monitor serum drug levels.

The best compromise between the pharmacologic-physiologic and institutional needs of our subjects was to give the drug twice a day and not only monitor blood serum levels for primidone, but also perform routine urine analyses to detect illicit-drug use, while having a nonblind researcher administer medications. A therapeutic regimen in a prison setting, of necessity, is a compromise between sound pharmacologic practice and an acceptable regimen to prisoners and security personnel.

The method for determination of anticonvulsant drug levels in serum was a Varian Aerograph (2700 series) equipped with a flame ionization detector coupled to a Varian A-25 Recorder. The column consisted of a three-foot one-eighth inch I.D. glass coil that is packed with 5 percent OV-7 coated on 80/100 mesh Gas Chrome-Q. Both the injector and the detector temperatures are held at 275 degrees centigrade. During an analysis the column oven temperature is varied between the limits of 190 degrees centigrade and 280 degrees centigrade at a rate of 12 degrees centigrade per minute. Nitrogen pressure of 16 PSI is maintained at the injector while flow rates of air and hydrogen are kept at 300 and 66 milliliters per minute respectively. The gas chromotograph is operated at a sensitivity of about 256×10^{-11} amps per millivolt. The serum is extracted with methylene chloride and after evaporation reconstituted in chloroform. Utilizing this technique the therapeutic range of primidone is considered to be 4.0 to 12.0 mcg. per milliliter.

Because medication in pill or capsule form can be easily hidden or manipulated, primidone was given as an elixir. The carrier was 200 mg. calcium sulfate per 5 cc., and the active elixir contained 50 mg. primidone per cc.[a] The carrier alone then provided the placebo medication. A careful observer could detect the slightly thicker, somewhat bitter active elixir from the placebo. The elixir was administered by the researcher who had the most contact with the prisoners. It was administered in the prison dispensary in front of the researcher, from a small clear plastic cup, after which the subject filled the cup with water to rinse down the medication.

The period of medication included eight weeks on placebo and eight weeks on active drug with a random crossover design. Subjects continued with their usual routines during the drug period except that twice a day they left their activities to come to the dispensary, a process that required seeking passes from guards and walking through a number of checkpoints. Thus, each trip might take up to one-half hour. Although more frequent medication might have been desirable from a pharmacologic point of view, it seemed impractical in this setting. Studies reported later in this chapter on blood serum levels indicate that patients maintained adequate therapeutic levels under this regimen, with a maximum primidone intake of 500 mg. two times a day. As Booker indicated, if patients started immediately with this level they complained of disconcerting side effects, particularly nausea, dizziness, sleepiness, and difficulty in concentration. Actually, our subjects would not tolerate side effects when medication started at 5 cc. (250 mg. per dose).

To avoid the initial side effect problems, the regimen started with a single 2 cc. dose once a day (100 mg.) for the first week followed by 5 cc. twice a day (500 mg. per day) the second week. The third week the individual received 5 cc. (250 mg.) in the morning and 10 cc. (500 mg.) in the afternoon while in the fourth week maximum dose was obtained, 10 cc. (500 mg.), twice a day and this was continued for the subsequent four weeks, allowing for a decrease during the last week of the medication phase (see Figure 3-2).

Primidone blood serum level was determined the third day of the fourth week; that is, when the individual had been receiving 500 mg. two times a day for the preceding two and a half days. The blood sample was taken six hours after the preceding dose and by this time on the average the subject had received

[a]Provided by Ayerst Laboratories, 685 Third Avenue, New York, New York 10017

152

a total of six grams of primidone over the preceding three weeks plus two days. On three occasions blood levels indicated that the subject was not taking the medication. In two instances the prisoners were given a second chance after admitting that they had avoided medication, and subsequent serum levels showed they cooperated with the drug regimen. A third individual had to be dropped from the study because he continued with his noncompliance despite warnings that he would be dropped.

Routinely subjects had two blood samples taken, one in each of the two drug phases. However, 9 subjects who were on active drug were monitored at weekly intervals over a period of ten weeks including one week following cessation of medication so that we could evaluate how quickly therapeutic levels built up and how long they were maintained after drug termination (Figure 11-1).

Subjects who started on placebo and shifted to active drug in the second phase were maintained on a constant volume of medication but the drug dose was initiated at the same low level of 100 mg. per day and gradually built up to the 1,000 mg. per day by mixing appropriate amounts of active and placebo elixir. Subjects verbally reported any side effects each day when they received

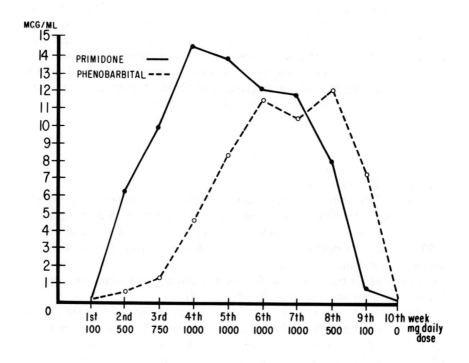

Figure 11-1. Mean Serum Levels of Primidone and Phenobarbital

their medication. The prison population is quite hypochondriacal or will often use either imagined or feigned symptoms for ulterior motives so it was imperative that the member of the research team administering drugs knew not only the prisoners but also the exact level of medication each prisoner was receiving.

One variation of this routine that soon became necessary was that weekend administration of medication had to be given in a double dose each morning; otherwise the routine would have interfered with the prisoners' recreational or visiting activities.

In the sixth and fourteenth week of the sixteen-week period, an EEG was done. At this time a urine sample was taken from the subject which was also analyzed for a wide range of drugs that might have been illicitly obtained in the prison. These included methadone, morphine, codeine, quinine, amphetamine, and barbiturates. It became apparent that illicit-drug use was not a problem, so routine urinalysis was discontinued. However, we continued to spot-check for illicit-drug use by urinalysis. Phenobarbital was found in the urine of subjects on active drug since it is one of the metabolites of primidone.

Ten subjects had some medication other than that prescribed by the research team during the study period. Two received antidepressants, one a benzodiazepine, one doxepin, and the rest various phenothiazines. However, in these ten instances it was felt that drug dosages used would have had no significant interaction with an anticonvulsant regimen. Several possible subjects who were on more complex regimens with high dose levels were rejected from the study.

Sixteen (23 percent) of the 69 subjects who dropped out of the study did so because they disliked the drug effects (see Chapter 4). The usual complaints regarding the drugs were dizziness, nausea, hyperirritability, drowsiness, or ataxia, and most of those who dropped out had two or more of these symptoms.

In the 93 subjects who completed the drug regimen the mean primidone level was 13.4 with a range of 5.5 to 34.2 and a standard deviation of 4.12. The means and standard deviations were not significantly different in those who received the medication first followed by placebo from those who received the placebo first followed by medication. Only 4 subjects showed primidone levels above 19. One had a level of 34.2, the second 23.0, a third 21.0, and a fourth 19.4. The particularly high level in one subject was never adequately explained but he had been on high levels of phenothiazines for an extended period of time before the study and voluntarily dropped out of the study because of preference for his chlorpromazine as compared to the research drug. Individuals showing relatively high blood serum levels did not particularly complain of drug side effects. In the 9 subjects who were followed at weekly intervals, the drug level peaked by the fourth week (at the time that we were measuring drug serum levels in all subjects) and persisted in all but 2 beyond the eighth week and then was zero one week after medication ceased. In all but 2 subjects serum levels had reached therapeutic point by the end of the second week and in all subjects such levels were present by the third week (Figure 11-1).

One of the striking findings with regard to the serum analysis of these patients was the phenobarbital range of 0 to 15 mcg. per milliliter with a mean of 3.15 and a standard deviation of 3.56. Compared to the findings of Booker and Gallagher, where their subjects' phenobarbital levels were three to four times those of primidone levels, our levels were just the reverse, usually one-third to one-quarter of the primidone levels. However, by the seventh week, in the 9 subjects studied, it had reached a ratio of approximately one. The marked difference between studies is explained by the different metabolic response of our pharmacologically "naive" subjects compared to subjects who are epileptic and have had a long history of anticonvulsant medication. It is also known that a combined phenytoin and primidone regimen increases the phenobarbital-primidone ratio (Gallagher 1970).

The data on primidone blood serum levels indicate that our complex drug regimen was successful in promoting adequate therapeutic levels and in reducing dropouts due to an intolerance for unpleasant side effects.

Analyses of Drug (Primidone) Effects

The Statistical Package for the Social Sciences (SPSS) was the analysis program used to code and analyze our data. Unfortunately, SPSS does not provide an analysis of variance (Anova) program which allows repeated measures with unequal Ns, although the program is flexible in other respects. The drug analysis could be pursued through the use of multiple regression analysis of coded dummy variables, an approach yielding potentially more information. A simpler approach, however, has been developed to allow the use of the (SPSS) Anova program to analyze this particular data set.

The four-way analysis of drug effects may be conceptually broken down into two subanalyses. The first of these subanalyses is the between-subjects analysis, comprised of those factors where independent groups of subjects may be established, namely, the Monroe Dyscontrol Scale score, EEG activation rating, and order dichotomies and their interactions. The second analysis, the within-subjects analysis, consists of those components that include the drug-placebo factor in any form. The between-subjects analysis is pursued simply as a three-way analysis in a conventional manner after drug effects are removed by summing the two drug conditions and using this sum as the individual score. The within-subjects analysis requires that the data be arranged as though each drug condition were an independent set of cases. Once this has been accomplished the data are analyzed using a four-way Anova approach. The error term obtained by such an approach, however, is inappropriate for use with those components that contain the repeated drug factor. Fortunately, since the drug factor is a dichotomy, and is the only repeated measure, the overall error sum-of-squares obtained in the second analysis need only be reduced by the between-subjects error sum-of-squares obtained from the first analysis in order to yield the appropriate error term for testing the drug components.

Examining the four main effects of the Monroe Dyscontrol Scale score, EEG activation, drug order, and primidone (Table 11-1), there is no evidence that the Monroe Dyscontrol Scale division into high and low alone effected a significant difference within any dependent variable. The implications of the Monroe Dyscontrol Scale are better realized by its combination with theta activation data and are reflected in its interaction effects to be presented later. The theta activation alone did, however, show a difference among the high and low groups in three variables, namely prison sex, Holtzman Form Definitiveness, and Holtzman Pathognomic Verbalization (Table 11-2). In all variables, the low theta groups (groups 2 and 4) had means significantly lower (more normal) than the high theta groups (groups 1 and 3, see Chapter 8). Regarding the theta activation results on the three variables reported earlier, we see that those with a high theta activation score on the EEG are more likely to act out sexually within the prison and show a tendency for concrete thinking.

In order effects alone across the variable pool, we notice three variables that showed significant placebo-active versus active-placebo effects. Somatic concerns were evidenced more in those subjects who started on placebo medication and then switched to active than in those who started on active. Secondly, there was less emotional lability noticed in the subjects starting on placebo than in those starting on active medication. Thirdly, the placebo-active group had more human responses on the Holtzman, possibly indicating less defensiveness.

Finally, in discussing drug effects alone, we notice five variables showing such effects, two of which are validity checks on the medication (primidone and phenobarbital levels). The remaining three variables showing pure drug effects were somatic concerns, psychophysiological reactions, and Holtzman Human Responses. The first two may reflect the side effect of primidone medication. More human responses on the Holtzman Inkblot in the drug group suggested that the subjects on primidone might have been less defensive with a better mental outlook than the placebo group.

Interaction Effects in the Four-group System

Recalling the four-group system (see Chapter 3), group 1, the "epileptoid" dyscontrol group, is composed of subjects with high dyscontrol scale scores, high activated theta; group 2, the "hysteroid" dyscontrol group, is composed of subjects with high dyscontrol scale scores, low activated theta; group 3, the "inadequate" psychopath group, is composed of subjects with low dyscontrol scale scores, high activated theta; and group 4, the "pure" psychopath group, is composed of subjects with low dyscontrol scale scores, low activated theta.

Table 11-1
Significant Variables in Drug Analysis
(p ≤ .05)

Variables	*Source*	*Mean Differences*			
		M	*E*	*O*	*D*[a]
Current: somatic concerns	(O) (D)			PA > AP	A > P
Current: psychophysiological reactions	(D)				A > P
Current: elated mood	(E-O)			Lo < Hi	PA > AP	
Current: suicide-self mutilation	(M-D)	Lo < Hi			A > P
Current: prison sex	(E) (M-E-O)	Lo < Hi	Lo < Hi	PA > AP	
Current: denial of illness	(E-O-D)		Lo < Hi	PA < AP	A < P
Primidone level	(D)				A > P
Phenobarbital level	(D)				A > P
Side Effects Number	(D) (M-E) (M-E-D)	Lo < Hi	Lo > Hi		A > p
Holtz: reaction time	(O-D)			PA < AP	A > p
Holtz: form definitiveness	(E)		Lo < Hi		
Holtz: pathognomic verbalization	(E)		Lo < Hi		
Holtz: human responses	(O) (D)			PA > AP	A > P
Holtz: abstract	(M-D)	Lo > Hi			A > P
Holtz: barrier	(M-E-O-D)	Lo > Hi	Lo < Hi	PA > AP	A > P
Holtz: balance	(M-E-D)	Lo < Hi	Lo < Hi		A > P
Auditory Discrimination Task: error quiet	(O-D)			PA < AP	A > P
Auditory Discrimination Task: error noise	(O-D) (M-O-D)	Lo < Hi		PA < AP	A > P
Mood: fatigue-inertia	(E-O-D)		Lo < Hi	PA > AP	A > P
Mood: confusion	(M-O)	Lo < Hi		PA > AP	
Affect: number of feelings	(E-O-D)		Lo> Hi	PA < AP	A > P
Affect: emotional lability	(O)			PA < AP	
Affect: impulsiveness	(M-D)	Lo < Hi			A > P
Lion Symptom Checklist	(O-D) (M-E-D) (M-E-O-D)	Lo > Hi	Lo < Hi	PA < AP	A > P
GRx: attendance	(M-O-D)	Lo > Hi		PA < AP	A < P
GRx: feelings for patient	(M-E-O)	Lo < Hi	Lo < Hi	PA < AP	
Time Estimation Task	(O-D)			PA > AP	A > P
Draw-a-Line	(O-D)			PA > AP	A > P
Porteus: test quotient	(O-D) (M-E-O-D)	Lo < Hi	Lo < Hi	PA > AP	A > P
Matching Familiar Figures: reaction time	(M-O) (O-D)	Lo < Hi		PA > AP	A > P
Matching Familiar Figures: total errors	(O-D)			PA < AP	A < P

aM – Monroe Dyscontrol Scale (Lo = < 20, Hi = ≥ 20)
  E – EEG Activation Rating (Lo = <5, Hi = ≥ 5)
  O – Order (PA = placebo-active, AP = active-placebo)
  D – Drug (A = active primidone, P = placebo)

Table 11-2
Summary of Main Effects

	EEG Activation Rating
Current:	prison sex (Lo < Hi)
Holtz:	form definitiveness (Lo < Hi)
Holtz:	pathognomic verbalization (Lo < Hi)

	Monroe Dyscontrol Scale
None	

	Order
Current:	somatic concerns (PA > AP)
Affect:	emotional lability (PA < AP)
Holtz:	human responses (PA > AP)

	Drug
Current:	somatic concerns (A > P)
Current:	psychophysiological reactions (A > P)
Primidone level (A > P)	
Phenobarbital level (A > P)	
Holtz:	human responses (A > P)

The results from Table 11-3 indicate that significant differences across groups reveal themselves in our target group 1 versus group 4 (four significant variables); group 2 versus group 3 (one significant variable); and group 3 versus group 4 (two significant variables). The variables that differentiate group 1 from group 4 are prison sex, Holtzman Balance, group therapist feeling for patient, and Porteus Maze Test Quotient. In all cases, the means of these variables were higher for group 1 than group 4. As it was predicted that group 1 would particularly respond to primidone, it is important to note that the Porteus Maze Test Quotient and Holtzman Balance response did improve on primidone although for the Porteus only in the placebo-active sequence.

Regarding group 2 versus group 3 differences, the one variable that differentiated the groups was number of side effects; group 2 ("hysteroid") reported more side effects than group 3 ("inadequate") if they were on primidone, which probably reflects neurotic dramatization of side effects.

Regarding group 3 versus group 4 differences, the two variables showing significant differences between the groups are Holtzman Barrier responses and Lion Symptom Checklist scores. There were more Barrier responses in group 3 ("inadequate") compared to group 4 ("pure") while on primidone if they were in the placebo-active sequence. Group 3 reported more symptoms while on primidone than group 4 if they were in the active-placebo sequence. The Lion Checklist responses will be discussed in more detail later.

Table 11-3
Summary of Interaction Effects in the Four-group Schema[1]

Variables	Mean Differences		
	Groups	Order	Drug
Current: prison sex	GP1 > GP4	PA > AP[a]	−
Side effects number	GP2 > GP3	−	A > P[b]
Holtz: barrier	GP3 > GP4	PA > AP	A > P
Holtz: balance (symmetry)	GP1 > GP4	−	A > P
Lion Symptom Checklist	GP3 > GP4	PA < AP	A > P
GR_x: dislikes patient	GP1 > GP4	PA < AP	−
Porteus: test quotient	GP1 > GP4	PA > AP	A > P

1. Group 1 = Hi Monroe Dyscontrol Scale, Hi Theta Activation Rating
   Group 2 = Hi Monroe Dyscontrol Scale, Lo Theta Activation Rating
   Group 3 = Lo Monroe Dyscontrol Scale, Hi Theta Activation Rating
   Group 4 = Lo Monroe Dyscontrol Scale, Lo Theta Activation Rating

[a]PA indicates the placebo-active sequence; AP indicates the active-placebo sequence.
[b]A indicates active medication; P indicates placebo.

In Table 11-4 the items marked by asterisks are interpreted as evidence of an improvement and only in the placebo-active sequence group was this improvement unequivocal. Three of the five indicators of improvement occurred in all groups and two more general indicators of improvement occurred in the active-placebo group. All these were psychological tests indicating improved performance, the only exception being auditory discrimination where errors increased in all groups on drug during the quiet subtest and also increased in the high dyscontrol group in the noise subtest. Thus, the drug must have had a general effect not determined by group assignment, in most instances improving intellectual performance. It is pertinent to report a finding that in the six-week follow-up those who identified correctly the drug period and claimed that the drug helped them would usually describe this in terms of "I think clearer," "I have it all together," "My mind is clearer," or "I see things in better perspective." This finding was a surprise to us, and no systematic data were collected on this factor in the Lion Symptom Checklist.

The high theta activation group suspected of hyperactivity (see Chapter 5) developed more inertia; hence this finding is considered an improvement. Additionally, this group showed less denial of illness, also an improvement. These occurred in the placebo-active and the active-placebo sequence respectively. The low dyscontrol group showed some suggestion of improvement in Abstractions on the Holtzman and in attendance at group therapy sessions, but the high dyscontrol group seemed to worsen behaviorally with the drug, that is, they were more impulsive and showed more suicidal thoughts or actions. In part, this is contrary to the prediction that at least the high dyscontrol, high theta

Table 11-4
Interactive Drug Effects

No Sequence Effects		Drug Effect
Suicide-self-mutilation	High dyscontrol	↑
Impulsiveness	High dyscontrol	↑
Holtzman Abstract responses	Low dyscontrol	↑*
Placebo-Active Sequence		
Mood: Fatigue-inertia	High theta	↑*
Time estimation	All groups	↑*
Draw-a-Line	All groups	↑*
Porteus Test Quotient	All groups	↑*
Matching Familiar Figures reaction time	High dyscontrol	↑*
Active-Placebo Sequence		
Denial of illness	High theta	↓*
Affect: No. of feelings	Low theta	↑*
Lion Symptom Checklist	All groups	↑
Holtzman reaction time	All groups	↓*
Auditory discrimination task: error quiet	All groups	↑
Matching Familiar Figures: total errors	All groups	↓*
Auditory discrimination task: error noise	High dyscontrol	↑
Group R_x: attendance	Low dyscontrol	↑*

*Indicates therapeutic improvement.

activation group 1 would show less impulsivity. This finding demands a closer look at the primidone regimen in the high dyscontrol, low theta activation group 2 in the future. Although it is not clear from the current study, it may be that the "hysteroid" group 2 responds adversely to anticonvulsants.

From the previous data it is not entirely clear but presumed that a greater number of feelings is an improvement for the low theta activation group.

Finally, it was hoped that the Lion Symptom Checklist would be an adequate measure of improvement on the primidone regimen. Actually, all subjects in the active-placebo sequence showed more symptoms and group 3 "inadequate" became worse in the placebo-active sequence (Table 11-3). Reviewing this list of symptoms on the Lion Symptom Checklist (Appendix F), it is clear that most of the statements (except item 11) reflect steady states and not episodic symptoms. Also, only late in the study did we add item 12A, "thinking clearly," which seemed to be the most frequently reported positive subjective response while on the drug.

160

Conclusion

We anticipated that in the controlled prison environment it would be hard to demonstrate drug effects compared to, for instance, a disturbed psychotic population (Monroe 1965). We did hope that by utilizing a number of measures that had proven useful in psychiatric inpatient and outpatient studies some might be found to be sensitive to drug effects, and a few were. The most direct measure of a target symptom would be infraction ratings—a measure of possible dyscontrol behavior. However, our population committed so few serious infractions per observation period (six weeks) that this proved to be an insensitive measure. The mental status designed for a psychiatric population was more sensitive than expected and evidenced four correlations with drug effects out of forty-one items, two of these probably discerning dysphoric side effects. Our symptom checklist omitted a factor that seemed to be of most importance, namely "clearer thinking," and was not a discriminating analysis of drug response. Mood and affect showed some changes as did group therapist observation. Psychometrics were more sensitive to change and indicated improvement under the drug condition, but our hope that the subgroups would respond differentially and thus enhance the clinical usefulness of our subtyping did not prove true except with regard to the Porteus Maze Test Quotient. However, we do not believe that this possibility can be rejected until it is tried on a group in a less structured environment (for example, this population when "back on the street"). It should be noted that 16 percent did report that the effect of medication was their primary reason for continuing the study (see Chapter 4).

References

Booker, H.E., Hosokowa, K., Burdette, R.D., et al. 1970. "A clinical study of serum primidone levels." *Epilepsia,* 11:395-402.

Gallagher, B.B., Smith, D.B., and Mattson, R.H. 1970. "The relationship of the anticonvulsant properties of primidone to phenobarbital." *Epilepsia,* 11:293-301.

Monroe, R.R., and Wise, S. 1965. "Combined phenothiazine, chlordiaze-poxide and primidone therapy for uncontrolled psychotic patients." *Am. J. of Psychiat.,* 122:694-698.

Tupin, J.E. 1972. "Lithium use in nomanic depressive conditions." *Comp. Psychiat.,* 13:209-214.

12 Summary of Findings
Russell R. Monroe

Utilizing the Monroe Dyscontrol Scale and activated theta activity ratings the 93 aggressive criminal subjects were assigned to four groups: group 1—high theta-high dyscontrol ("epileptoid" dyscontrol); group 2—low theta-high dyscontrol ("hysteroid" dyscontrol); group 3—high theta-low dyscontrol ("inadequate" psychopath); group 4—low theta-low dyscontrol ("pure" psychopath).

The criterion variables were sufficiently powerful to separate unique clinical entities, although routine psychometric and psychiatric data alone were insufficient to define these groups adequately. Although pairing group 1 with group 2 and group 3 with group 4 yielded similar MMPI profiles, the former pair (high dyscontrol groups) showed significant differences from the latter pair (low dyscontrol groups). This was particularly true of group 1 ("epileptoid" dyscontrol) which showed significantly elevated scores on the psychotic tetrad, paranoia (Pa), psychasthenia (Pt), schizophrenia (Sc) and mania (Ma), while all four groups showed elevated psychopathic deviate (Pd) scores. There were no significant differences on the MMPI between the high and low activated theta groups. On the other hand, the psychiatric profiles on the Current and Past Psychiatric Scales (CAPPS) did show some significant differences between the high and low activated theta groups. For instance, group 1 was significantly higher than group 2 on the CAPPS scale labeled "organicity." We feel that a better label for this would have been "CNS impairment." Group 3 was significantly higher than group 4 on the scales labeled "poor impulse control" and "dependency." These scales measured inadequate behavior, antisocial acts, and drug abuse. Neither the MMPI nor the CAPPS, however, adequately described all four groups.

Among measures distinguishing group 1 ("epileptoid" dyscontrol) from the others, a neurologic scale (see Chapter 10) consisting of eleven items provided a score that differentiated our particular target group (group 1 "epileptoid" dyscontrol) from all other groups. This neurologic scale included a history of possible (1) birth trauma, (2) head injury, (3) formes frustes of epilepsy, and (4) CNS insult, such as infection, excessive drug use. The neurologic examination contributed to this score in terms of physical evidence of (1) congenital stigmata, (2) hyperacusis, (3) photophobia, (4) apraxia, and (5) asymmetries in motor strength. On the other hand, this group actually performed better than the other three groups on (6) gross coordination and (7) sensory discrimination. These data, plus the fact that both the psychiatrist and the neurologist made a global estimate that these individuals were likely to have an epileptoid mechanism as at least a partial explanation of their behavior, seem to indicate that the label "epileptoid" is an appropriate one. However, the psychiatric data gave little information that clearly differentiated the "epileptoid" from the others in terms of either the psychiatric history or the mental status examination, except that this group appeared to be more sexually active and perverse, both within the prison and in their past lives. This group was also identified by their group therapist as more likely to show impulsive and aggressive behavior during therapeutic sessions.

Group 2 ("hysteroid" dyscontrol) in comparison to one or the other of groups 1, 3, and 4 appeared to be as aggressive as group 1 during their dyscontrol acts, but more likely to be amnesic following the act. This finding, in association with the lack of neurologic symptoms or history suggesting an epileptoid mechanism, as well as the increased somatic concerns and tendency to exaggerate drug side effects, seems to indicate that "hysteroid" is an appropriate label for this group.

Group 4 ("pure" psychopath) was the "normal" group; that is, in a random sample of the population it would be assumed that this group as a whole would demonstrate less psychopathology than the other groups. This was true also for this study group but, of course, with our prison population, these individuals gave both projective and psychiatric anamnestic data for antisocial behavior. Thus, the label "psychopath" seems appropriate for this group in this particular study.

Group 3 ("inadequate" psychopath) was a surprise in terms of the lack of neurologic signs and symptoms (except for EEG theta) and in terms of the minimal psychometric evidence for organicity. This group is identified, however, by the psychiatric history, particularly such factors as poor adaptation to stress, impaired judgment, emotional unresponsiveness, hypersensitivity, fluctuation of feelings, lack of responsibility, grandiosity, aimlessness, alcohol abuse, brooding, agitation, and severity of symptoms. For this reason it seemed to us that the label "inadequate" personality or "inadequate" psychopath was appropriate.

The psychometric battery selected to measure behavioral control, central nervous system integration, and cognitive control did not show differences between these four groups, although the psychometric battery did reveal some differences in those individuals with EEG abnormalities (drug-activated generalized theta waves and/or specific abnormalities, most often random spikes or sharp waves). The group with unequivocally normal electroencephalograms even after physiologic (sleep and hyperventilation) and drug (alpha chloralose) activation had a greater capacity in planning and more deliberation in responding to ambiguous stimuli as measured by the psychometric evaluation.

A multiple regression analysis of our data revealed that the MMPI and the psychiatric scales could be utilized to predict group membership correctly in 89 percent of our subjects if the grouping was collapsed into a three-group schema as follows: group 1–"epileptoid" dyscontrol; group 3–"inadequate" psychopath. (These groups showed equal evidence for drug-activated generalized theta waves); group 2 + 4—a combination of the former group 2, "hysteroid" dyscontrol, and group 4, "pure" psychopath (in other words, group 2 + 4 represented those individuals where the criminal behavior is presumed to be psychosocially determined, with both lacking evidence for central nervous system instability in the form of drug-activated theta waves or "soft" neurologic signs).

This discrimination depends upon two functions. The first includes fatigue-inertia and level of tension on the Mood and Affect Scale respectively, and the second function includes poor social-sexual relations, poor scholastic performance, and poor scores on the WAIS subtests of similarities and block design. The fact that group 2 and group 4 are difficult to differentiate is not surprising when one considers that our data source and collection system did not emphasize the psychodynamic features that would differentiate between them.

Table 12-1 summarizes the global characteristics of our four groups. Perusal of this suggests some speculation. First, group 1 ("epileptoid" dyscontrol) may be an adult version of the hyperkinetic or minimal brain dysfunction of childhood. This conjecture plus the suspicion of an epileptoid brain activity leads one to predict not only that there may be a significant genetic component behind this group, but also that perinatal and early childhood CNS "insult" may contribute to this disorder.

Table 12-1
Summary of Four-group Characteristics

	Group 1	Group 2	Group 3	Group 4
Suspicion of epilepsy	+			
Neurologic dysfunction	+			
Excessive motor activity	+			
Deviant thinking	+			
Sexual aggression	+			
Hostility	+			
Poor academic performance	+			
Passive-aggressive		+		
Amnesia		+		
Less overt guilt		+		
Socially inept			+	
Irresponsible			+	
Poor judgment			+	
Aimless			+	
Poor interpersonal relations			+	
Alcohol abuse			+	
Better abstract thinking				+

On the other hand, group 3 seems to be the most severely ill and socially deviant group. The fact that this group shows equal evidence of CNS instability with group 1 in terms of the activated theta waves, but does not manifest other evidence of neurologic disorder nor suspicion of epilepsy, has some important implications. The "inadequate" group is not significantly characterized by early childhood central nervous system "insult" but rather by a CNS dysfunction fundamentally different than that manifested by group 1 despite EEG similarities. Perhaps this reflects a maturational lag rather than the epileptoid mechanism proposed for group 1.

Finally, group 2 ("hysteroid" dyscontrol) may represent the neurotically overcontrolled and generally inhibited person who manifests explosive aggression as described by Megargee (1966).

Because of our preliminary success in identifying four reasonably distinct groups among subjects who within the criminal justice system were seen as a homogeneous group, it was a disappointment that we could not document more dramatic changes on anticonvulsant medication, particularly in our target group (group 1 "epileptoid" dyscontrol). Our research design was confounded by the lack of dyscontrol behavior even in prone individuals when they live under strictly imposed external restraints. Additionally, our results are confused by a strong order effect with most therapeutic responses occurring in the placebo-active sequence. There is a suggestion that the target group (group 1) may function better intellectually under anticonvulsants, since both the Porteus Test Quotient and the symmetry or Balance responses on the Holtzman increased. There is evidence, however, on other intellectual measures that all groups showed increased functioning on the drug regimen. It is interesting that the most common statement by those who differentiated drug from placebo and who felt they had benefited from the medication was the remark that they "thought more clearly." These meager positive findings have to be balanced against the fact that under medication some patients actually felt more impulsive and suicidal, while others had numerous somatic complaints, probably reflecting the side effects of primidone, but this response was more likely to occur in the "hysteroid" group. It is obvious, then, that testing the heuristic value of this grouping as an aid in planning an appropriate pharmacologic regimen will depend upon an analysis of dyscontrol subjects in a less restricted environment, either prisoners who have returned to the street or psychotic patients whose dyscontrol behavior, for whatever reason, is less restrained.

Reference

Megargee, E.I. "Undercontrolled and overcontrolled personality types in extreme antisocial aggression." *Psychological Monographs.* 80/3: (Whole No. 611), 1966.

13

Implication of Findings

Russell R. Monroe,
George U. Balis, and
John R. Lion

Three assumptions underlying this study have up to this point remained implicit. For the discussion that follows regarding the implications of our findings in light of other studies on criminality, these assumptions must be made explicit. First, this study is one of aggression, not of criminality per se. In fact, we are concerned particularly with a primitive, explosive type of aggression. This type of aggression was indeed a critical factor in selecting our research population. We thought that a group of recidivist aggressors such as those found at Patuxent Institution would yield a source of subjects manifesting aggressive dyscontrol defined by our research criteria. This proved to be the case in 60 percent of our subjects and we feel that our findings contribute to the understanding of criminal behavior relevant to aggressive dyscontrol.

Second, underlying the research was the assumption of heterogeneity of psychiatric diagnoses. Currently, there has been reexamination of diagnostic categorizations that have heretofore been considered homogeneous (for example, schizophrenia and manic-depressive psychosis), not to mention the wastebasket category of antisocial behavior. Furthermore, because our view of aggression as a target symptom was itself heterogeneous, this research cannot be considered to be a comprehensive study of aggression, but rather a study of aggression by men who have been repeatedly violent in their past criminal acts, and who have been given indeterminate sentences until such time treatment may render them able to reenter society.

Third, our research was based on a multivariate approach to understanding behavior. This concept ideally considers genetic, perinatal, developmental trauma (both psychologic and medical) and socioeconomic-cultural factors; however, it is virtually impossible to design a protocol that will give appropriate weights to all factors involved. For example, the selection of our research population probably established a homogeneous group regarding inheritable and socioeconomic factors, while it magnified the significance of psychiatric, neurologic, neurophysiologic, and neuropsychologic factors. The complexity of analyzing such a population centers on the validity and reliability of measurement, for if the instruments are sound, the skewness of the results may indeed be caused by a critical single factor in that multivariate formula. In our research, we found that one single factor stood above the rest in accounting for most of the variance among this "homogeneous" population, and that was some undefined neuropsychiatric syndrome which possibly has specific prognostic and

165

therapeutic implications. It was with this in mind that we defined subgroups of aggressive (criminal) individuals. In this way we were able to explore the use of the medical model in investigating socially destructive behavior.

The integration of our findings with other studies of antisocial behavior encourages a better understanding of this important area; however, the limitations of our study for making broader generalizations regarding antisocial behavior should be kept in mind.

The complexity of our analysis demanded a hypothesis, which simply stated was that an episodic recurring central nervous instability could result in recurrent aggressive behavior. Defining a dyscontrol group on the basis of a self-rated dyscontrol scale and activated EEG theta waves, we found that such a group could be identified by other measuring instruments as long as these consisted of data from the neurologic examination, psychiatric history, current behavior (both in and out of therapy), psychometric tests, and to some degree, response to a medical regimen. Further, we discovered and characterized a second group, ("inadequate" psychopath) not predicted on the basis of our hypothesis, which showed equal evidence for central nervous system dysfunction in terms of activated EEG theta waves, but less impulsiveness and less neurologic dysfunction. This group showed more psychosocial impairment. These two groups were contrasted with a third and fourth group that seemed to be determined more by psychodynamic and social factors.

The pivotal aspect of this chapter will be the neurologic dysfunctions reported both in this study and in those of other investigators. Such studies have focused on three areas: (1) aggression as a sequela to head trauma, (2) dysfunction in the dominant hemisphere as a characteristic of psychopathy, and (3) the relationship of temporal lobe abnormalities, or psychomotor epilepsy, to criminality. Studies related to aggression were reviewed in Chapter 2; in this chapter emphasis will be placed not on aggressiveness alone but psychopathy in general.

Flor-Henry (1974) observed that dysfunction in the dominant hemisphere seemed to be related not only to learning and reading difficulties but also to psychopathology, including childhood autism, schizophrenia, as well as psychopathy. In contrast, dysfunction of the nondominant hemisphere was related to affective disorders. His observations have resulted in an intense interest in measuring hemispheric dysfunctions. Yeudall (1977a, 1977b) utilizing a neuropsychiatric battery and a spectral analysis of the electroencephalogram, confirmed Flor-Henry's findings and specifically focused on criminal behavior. Utilizing these techniques, he could predict recidivist and nonrecidivist groups with over 70 percent accuracy, far exceeding previously published predictive measures. Earlier, Serafetinides (1965) found that in patients selected for anterior temporal lobectomy, aggressive behavior was associated with left (dominant) temporal lobe involvement as well as with early onset of epilepsy and male gender. Taylor (1972) also concluded, on the basis of follow-up studies of temporal lobectomized patients, that lesions in the left temporal lobe were more likely to be associated with aggressive behavior.

Since Wechsler in 1958 made the statement that sociopathic populations score higher on the WAIS Performance Test than on the Verbal Test, there have been a number of studies (reviewed by Yeudall 1977a, 1977b) supporting this finding as well as almost an equal number that failed to show this disparity between performance and verbal scores. The verbal impairment in psychopaths would tend to support, then, the hypothesis that dysfunction in the dominant hemisphere correlates highly with criminal activity. However, such a finding is compounded by the learning and reading disabilities manifested by dominant lobe dysfunction as well. There may be a complex interaction between this intellectual dysfunction and delinquency as there have been a number of studies suggesting that the severity of delinquent behavior is proportionate to the severity of the reading disability (Yeudall 1977a, 1977b).

Although we did not systematically test for hemispheric function, it is important to note that in our sample, there was no difference in the WAIS performance and verbal scores. On our discriminant function analysis, WAIS Similarities and Block Design, which should measure left-right dysfunction respectively, did turn up as discriminating variables of a low power, but this did not suggest left (dominant) hemisphere dysfunction in our subjects. Despite Yeudall's findings in predicting recidivism, one wonders whether the dominant hemisphere dysfunction, supposedly associated with psychopathy, may be a secondary rather than a primary etiologic mechanism contributing to the criminal behavior of only a small group of incarcerated individuals.

Frontal Lobe–Limbic System Dysfunction

In Chapter 2 we reviewed the current literature on the relationship of aggressive behavior and epilepsy, particularly temporal lobe epilepsy. We also pointed out in Chapter 6 and Chapter 10 that while the prevalence of aggressive behavior may be more common in epileptic subjects, particularly temporal lobe epileptics, in our group of aggressive individuals we found only 1 subject with a significant history of typical seizures and only 5 of the 93 showed evidence for a temporal lobe focus, either spike or slow wave. Thus, it is our conclusion that among a group of incarcerated aggressive criminals, very few will manifest temporal lobe epilepsy.

Here we would like to discuss a complex neurophysiologic and neuroanatomic concept proposed by Yeudall (1977a, 1977b) to explain psychopathic behavior in general. He proposes a three-dimensional brain model with dysfunction in any one of these dimensions or combination of these dimensions as likely to lead to characteristically unique subgroups of psychopathic behavior. The behavioral correlates and the neurophysiologic explanation of this behavior are not entirely clear but ultimately he thinks he can identify the following subgroups: (1) a frontal-limbic psychopath, (2) a temporal-limbic psychopath, (3) a neocortical temporal psychopath, (4) dorsal-lateral frontal lobe psychopath. A simplified behavioral description of these "neuroanatomical psychopaths" describes behavior reminiscent of two of our four groups as follows: (A) dysfunction of dorsal-lateral convexity of the frontal lobes, behaviorally characterized by

1. impairment in planning and intention
2. inability to predict consequences of one's actions
3. reduction in abstract reasoning
4. reduction in concentration and motivation
5. reduction of language as a means of regulating foresight
6. distractibility
7. impulsivity, disinhibition, and euphoria;

(B) dysfunction of orbital surface (limbic projection) of the frontal lobe, behaviorally characterized by

1. lack of self-control
2. emotional outbursts
3. changes in personality
4. lack of guilt and remorse
5. increase in sexual and aggressive drives
6. more psychopathic type behavior
7. affective disorders
8. increased sensitivity to alcohol.

Yeudall's group B fits most closely with our group 1, "epileptoid" dyscontrol, while his group A fits most closely with our group 3, "inadequate" psychopaths. In both groups 1 and 3 our studies indicated CNS instability in the form of activated theta frequencies. As the orbital surface of the frontal lobe is the primary projection of the limbic system to the frontal lobe, and Yeudall, furthermore, points out a variance of a limbic system dysfunction wherein the psychopaths manifest an overactivation of facilitory mechanisms manifested by explosive dyscontrol acts, it would seem that he comes close to recognizing our limbic system dysfunctions and characterizing them in much the same way that we have in this study.

It is certainly true, as Yeudall points out, that dysfunctions in the limbic system and the prefrontal cortex alone or in combination could result in a typical psychopathic behavior. For instance, stimulation of the limbic system elicits intense affects often with impulsive actions, appropriate autonomic responses to these intense affects, as well as confusion and blocking of memory.

Bilateral lesions within the limbic system, depending upon their location and extent, exert a "taming" effect on the individual (Monroe 1970). Williams (1962 p. 701) succinctly states that the functions of the temporal lobe are "much more closely identified with the subject himself; they involve his emotional life, his instinctive feelings and activities and his visceral response to environmental change. . . . that is to say they include his social as well as his physical milieu."

Prefrontal functions may also play a decisive role in the expression of psychopathic behavior in that, as Luria (1973) points out, "it is this area that seems responsible for the regulation of man's intentions, strategies, and planning all necessary to correct mistakes he has made in the past and to check whether future actions are following the right course." Nauta (1971) further elaborated on the role of the frontal lobes in terms of that area monitoring and modulating activity in both the neocortical regions and the limbic system, adding that it is the reciprocal relationship between the frontal lobes and the limbic system that is responsible for anticipation of the future.

Although Yeudall (1977a, 1977b) mentions the caveat that one cannot anatomically localize psychopathy within the brain and points out that an individual's behavior represents a complex interaction among neurophysiologic systems rather than any simple dysfunction of one area or another, this type of neuroanatomical thinking usually rests on extreme extrapolations from minute bits of neuropsychologic data. We have tried to keep such extrapolations to a minimum in the development of our own hypotheses which are the following.

1. With the present state of our neurophysiologic knowledge, it is impossible comprehensively to explain behavior in neurophysiologic terms.

2. In view of this, we make no attempt to describe the neurophysiology of psychopathy but rather look at a group of psychopathic individuals to see whether a subgroup could be identified that has either EEG evidence and/or neurologic evidence for CNS dysfunction.

3. We hypothesize that there are individuals with an intermittent dysfunction of neuronal mechanisms, best described as a focal ictal activity in subcortical areas of the brain, without typical epilepsy, but associated with intermittent behavioral disturbances. This intermittent hyperexcitability of neurons, which we call an "epileptoid" mechanism, is probably most often localized in the limbic system because of its low seizural threshold. On the basis of our present knowledge we have no idea what other areas may be included in the subcortical focal seizure.

4. On the basis of factual evidence we are in no position to decide whether such focal ictal activity is the result of heredity, trauma, toxic, maturational, or psychological mechanisms. It could be any one of these or more likely some combination of these that result in the lowered threshold and ictal response.

5. As direct evidence for this subcortical focal activity is limited to a few patients monitored by chronically implanted subcortical electrodes, we are forced to infer such activity on the basis of behavioral characteristics or induced

electroencephalographic abnormalities through the use of activating drugs. For this reason, we often refer to the potential for a lowered threshold as "central nervous system instability." Furthermore, in avoiding overly inclusive and specific neuroanatomical and neurophysiologic theorizing, we propose that a certain number of our aggressive criminals would show evidence for soft neurologic signs and symptoms on the neurologic examination and give a significant history of past neurologic insult. Yeudall (1977a, 1977b) found that based on medical records and interviews with his patients, 70 percent gave a history of head injuries, unconsciousness, and blackouts, data similar to ours, and that 90 percent of them showed deficits on his neuropsychologic battery suggesting frontal and/or temporal defects. Others have reported similar findings, including Elliott (1976), Feldman (1976), Freides (1976), Lorimer (1972), and Mark (1975).

Theoretical Formulation of Aggressive Dyscontrol Acts

This formulation is based on Monroe's 1970 phenomenologic analysis of the "act as a unit" summarized diagrammatically in Figure 1-2. He hypothesized that dyscontrol acts reflect an absence or distortion of the reflective delay, which is normally interposed between the environmental stimulus and the behavioral response to that stimulus. Monroe stated that reflective delay "is the time involved in trial action through thought, the time needed for establishing the uniqueness and the familiarity of external reality by associative connections with past experiences, the time necessary to contemplate a series of alternate courses of action, the time necessary to project into the future and predict the outcome of alternative actions." If one looks at the middle column of Figure 1-2, labeled "Reflective Delay," one can see that the component parts are (1) affects, (2) memory, (3) anticipation, (4) reason, and (5) conscience. A severe deficit in any one component or what is a more likely situation, some deficit involving several or all of these components, leads to the absence or distortion of this reflective delay. Monroe pointed out that the failure of the central integrative mechanism involving reflective delay resulted from two possibilities, either "faulty equipment," that is dysfunction of the central nervous system, or "faulty learning," that is failure in the developmental educational process. He postulated that the former was more likely related to an absence of reflection and the latter to a distortion of reflection based on idiosyncratic personal and social factors. Examining these component aspects in more detail, Monroe proposed the following.

    1. *Affective disturbances:* whether the dysfunction is learned or is the result of focal seizural activity in the limbic system, the outstanding affective distortion is intense dysphoric feelings, particularly of the emergency emotions, fear and rage, which would not only overwhelm what otherwise might be normal

control (inhibitory) mechanisms but also distort the evaluation of the objective reality and demand an explosive escape or attack response. What Monroe did not consider was the alternative extreme, that is the lack of affective responsiveness and the implication of such lack on the socializing process. For instance, there is some evidence from skin conductance studies that a number of behavioral disorders, including psychopathy, can be divided into two large groups, an overreactive and an underreactive group (Hare 1977). Monroe did mention that a lack of inhibitory anxiety would seriously interfere with the development of appropriate conscience mechanisms.

2. *Memory:* adaptive behavior depends upon intact memory as illustrated by the incapacity of the severely demented patient. Equally important is the consolidation of new learning and the recall of appropriate past experiences, all seemingly related to normal limbic system function. It is the affective component of the stored memory that is probably the link between the current perception (with its concomitant affects) and the recollection of appropriate stored memories with similar affects.

3. *Anticipation:* Monroe (1970) pointed out that one of the most unique characteristics of homosapiens is the anticipation not just of the immediate future but of the far distant future as well, that is, anticipation not only of one's existence but of the world beyond one's existence, the very essence of the so-called existential anxiety. This seems to be a function of the prefrontal cortex and is phylogenetically represented by the dramatic increase in the size of the prefrontal lobes in man compared to even the highest primates. As Nauta (1971) states, "the reciprocal frontal-limbic relationship could be centrally involved in the phenomenon of behavior anticipations. This anticipatory mechanism is necessary if the prefrontal region is to play a decisive role in the formation of intentions and programs in the regulation and verification of the most complex forms of human behavior." Nauta further states that the frontal lobes "allow for comparison of the effective action with the original intention." This is why, if this mechanism is impaired, the patient "loses the power to look critically at the results of his actions, to correct mistakes he has made, and to check whether his actions are following the right course" (Luria 1968). Monroe (1970) pointed out that the development of the prefrontal cortex not only is a late phylogenetic development but also is functionally a late ontogenetic development. That is, "anticipatory mechanisms of seeing the distant future are obviously quite rudimentary in the preschool child. What is equally true is that such anticipation does not develop fully until late adolescence and early adulthood, perhaps not until the resolution of the adolescent "identity crisis." As this anticipatory mechanism is a prerequisite of socialized behavior, then, the concept of a maturational lag in some individuals demonstrating antisocial behavior is appropriate (Monroe 1970).

4. *Reason:* the reflective delay, as here described has been referred to in the psychoanalytic literature as "thought as trial action." This thinking is often if

not always talking to oneself, suggesting the possibility of a correlation between the failure in reflective delay in those individuals that have language or learning disabilities on the basis of dominant hemispheric dysfunction.

5. *Conscience mechanism:* the development of conscience depends upon all components mentioned above, that is, the memory of what has been rewarded and what has been punished in the past, probably etched into the memory systems by the affects of pleasure with reward and pain with punishment. Anticipation of the future consequences of our behavior in terms of the reward-punishment system associated with the automatization of the conscience mechanisms based on the reasoning process is necessary if the conscience is to operate when a policeman is not at our elbow (Monroe 1970).

Finally, Monroe (1970) pointed out that there was another delay process. This he referred to as "choice" delay which could operate only following reflective delay, that is, when alternatives were envisioned regarding the possible consequences of anticipated behavior. Monroe says, "choice delay implies postponement of immediate gratification for long term rewards. It is a decision regarding possible devious actions or preparatory actions; that is waiting for the 'opportune time' or 'biding one's time.'" He points out that even though reflective delay does occur, choice delay may not, particularly when the urges are so strong as to lead the individual to seek gratification, "the consequences be damned." This is reflected in such statements as "I will take my chances" or "I will pay the price" or "I will suffer the consequences." This attitude implying a lack of choice delay undoubtedly characterizes a number of psychopaths but is at a completely different level of central integration than the lack of or distortion in reflective delay discussed earlier. Choice delay must be influenced more by learned behavior.

It must be remembered that sometimes the short circuit of reflective delay and the absence of choice delay may be an adaptive response rather than a maladaptive one. In such instances, we refer to the individual's spontaneity or his spontaneous act. A given situation may demand an instantaneous act or at other times such an instantaneous act (or thought) is a creative inspiration. This spontaneous behavior has adaptive and creative potential, particularly in those individuals whose life otherwise is disciplined or governed by the long-term development of particular skills or talents (Monroe 1978). Most often, however, the failure of delay between the stimulus and the response leads to either self- or socially destructive behavior.

The complexity of the act as a unit is such that simple neurologizing of psychopathic behavior leads to theories that are far removed from clinical experience. Our analysis would suggest that the presence of neurologic stigmata or a history of central nervous system insult would not be a surprising finding in many psychopaths. On the other hand, complex psychodynamics and social considerations would make it equally surprising if all antisocial individuals showed such neurologic defects. For example, our own research project which undoubtedly maximized the finding of neuropsychiatric disorders among a group of criminals still indicated that only 40 percent had EEG and/or significant neurologic abnormalities.

Mednick's study (1975a, 1975b) of genetic factors in criminal behavior would suggest that virtually all our subjects were at high risk for criminal activities; namely, both biologic as well as rearing fathers were criminals. Social dysfunction is also complicated by assortive mating which could only increase the high risk characteristics of our group. This is indicated by the frequency of mental illness and alcoholism in parents, siblings, and other relatives in our subjects. Furthermore, Gordon's (1976) study on the correlation of low intelligence with delinquency, and Mednick's finding that the only significant factor that seems to protect high risk individuals from developing criminal behavior is intelligence, would further indicate the potential high risk of our group whose mean IQ was low normal.

Clarifying the interactive affects in criminality, then, will necessitate an analysis of neurologic, psychiatric, and psychometric data in an unselected group of subjects who are first entering the criminal justice system. We did uncover one interesting demographic variable in our study, namely, that our subjects had a mean educational level that was at least two years lower than the level of their fathers. This was a surprising finding and the interpretation of this remains unclear. It is possible that even though the fathers of our subjects were equally deprived from a social-economic point of view, the children's (our subjects') poor school achievement might be explained on the basis of some central nervous insult during birth or their early developmental years. Unfortunately, our data did not clarify such a hypothesis.

The most significant finding in our study is that the concept of episodic dyscontrol with an "epileptoid" mechanism could be established on the basis of a careful phenomenologic analysis of behavior in almost 30 percent of our population. On the basis of this and previous studies, one must remember that between episodes, integrative adaptive behavior is often intact, and during these periods the individual is responsive to psychotherapeutic and reeducational intervention. Also on the basis of this and previous studies it is possible to design a drug regimen that raises the seizural threshold, particularly of the limbic system, which in turn could reduce or eliminate dyscontrol acts. Because of these characteristics, the "epileptoid" dyscontrol group of criminals must be identified as they will respond favorably to an appropriate therapeutic program.

References

Elliott, F.A. 1976. "The neurology of explosive rage. The dyscontrol syndrome." *Practitioner,* 217:51.

Feldman, R.G., and Paul N. 1976. "Identity of emotional triggers in epilepsy," lecture delivered at the University of Maryland School of Medicine.

174

Flor-Henry, P. 1974. "Psychosis, neurosis, and epilepsy. Developmental and gender-related effects and their etiological contribution." *Brit. J. Psychiat.*, 124:144.

Freides, D. 1976. "A new diagnostic scheme for disorders of behavior, emotion, and learning based on organism environment interaction," Part I and II, *Schizo. Bull.*, 2:218.

Gordon, R.A. 1976. "Prevalence: The rare datum in delinquency measurement and its implications for the theory of delinquency," (Chapter 8), in Klein, M.W. (Ed.). *The juvenile justice system, Vol. V. Sage criminal justice system.* Beverly Hills: Sage Publications.

Hare, R. 1977. "Electrodermal and cardiovascular correlate of psychopathy," (Chapter 7), in Hare, R.D., and Schalling, D. (Eds.). *Psychopathic behavior: Approaches to research.* London: Wiley.

Lorimer, F.M. 1972. "Violent behavior and the electroencephalogram," *Clin. Electroencephal.*, 3:193.

Luria, A.R. 1968. "The complex mechanisms of psychological processes," *Impact of Science on Society,* 18:141.

_____. 1973. *The working brain. An introduction to neuropsychology.* New York: Basic Books.

Mark, V.H., Sweet, W., and Ervin, F.R. 1975. "Deep temporal lobe stimulation and destructive lesions in episodically violent temporal lobe epileptics," in Fields, W.S., and Sweet, W.D. (Eds.). *Neural bases of violence and aggression.* St. Louis: Warren H. Green.

Mednick, S.A. 1975a. "A bio-social theory of the learning of law-abiding behavior," presented at the Proceedings of the II International Symposium on Criminology, Sao Paulo, Brazil.

_____. 1975b. "Considerations regarding the role of biological factors in the etiology of criminality," presented at the Proceedings of the II International Symposium on Criminology, Sao Paulo, Brazil.

Monroe, R.R. 1970. *Episodic behavioral disorders.* Cambridge: Harvard University Press.

_____. 1978. "The episodic psychoses of Vincent van Gogh," *J. Nerv. Ment. Dis.,* 166: (July in press).

Nauta, W.J.H. 1971. "The problem of the frontal lobe: A reinterpretation," *J. Psychiat. Res.,* 8:167.

Serafetinides, F.A. 1965. "Aggressiveness in temporal lobe epileptics and its relation to cerebral dysfunction and environmental factors," *Epilepsia,* 6:33.

Taylor, D.C. 1972. "Mental state and temporal lobe epilepsy: A correlative account of 100 patients treated surgically," *Epilepsia,* 13:727.

Williams, D. 1962. "Temporal lobe syndromes," in Vinken, P.J., and Bruyn, G.W. (Eds.). *Handbook of clinical neurology. Vol. 2: Localization in clinical neurology.* Amsterdam: North Holland.

Yeudall, L.T. 1977a. "Neuropsychological correlates of criminal psychopathy: Part I. Differential diagnosis," presented at the 5th International Seminar in Comparative Clinical Criminology, Montreal.

Yeudall, L.T., and Wardell, D.M. 1977b. "Neuropsychological correlates of criminal psychopathy: Part II. Discrimination and prediction of dangerous and recidivistic offenders," presented at the 5th International Seminar in Comparative Clinical Criminology, Montreal.

Appendixes

Appendix A
Current and Past
Psychopathology Scale
(CAPPS) with
Modification

Modified CAPPS—Diagnosis

A. DMS-II (Nonepisodic)

   1. Symptomatic (behavioral)_____

   2. Characterologic_____

   3. Psychophysiologic_____

B. Episodic behavior disorder

   1. Episodic dyscontrol (behavioral)—Ratio score
      Primary total/Secondary Total

C. Estimated epileptoid mechanism

?	1	2	3	4	5	6	7
	solely	predominantly	often	equally	occasionally	rarely	never

Modified CAPPS—Psychiatric Evaluation Form
(Subject's Functioning During Past Month)

SCALE

?	1	2	3	4	5	6
	None	Minimal	Mild	Moderate	Severe	Extreme

Physical Health

214 Somatic concerns

215 Conversion reaction

216 Psychophysiological reactions

Mood

217 Elated mood

218 Anxiety (reported)

219 Phobia

220 Depression

221 Guilt

222 Obsessions-compulsions

223 Suicide-self-mutilation

Social Isolation and Suspicion-Persecution

224 Social isolation

225 Suspicion-persecution

226 Grandiosity

Hallucinations-Dissociation

227 Hallucinations

228 Auditory hallucinations

229 Visual hallucinations

230 Dissociation

231 Alcohol abuse

232 Daily routine-leisure time impairment

233 Narcotics-drugs

234 Antisocial attitudes or acts

235 Sex deviation

236 Belligerence-negativism

237 Inappropriate affect, appearance, or behavior

238 Posturing

239 Silliness

240 Retardation-lack of emotion

Roles

241 Participation in group therapy

Not

?

1   Regular attendance-good improvement

2   Regular attendance-slight improvement
3   Regular attendance-no improvement
4   Irregular or disruptive
5   Rarely attends
6   Refuses therapy

242 Prison assignment

Not
?
1   Full parole
2   Half-way house
3   Work release
4   Holiday and weekends
5   Level 3 or 4
6   Level 1 or 2

243 Prison adjustment

Not
?
1   Good
2   Minimal difficulties
3   Mild difficulties
4   Moderate difficulties
5   Severe difficulties
6   Extreme difficulties

244 Work and/or rating

?   Refuses work
1   Poor
2   Satisfactory
3   Good

245 Mate

246 Parent

247 Agitation-excitement

248 Speech disorganization

249 Disorientation-memory

250 Delusions

251 Denial of illness

Modified CAPPS–Psychiatric History Schedule

SCALE

?	1	2	3	4	5	6
	None	Minimal	Mild	Moderate	Severe	Extreme

Childhood

314   Neurotic traits in childhood

315   Antisocial traits in childhood

Adolescent Friendship Pattern

316   Adolescent friendship pattern (ages 12-18)

    ?
    1   Superior. Spent a good deal of time with many special friends and groups of friends he enjoyed being with. He often initiated the interaction and was asked to join social activities by others.
    2   Very good
    3   Good
    4   Fair. Had a few special friends but either avoided or did not enjoy group activities
    5   Poor. Had no special friends and preferred to be by himself most of the time or was actively avoided by peers.
    6   Grossly inadequate. Had practically no social contact.

School

317   Highest Completed School Grade

    ?
    1   Professional (M.A.,M.S.,M.E.,B.Ms.,M.D.,Ph.D.,LL.B.)
    2   Four years college graduate (B.A.,B.S.)
    3   1-3 years college or business school
    4   High school graduate
    5   10-11 years of school (part high school)
    6   7-9 years of school
    7   Under 7 years of school

318   Overall academic performance

    ?   No information or never attended
    1   Superior
    2   Very good
    3   Average

4   Fair

5   Poor

6   Failing or never went to school because of his psychopathology

319 Nonacademic school difficulties

320 Establishment of independent residence

?

1   Less than 16 years old

2   16 to 24

3   25 to 34

4   35 to 44

5   45 and over

6   Never (still there at time of interview)

Outpatient Treatment

321 Outpatient treatment

?

1   No contact

2   Consultation or brief period of treatment

3   Continuous treatment for at least 6 months or several brief periods

4   Continuous treatment lasting several years or numerous brief periods

Hospitalization, Institutionalization, Incarceration

322 Psychiatric hospitalizations, institutionalizations, or incarcerations

?

1   No

2   Yes

If yes: age of first hospitalization, etc. was

323 (First digit of age)

324 (Second digit of age)

325 Total time of hospitalization, institutionalization, incarceration

?

1   None (never hospitalized, etc.)

2   Less than 6 months

3   Less than 1 year

4   Less than 2 years

5   Less than 5 years
6   5 or more years

326 Number of previous psychiatric hospitalizations, institutionalizations, incarcerations

? 0 1 2 3 4 5 6 7 8+

Treatment Modalities

327 Received treatments for psychopathology

?
1   No
2   Yes

If yes, check all that apply:

328 Electric shock treatment

329 Brain surgery

330 Insulin coma

331 Drugs

332 Brief psychotherapy or counseling (fewer than 15 sessions)

333 Psychotherapy or counseling (at least 15 sessions)

Other

Occupation

334 Highest occupational level ever attained (include military service)

?   No information; housekeeper or student only
1   Higher executive, proprietor of large concern or major professional
2   Business manager, proprietor of medium sized business or
lesser professional
3   Administrative personnel, small independent business or minor
professional
4   Clerical or sales worker, technician or owner of a little business
5   Skilled manual employee
6   Machine operator or semiskilled employee
7   Unskilled employee
8   Adult not working at job, school, or housework

335 Stability and performance

    ?   No information, did not work at all for nonpsychopathological reason (retired, physically ill, housekeeper, student)
    1   Superior
    2   Very good
    3   Average
    4   Fair
    5   Poor
    6   Did not work at all because of psychopathology

336 Change in occupational status or responsibility

    ?   No information or did not work at all
    1   Marked elevation
    2   Some elevation
    3   No change
    4   Some decline
    5   Marked decline

337 Has tended to have no long-term goals or plans for his life, or has kept changing them (aimless)

338 Efforts to improve

    ?
    1   Superior
    2   Very good
    3   Average
    4   Fair
    5   Poor
    6   Grossly inadequate

Sexual Adjustment

339 Adolescent sexual adjustment (Ages 12-18)

    ?
    1   Superior. Showed a strong healthy interest in members of the opposite sex and at some time had an emotionally intimate relationship with someone whom he dated and had some sexual physical contact.
    2   Very good
    3   Good. Showed a strong healthy interest in members of the opposite sex and frequently dated with some sexual physical contact.

4 Fair
5 Poor. Had little sexual physical contact with opposite sex, or engaged in promiscuous or homosexual or other perverse sexual activity.
6 Grossly inadequate. Practically no curiosity about sex or markedly negative feelings about sex or engaged in no form of sexual activity with himself or others.

340 Highest level of adult heterosexual adjustment

?
1 Superior. Has had long-standing, satisfying heterosexual relationship(s) involving emotional initimacy and relatively symptom-free sexual physical contact.
2 Very good
3 Good. Has had long standing generally satisfying heterosexual relationship(s) with no more than minor impairment in sexual interest, enjoyment, or performance.
4 Fair. Has had some heterosexual relationship(s) with some sexual activity and with no more than minor impairment in sexual interest or activity.
5 Poor. Has had some heterosexual relationship(s) but with considerable impairment in either interest, performance, or enjoyment.
6 Grossly inadequate. Practically no heterosexual activity or interest.

341 Perversion

342 Homosexual

343 Preoccupied with sex or perverse sexual impulses

Physical Health-Somatic Symptoms

344 Physical health (after age 12)

?
1 Excellent. Practically never sick and almost always feels good.
2 Very good. Only minor complaints, colds, allergies, etc.
3 Good. Occasional illness requiring medical care.
4 Fair. Numerous minor ailments or a chronic condition with little impairment (e.g., diabetes well controlled).
5 Poor. Often seriously ill requiring medical attention (e.g., cirrhosis, angina, pneumonia).
6 Extremely poor. Frequently seriously ill or extreme impairment from a chronic disease (e.g., uncontrolled diabetes, liver failure, emphysema).

345 Impairment due to a CNS disease or physical illness or injury which most likely resulted in some permanent damage to CNS

346 Epileptic attacks

347 Amnesia, fugue, dissociative state

348 Hypochondriasis

349 Psychophysiological reactions to stress

350 Conversion reaction

351 Tiredness

352 Loss of appetite or weight

353 Insomnia

Narcotics-Drugs

354 Problem with narcotics-drugs

Note type(s):

355 Heroin

356 Codeine, Demerol, morphine

357 Cocaine, opium, other narcotic

358 Marijuana

359 LSD, mescaline, peyote, or other consciousness-expanding substance

360 Barbiturate

361 Amphetamine

362 Tranquilizer

363 Antidepressant

364 Other or nonspecified

Note characteristic:

365 Toxic psychosis

Alcohol Abuse

366 Alcohol abuse

Note characteristic:

367 Delusions or hallucinations

Illegal Acts

368 Law enforcement

369 Antisocial

Brooding

370 Broods or preoccupied with unpleasant thoughts or feelings

Depression

371 Depression

Guilt

372 Guilt

Suicide

373 Suicide

Anxiety

374 Anxiety

Phobia

375 Phobia

Obsessions-Compulsions

376 Obsessions-compulsions

Interest-Enjoyment

377 Loss of interest or enjoyment

Agitation

378 Periods of agitation and restlessness

Elation

379 Elated mood, overtalkativeness, and overactivity

380 Alternating periods of elated mood and sadness

Retardation

414 Retardation in speech and voluntary movements

Control of Affect

415   Overreact emotionally

416   Histrionic

417   Sullen or pouting

418   Stubborn

419   Inhibited

420   Hostility or anger

421   Violent against people or things

Compulsivity

422   Compulsivity

423   Unduly concerned or involved with work or getting things done

Impulsivity

424   Impulsivity

Adapting to Stress

425   Ineffectual when confronted with stress or difficulty adapting

Judgment

426   Poor judgment

Self-defeating Behavior

427   Self-defeating and demonstrating a failure to learn from experience

Adult Friendship Pattern

428   Adult friendship pattern during last five years under study

    ?

    1   Superior. Has a number of special friends and groups of friends that he enjoys being with and has regular contact with. Has at least one close friend that he confides in and with whom he shares common interests.

    2   Very good

    3   Good

    4   Fair. Had a few special friends but either avoided or did not enjoy group activities.

5 Poor. Had no special friends and preferred to be by himself most of the time.

6 Grossly inadequate. Had practically no social contact.

Interpersonal Relationships

429 Unduly sensitive

430 Emotionally distant and unresponsive

431 Painful relations

432 Extreme fluctuation of feelings towards people

433 Dependency

434 Cling to other people

435 Lack of responsibility

436 Passive aggressive

437 Blame others

438 Suspicious and distrustful

Pleasure Capacity

439 Pleasure and satisfaction in activities, relationships, or interests has been:

?
1 Superior
2 Very good
3 Good
4 Fair
5 Poor
6 Inadequate

440 Superficial and excessive involvement

Religion

441 Preoccupied with religion or some metaphysical or abstract question or problem

Grandiosity

442 Grandiosity

Ideas of Reference

443 Ideas of reference

Delusions

444 Delusions

Note type(s):

445 Persecutory (e.g., attacked, harassed, cheated, conspiracy, talked about)

446 Grandiose (e.g., identity, power, knowledge, relationships)

447 Influence (e.g., believed mind, thoughts, body or actions controlled or influenced by outside force)

448 Sexual (e.g., sexual identity, feelings, or activity)

449 Somatic (e.g., body or organ diseased or changed)

450 Poverty or guilt (e.g., financial ruin, sinful, responsible for disaster)

451 Other

Note characteristic(s):

452 Systematized delusion

453 Period(s) lasting more than one week in which delusions were moderate, severe, or extreme

Perceptual Distortions, Hallucinations

454 Depersonalization, derealization

455 Illusions

456 Hallucinations

Note Types:

457 Visual

458 Auditory

459 Somatic or tactile (e.g., feels things creeping, electrical or other weird sensations)

460 Olfactory

Memory-Orientation

461 Orientation to time, place, or person or memory for recent or past events

Speech

462 Incoherent

Inappropriate-Eccentric

463 Disheveled

464 Eccentric, odd, or idiosyncratic

Intellectual Capacity

465 Estimate of intellectual capacity

    ?
1 Superior (I.Q. 120 plus)
2 Bright normal (110-119)
3 Average (90-109)
4 Dull normal (80-89)
5 Borderline (70-79)
6 Mental defective (69 and below)

Course of Psychopathology

466 Course of psychopathology
(Check the category that is most descriptive)

    ? No information, no significant psychopathology
1 After onset, no clear cut episode(s) and no periods of marked change
2 After onset, no clear cut episode(s) but many periods of worsening and/or improving
3 One or more fairly clear cut episodic reactions. (Episodes may be superimposed upon a chronic illness. Include present illness if it began during the period under study and is judged to be the beginning of an episode.)
4 Dyscontrol acts

Characteristics of Previous Episodes
(Skip to *Overall Severity* if no previous episodes, i.e., item 466 is not 3.)

467 Number of previous episodes of all kinds

    ? 1 2 3 4 5 6 7 8+

468 Number of previous episodes lasting more than one week where depressed or elated mood of at least moderate intensity was the predominant disturbance.

    ? 0 1 2 3 4 5 6 7+

469 Usual level of psychopathology after episode or between episodes

    ? 1 2 3 4 5 6

470 Usual stress of precipitating events for previous episode(s). (Consider both the number of stressful events and context in which they occur. For example, stress associated with the death of a relative depends upon the closeness of the relationship. Similarly, the joint occurrence of a number of events, each of which is only moderately stressful, may result in a severely stressful situation.) A rating of ? should be used when the item is not applicable. Examples: drug reaction, CNS injury.

? 1 2 3 4 5 6

Overall Severity

471 Overall severity of illness during period under study

472 Age at which he first exhibited psychopathology of at least moderate
473 severity which lasted more than one week. (Leave blank if never.)

474 Has had a period lasting more than one week where he was either markedly delusional, incoherent, or hallucinating or was grossly impaired in carrying out his occupational role, or acted in a bizarre manner.

?

1 Yes
2 No

If yes, note age of first occurrence.
(Leave blank if never.)

475 (First digit of age)
476 (Second digit of age)

477 During the period under study his condition has:

?

1 Improved markedly
2 Improved slightly
3 Remained fairly stable
4 Been variable but without deterioration (e.g., now is recovering from an episode with no deterioration)
5 Worsened slightly
6 Worsened markedly

Quality of Information

478 Accuracy and completeness

?

1 Extremely accurate

2   Very good
3   Good
4   Fair
5   Poor
6   Grossly unreliable or incomplete

Modification CAPPS for Episodic Behavior
(Psychiatric History Schedule)

Scales

467.10 Number of previous episodic reactions of all kinds:

? 0 1 2 3 4 5 6 7+

467.11 Average duration of episodic reactions:

?
1 momentary
2 less than 1 hour
3 less than 1 week
4 less than 1 month
5 less than 1 year
6 a year or longer

467.12 Average severity of episodic reactions

? 0 1 2 3 4 5 6

467.20 Number of previous dyscontrol acts of all kinds

? 0 1 2 3 4 5 6 7+

467.21 Severity of dyscontrol act

1 wish (only) to be impulsive
2 concern of loss of control only
3 acts recognizable by others as impulsive
4 work incapacity
5 acts requiring hospitalization or incarceration
6 permanent damage to self or others

467.22 Premeditated acts

?
1 never
2 rarely
3 occasionally

4 often
5 usually
6 always

467.23 Conscious premeditation
(Rate as 467.22)

467.24 Unconscious premeditation
(Rate as 467.22)

467.25 Specificity of affect

?
0 no affect
1 diffuse chaotic affect through
3 rapid variation in affect to
5 discrete consistent affect
? 0 1 2 3 4 5 6

467.26 Aggressive affect during act
(Rate as 467.22)

467.27 Fear-panic affect during act
(Rate as 467.22)

467.28 Sexual affect during act
(Rate as 467.22)

467.29 Affection-closeness expressed during act
(Rate as 467.22)

467.30 Coordination of act

?
0 inhibition of act when act called for
1 flailing uncoordinated act
3 crude brute force
5 subtly finely coordinated act
? 0 1 2 3 4 5 6

467.31 Clear sensorium during act
(Rate as 467.22)

467.32 Amnesia for act
(Rate as 467.22)

467.33 Loss of personal identity
(Rate as 467.22)

467.34 Denies responsibility for act
(Rate as 467.22)

467.35   Personal discomfort regarding act
         (Rate as 467.22)

467.4   Secondary gains of behavior
         (Rate as 467.22)

467.5   *Prodromal* symptoms for either episodic reactions or episodic dyscon-
         trol acts as listed below

467.51   Irritability
         (Rate as 467.22)

467.52   Motor restlessness
         (Rate as 467.22)

467.53   Depression
         (Rate as 467.22)

467.54   Anger
         (Rate as 467.22)

467.55   Thinking disturbance
         (Rate as 467.22)

467.56   Sexual
         (Rate as 467.22)

467.57   Perceptual
         (Rate as 467.22)

467.58   Autonomic
         (Rate as 467.22)

467.59   Neurologic
         (Rate as 467.22)

Source: Portions from R.L. Spitzer and J. Endicott, *Current and Past Psychopathology Scales* © 1968 by Evaluation Unit Biometrics Research, New York State Department of Mental Hygiene, New York State Psychiatric Institute. Reprinted by permission.

Appendix B
Psychometrics

Bender Standard and Center Background Interference Procedure

Memory for Design

MMPI

WAIS (collected from institution records)

Auditory Discrimination Task

Matching Familiar Figures

Holtzman Inkblot

Porteus Maze

Slow Writing, Time Estimation, Draw-a-Line

Bender and the Canter Background Interference Procedure
for the Bender Gestalt Test

This psychometric instrument employs the standard nine-card designs on the Bender Gestalt Test except testing is repeated after an interval of another task on a special "interference" sheet of paper. The purpose of the test is to approximate degree of organic brain impairment. The variables relating to the Canter BIP procedure are (1) total deviation scores on the standard administration, (2) total deviation scores on the background interference administration, (3) the BIP difference score which is simply the total deviation score on the standard mode subtracted from the total deviation on the BIP mode, (4) the number of positives which is an index to the number of designs showing a significantly positive BIP effect, that is, where total deviations on the BIP mode exceeded total deviations on the standard mode by at least two points; (5) design overlap difference score, derived by recording design overlaps in each of the two modes and subtracting the number of D.O. in the standard mode from the number of D.O. in the BIP mode, (6) the base level of performance, which is an index to the general level of performance under standard conditions, is a seven-point scale ranging from I-relatively error free to VII-markedly impaired, and (7) the classification for the base level which is a system of interpreting base level performance with regard to BIP effect and ranges from 1 = no organic brain disorder, 2 = borderline, to 3 = organic brain disorder.

Some of the data collected on the Canter BIP indicate a positive BIP effect for adults who have organic brain disease regardless of presence of psychiatric disorder or mental retardation. The **BIP** difference score appears uncorrelated with I.Q. The likelihood of missing a diagnosis of OBD (false-negatives) is most likely in convulsive disorders, without brain damage. False-positives appear more likely from the manic disorders.

Graham-Kendall Memory-for-Design-Test

This test used in between the Canter-Bender segments involves the presentation of simple geometric designs and the reproduction of these designs from immediate memory (five-second delay). The aim of this test is to index brain damage.

The MMPI[a]

Validity Scales

L Scale—a high score indicates concealment or misrepresentation in a subject's desire to appear socially acceptable, a low scorer tends to be independent, socially responsible.

F Scale—high score suggests test is invalid for reason of subject's not understanding questions or attempting to appear disturbed; low F indicates test taken according to instructions.

K Scales—high score suggests subject is defensive, moderate elevations (55-65) may suggest adaptiveness and ego strength; low K suggests subject is self-critical and willing to admit symptoms and failings.

Clinical Scales

Hs—high scores indicate subject is unduly concerned with bodily functions and tends to be egocentric, irritable, and complaining; low scores suggest ambitious, energetic, responsible person.

D—high scores suggest depression, worry; low scores associated with absence of depression.

Hy—high scores suggest emotional lability, immaturity; low scores suggest a constricted, guarded, and socially nonparticipating person.

[a]Sources: Portion of Item C of this Appendix abstracted from Raymond D. Fowler, Jr., *The Clinical Use of the Automated MMPI* © 1976 Roche Psychiatric Service Institute, New Jersey, pp. 2-5.

Pd—high scores suggest impulsiveness, resentfulness, lack of deep emotional responses; moderate is characteristic of normals; low scores suggest a conforming unassuming person who is overaccepting of authority.

Mf—high scores in males suggest sensitivity and femininity of interests; low scores suggest an adventurous person who prefers action to contemplation.

Pa—high scores suggest a suspicious, overly sensitive person who utilizes projection as a defense, tends to be self-centered; low scorers are suspicious accompanied by lack of concern with social contact, stubbornness, and evasiveness.

Pt—high scores are associated with anxiety, rigidity, tension, fears, and excessive doubt; low scores suggest a well-organized, persistent, and realistic person who can mobilize resources.

Sc—high scores suggest social withdrawal, unusual thought processes; low scores suggest a person who is conventional, controlled, and somewhat compliant.

Ma—high score suggests high energy level, restlessness, and hyperactivity; low score suggests low energy level, lack of self-confidence.

Si—high score suggests a shy, sensitive person who is hesitant to become involved in social situations; low score suggests a sociable person who is outgoing and assertive.

WAIS[b]

The Wechsler Adult Intelligence Scale, aside from its merit as a test of intelligence, is also a diagnostic instrument. The I.Q. score interprets as follows:

130 and above

120-129	very superior (2.2 percent)
110-119	bright normal (16.1 percent)
90-109	average (50.0 percent)
80-89	dull normal (16.1 percent)
70-79	borderline (6 percent)
69 and below	mental defective (2.2 percent)

[b]Portion of Item D of this Appendix from David Wechsler, *WAIS Manual: Wechsler Adult Intelligence Scale*, Table 12 © 1955 by the Psychological Corporation, New York. Reprinted by permission.

The eleven subtests are broken into six verbal tests: information, comprehension, arithmetic, similarities, digit span, and vocabulary; and five performance tests: digit symbol, picture completion, block design, picture arrangement, and object assembly.

Information measures amount of general knowledge that the individual has absorbed from his environment, rather than the way he utilizes that knowledge. It can provide clues to personality organization.

Comprehension measures the degree to which the subject has been able to evaluate accurately a sample of past experiences and apply it to everyday social situations. It assesses a degree of social acculturation. The response may reveal coping styles such as passive, dependent, and so on. High scores indicate adequate judgment. Pathological groups (brain damaged, retarded, anxiety state) do relatively well. Subjects preoccupied with hostility and guilt are apt to score lower. Sociopathic ideas may result in low scores.

Arithmetic measures cognitive development of number and measures concentration. It provides clues to memory and concentration, particularly when paired with digit span. High scores show success and sometimes obsessiveness; failures may indicate a variety of problems.

Similarities measure a subject's ability to classify objects, facts, and ideas. Memory, comprehension, and capability for associative thinking are called into play. This subtest can relate to academic success. There is a relationship to creativity. If similarities score is higher than comprehension, this is sometimes indicative of the dreamer. The test is vulnerable to disturbance.

Digit span measures immediate auditory recall. Basically it measures attention and freedom from distractibility, particularly from bizarre effects or confused thought processes. In schizoid cases, digit span may surpass arithmetic. Low scores can indicate the vulnerability of attention.

Vocabulary measures classificatory and conceptualizing skills. This subtest can give clues to subject's status and background. The range and richness of his ideas and the level of abstract thinking can be tapped. Some pathological groups do well on this test (obsessives, paranoids, anxiety and depressive patients and certain preschizophrenic patients). Language and thought disturbances may be reflected in low scores.

Digit symbol measures ability to learn an unfamiliar task. Motor behavior is more important than in any other subtest. Low scores may indicate a dominance problem. Low scores may reflect brain damage, anxiousness, depression, dissociation, schizophrenia, and hyperactivity.

Picture completion measures personality integration. High scores may indicate good perception and concentration and interest in the environment.

Block design measures reasoning rather than memory. Intellectual functioning can be tapped. Visual-motor integration and speed of performance are also measured. Low scores may reflect a speedy, careless approach or a lack of reflectiveness in performance. Those with "failure" orientation may refuse to try or give up readily.

Picture arrangement measures visual perception, synthesis into wholes through planning, and ability to see cause-effect relationships. This subtest furnishes clues to a person's interpersonal relationships, as well as his ability to gauge social situations. Cultural background is important here. High scores reflect an ability to delay a solution until all components are perceived and implications understood.

Object assembly measures visual analysis and its coordination with simple assembly skills. Modes of thinking may be revealed here. This subtest calls for mental organization and planning. There is some emotional loading on object assembly, and chronic anxiety in general tends to lower the score.

Goldman, Fristoe, Woodcock Test of Auditory Discrimination

The focus of this test is on primary age levels for the identification and assessment of auditory discrimination deficits. For the purpose of this study, the test was employed as a measure of distractibility using the quiet subtest as a baseline and the noise subtest as a controlled measure for distraction. Due to the pictorial nature of the test, vocabulary development is not a factor in test performance. Essentially, the test is comprised of a training procedure, a quiet subtest, and a noise subtest. Scores are derived in terms of errors on each of the two subtests.

Matching Familiar Figures

This test consists of fourteen items whereby the subject is presented with one main picture and six other pictures five of which look similar to the main one and one of which is identical. The subject is asked to find the one (of the six pictures) that is identical to the main one as fast as he can. For the purposes of this study, the figures were split into two forms (odds and evens) so that at the end of the two phases, each subject would have completed all fourteen items. Subjects were scored on reaction time in seconds and total number of errors made. The purpose of the test was to provide an index to impulsiveness and delay control.

Holtzman Inkblot Technique

The Holtzman Inkblot Technique is a standardized approach to the assessment of personality through projective technique and is more objectively scored than the Rorschach. There are twenty-two scored categories for each of the forty-five inkblots, the first eleven pertaining to the nature of the response and the remaining eleven pertaining to the content. A numerical score is obtained in each of the following categories:

Reaction time (RT)

Rejection (R)

Location (L)

Space (S)

Form definitiveness (FD)

Form appropriateness (FA)

Color (C)

Shading (Sh)

Movement (M)

Pathognomic verbalization (V)

Integration (I)

Human (H)

Animal (A)

Anatomy (At)

Sex (Sx)

Abstract (Ab)

Anxiety (Ax)

Hostility (Hs)

Barrier (Br)

Penetration (Pn)

Balance (B)

Popular (P)

Porteus Maze Tests

The Porteus Maze Tests used in this study were the Standard Vineland Revision Mazes, years VII, VIII, IX, X, XI, XII, XIV, adult one. All rules for scoring performances were based on Porteus's procedures. The same version was repeated in both phases of this study, and the results reported represent an average, except as otherwise noted. It is believed that the quality scores differentiate delinquent from nondelinquent groups. Quality of performance is higher (lower score) in those who delay gratification than those who choose immediate gratification.

Slow Writing, Time Estimation, Draw-a-line

The slow writing task was designed using the year III design from the Porteus Maze-Vineland Revision. The subject was asked to start at the arrow with his pencil and draw a line inside the concentric diamond to the point where he began as slowly as he possibly could, without stopping.

Although we do not have normative data, we are measuring "delay" in the motor area. Recorded as a single score was the number of seconds it took to complete the task.

The time estimation task consisted of asking the subject to estimate how long he thought a minute was and simply recording the number of seconds of elapsed time from start to when subject indicated stop. It was hypothesized that any prison population would tend to underestimate the time, especially a group of impulsive prisoners. Again, the scores were based on an average of the two performances.

The draw-a-line task was inserted in the test battery by the research psychometrician to see if it reflected a trend similar to the time estimation task. The instructions to the subject were to draw a line approximately one inch on a sheet of paper. Scoring was recorded on the basis of decimal equivalents to the inch (1.0).

Appendix C
Mood and Affect
Scales

Mood Scale

1. *Factor T*: Tension-anxiety
   (Subject can be defined as feeling tense, nervous, on edge, shaky, restless, etc.)

   Not at all tense - 1 2 3 4 5 6 7 - Extremely tense

2. *Factor A*: Anger-hostility
   (Subject can be defined as feeling angry, furious, ready to fight, grouchy, etc.)

   Not at all angry - 1 2 3 4 5 6 7 - Extremely angry

3. *Factor D*: Depression-dejection
   (Subject can be defined as feeling worthless, helpless, unhappy, discouraged, etc.)

   Not at all worthless - 1 2 3 4 5 6 7 - Extremely worthless

4. *Factor V*: Vigor-activity
   (Subject can be defined as feeling lively, vigorous, full of pep, active, etc.)

   Not at all lively - 1 2 3 4 5 6 7 - Extremely lively

5. *Factor F*: Fatigue-inertia
   (Subject can be defined as feeling tired, fatigued, worn out, sluggish, etc.)

   Not at all tired - 1 2 3 4 5 6 7 - Extremely tired

6. *Factor Fr*: Friendliness
   (Subject can be defined as feeling friendly, cooperative, good-natured, etc.)

   Not at all friendly - 1 2 3 4 5 6 7 - Extremely friendly

7. *Factor C*: Confusion
   (Subject can be defined as feeling forgetful, not able to concentrate, not able to think clear, not efficient, etc.)

   Not at all forgetful - 1 2 3 4 5 6 7 - Extremely forgetful

Affects Observation Scale

Instructions: Your ratings on this form are to be based upon the subject's verbal report and observations of his behavior.

1. *Level of tension*—Rate on the basis of physical and motor manifestations of tension, "nervousness", and heightened activation level (fidgeting, tremors, twitches, sweating, frequent changing of posture, hypertonicity of movement and heightened muscle tone).

   Not at all tense - 1 2 3 4 5 6 7 8 - Very tense

2. *Level of anxiety*—Rate solely on the basis of the subject's verbal report of worry, fear, or over-concern for the present or future. Do not infer anxiety from physical signs.

   Not at all anxious - 1 2 3 4 5 6 7 8 - Very anxious

3. *Number of feelings*—How many kinds of feelings or moods does he express (e.g., anger, sadness, disappointment, fear, happiness, etc.)?

   Expresses hardly any feelings - 1 2 3 4 5 6 7 8 - Expresses many feelings

4. *Emotional responsiveness*—How easily are his feelings aroused (e.g., does it take much to make him feel sad or happy, angry or upset, etc.)?

   Very difficult to arouse - 1 2 3 4 5 6 7 8 - Very easy to arouse

5. *Intensity of emotions*—How intensely does he seem to experience different feelings (e.g., when he is angry, is he *very* angry; when he is sad, is he *very* sad, etc.)?

   Not intensely at all - 1 2 3 4 5 6 7 8 - Very intensely

6. *Emotional lability*—Do his feelings or moods show marked fluctuations (e.g., does he very easily shift from feeling sad to feeling happy, etc.)?

   No fluctuation - 1 2 3 4 5 6 7 8 - A great deal of fluctuation

7. *Speed of reaction*—How quickly does he react to things?

   Very slow to react - 1 2 3 4 5 6 7 8 - Very fast to react

8. *Impulsiveness*—How impulsive is he, i.e., how prone is he to react or to act without thinking before hand?

   Not at all impulsive - 1 2 3 4 5 6 7 8 - Very impulsive

Appendix D
Group Therapist
Questionnaire

(for events during the preceding month)

1. Patient attends group
   regularly and on time   always   1 2 3 4 5 6   never

2. Participates meaningfully
   in sessions; active and verbal   always   1 2 3 4 5 6   never

3. Range of emotional responses   flat   1 2 3 4 5 6   volatile

4. Speech or action is impulsive   thoughtful 1 2 3 4 5 6   impulsive

5. A. Is verbally hostile to
       group members   never   1 2 3 4 5 6   extreme

   B. Is verbally hostile to
       therapist   never   1 2 3 4 5 6   extreme

6. Physically hostile in group   never   1 2 3 4 5 6   usually

7. Motor activity in group   quiet   1 2 3 4 5 6   agitated

8. A. Thinking has been   positively   negatively
       modified by group   influenced 1 2 3 4 5 6   influenced

   B. Behavior has been   positively   negatively
       modified by group   influenced 1 2 3 4 5 6   influenced

9. Acceptance by others in group   liked   1 2 3 4 5 6   disliked

10. Your feelings for patient   like   1 2 3 4 5 6   dislike

11. Your prognosis of group   much
    effect   benefit   1 2 3 4 5 6   none

Source: From Russell R. Monroe, et al., "Neurologic Findings in Recidivist Aggressors," in *Psychopathology and Brain Dysfunction* edited by C. Shagass, S. Gershon, and A.J. Friedhoff © 1977 by Raven Press, New York. Reprinted by permission.

Appendix E
Infraction Ratings

Rule Infractions	Weight
Escape, break-out	10
Assault with weapon on officer	10
Assault on officer, no weapon	9
Assault with weapon on inmate	9
Possession of weapon	7
Possession of means of escape	7
Escape, walk-off	6
Assault on inmate with force, no weapon or perversion	4
Possession of contraband drug, alcohol, or under influence of same	3
Destruction of state property—very serious	3
Sexual perversion without force	3
Refusal to obey or insolence	2
Out of bounds	2
Possession of unauthorized items	2
Arguing with other inmates	2
Destruction of state property—minor	1
Other minor infractions of rules	1

Incident Reports	Weight
Argued with other inmates	2
Warning given	2
Uncooperative behavior	2
Refused to work	2
Reports of problems with other inmates	2
Cutting himself	1
Physical complaints	1
Griping	1
Unauthorized items	1
Refused medication	0
Sleeping reports	0

Source: Appendix B from Russell R. Monroe, et al., "Neurologic Findings in Recidivist Aggressors," in *Psychopathology and Brain Dysfunction* edited by C. Shagass, S. Gershon, and A.J. Friedhoff © 1977 by Raven Press, New York. Reprinted by permission.

Appendix F
Lion Symptom
Checklist

Name _____

Date _____

Since I have been on this new medication, I have felt

1. Less irritable____   More irritable____   Irritability is the same____

2. More angry____   Less angry____   Anger the same____

3. More moody____   Less moody____   Same____

4. More easily annoyed____   Less easily annoyed____   Same____

5. Sleep better____   Sleep worse____   Sleep unchanged____

6. More anxious____   Less anxious____   Anxiety the same____

7. More appetite____   Less appetite____   Same____

8. More depressed____   Less depressed____   Same____

9. More friendly____   Less friendly____   Same____

10. More sad____   Less sad____   Same____

11. More in control____   Less in control____   Same____

12. Better____   Worse____   Same____

12a. Thinking more clearly[a]____   Thinking less clearly____   Same____

_____

[a]This item added later in study

Indexes

Name Index

Subject Index

Acting out, 3-6, 48

Affective disturbances, 170-171

Affect Scale, 95, 96, 140, 144; description of, 206

Aggression, 20; homicidal, 21; implication of findings on, 165; instrumental versus expressive, 19; surgical studies of, 37-42. *See also* Episodic behavioral disorders

Aggression: A Social Learning Analysis (Bandura), 19

Aggressive Behavior (Garattini and Sigg, eds.), 19

Akinetic mutism, 1

Alcohol, 35; relation between episodic behavioral disorders and, 16, 17, 20

Alpha chloralose: activation, 6-7, 32, 37, 61, 105-106, 109; administration of, 107, 108, 115; experimental use of, 68; reactions to use of, 68

American Psychiatric Association (APA), 74

Amphetamines, 20, 47

Amygdala: aggression and, 23; epilepsy and, 24

Amygdalectomy, 23

Amygdalotomy, 39-41, 42

Anticipation, 170, 171

Anticonvulsants, 43-45, 46, 47, 50. *See also* Primidone

Antidepressants, 47

Antiepileptic agents, 46

Antiparkinson agents, 46

Antipsychotic medications, 46

Antisocial behavior, 79-80, 165, 166

Aphora, 16

Apraxia, 142, 143, 161

Assassinations, 19

Auditory Discrimination (ADT), Goldman, Fristoe, Woodcock Test of, 11-12, 65; description of, 201; mean scores on, 90

Background Interference Procedure (BIP), for Bender Gestalt Test, 11, 89-90, 116-118, 144, 197-198

Bender Visual Motor Gestalt Test (Bender Gestalt), 11, 34, 65, 89-90, 197-198. *See also* Background Interference Procedure

Benzodiazepines, 45-46, 50

BIP. *See* Background Interference Procedure

Birth data, 141, 143, 161

Brain Changers, The (Pines), 37

Brain Control (Valenstein), 37

Brain dysfunction, 17-18

Brain Revolution, The (Ferguson), 37

Brevital. *See* Methoxyhexital

Brief Psychiatric Rating Scale, 43

CAPPS. *See* Current and Past Psychopathology Scales

Carbachol, 23

Carbamazepine (Tegretol), 44, 45, 50

Catalepsy, 1

Catatonia, periodic, 1

Central nervous system (CNS): function, disordered, 17; instability, 61, 170; insult, 141-142, 143, 161; integration, 7, 10-12

Chlordiazepoxide (Librium), 45, 50, 69, 107

Chlorpromazine, 45

"Choice delay," defined, 3, 172

Cingulotomy, 42

Clonazepam, 46

CNS. *See* Central nervous system

Cognitive control, 7; assessment of, 12

Congenital (neurologic) stigmata, 142, 143, 161

Conscience mechanism, 170, 172

Consent, procedure for obtaining informed, 68-69

Coordination, 142, 143, 161

Cornell Medical Index, 33

Crimes committed, resulting in incarceration, 75
Current and Past Psychopathology Scales (CAPPS), 62, 64, 66, 125-126; assessment of psychiatric adjustment and social behavior by, 79-81; and Memory for Designs Test, 89; with modification, 179-196; and Monroe Dyscontrol Scale, 93, 96

Delta activity, 109; product-moment analysis of theta and, 115-120
Demographic data, on study population, 75-78, 173
Diagnoses, psychiatric, of subject population, 78
Diaphoria, defined, 16
Diazepam (Valium), 45, 46, 50
Dilantin. See Phenytoin
Diphenylhydantoin, 44
Discriminant analysis: with four-group schema, 133-134; with three-group schema, 136-137
Draw-a-Line, 90, 203
Drugs. See Pharmacologic treatment of episodic behavioral disorders
Dynamics of Violence, The (Fawcett), 19
Dyscontrol, episodic, 1, 3, 6, 9, 13, 50; primary (seizure or instinct), 3, 6, 18-19; secondary (impulse and acting out), 3-6; violence and, 15, 18-22. See also Episodic behavioral disorders
Dyscontrol acts, theoretical formulation of aggressive, 170-173
Dyscontrol behavior, psychological measurement of, 7-9, 61; and behavioral inhibition sampling technique, 9-10; and central nervous system integration, 10-12; and cognitive control, 12; and personality characteristics, 12-13. See also "Epileptoid" dyscontrol; "Hysteroid" dyscontrol; "Inadequate" psychopath; "Pure" psychopath

ECT. See Electroconvulsive therapy
EEG (electroencephalogram): abnormalities, 6, 19, 30-34, 105, 109-111, 120; activation procedures, 34-37, 61, 106-107; analysis, 107-109; patterns and behavior, comparisons of specific and nonspecific, 112-115
Electroconvulsive therapy (ECT), 44, 48
Electroencephalogram. See EEG
Epilepsy: relation between episodic behavioral disorders and, 16, 23-30, 167; suspect, range of symptoms of, 141, 143, 161
"Epileptoid" dyscontrol (group 1), 93, 133-138, 168, 169; group differences in, 121-132 passim; versus group 2 + 4 ("functional"), 138-139; versus group 3 ("inadequate"), 139; interaction effects of primidone on, 155-159; summary of findings on, 161-164, 173
Episodic behavioral disorders (EBD): with abnormal EEGs, 30-34; activated electroencephalography in, 34-37; concept of, 15-18; defined, 1; discussion of, 1-7; epilepsy and, 23-30; neurophysiologic and nueroanatomic considerations in, 22-23; pharmacologic treatment of, 43-48; psychotherapy of, 48-49; summarized, 50-51; and surgical studies of aggression, 37-42. See also Aggression
Episodic disinhibitions, 1
Episodic dyscontrol, 1, 3, 6, 9, 13, 50; primary (seizure or instinct), 3, 6, 18-19; secondary (impulse and acting out), 3-6; violence and, 15, 18-22
Episodic inhibitions, 1
Episodic reactions, 1, 6, 13, 17, 18, 50
Explosive personality, 21, 47
Eysenck Personality Inventory, 27

Faulty equipment and faulty learning, 9, 30, 105, 121; defined, 3, 6, 170

About the Authors

Russell R. Monroe is professor of psychiatry, chairman of the department, chairman of the Executive Committee of the Maryland Psychiatric Research Center, and director of the Institute of Psychiatry and Human Behavior, all at the University of Maryland School of Medicine, Baltimore. He received the B.S. and M.D. degrees from Yale University and psychiatric and psychoanalytic training at Columbia University. He has published two books, *Psychiatric Epidemiology and Mental Health Planning* (Russell R. Monroe, Gerald D. Klee, and Eugene B. Brody), American Psychiatric Association, Research Report #22, 1967, and *Episodic Behavioral Disorders*, a Commonwealth Fund book, Harvard University Press, 1970. Dr. Monroe has also published more than 75 articles in professional journals, many related to the area of brain mechanisms and behavior.

George U. Balis is professor of psychiatry at the University of Maryland School of Medicine and director of Undergraduate Medical Education and Editor-in-Chief of a six-volume textbook entitled, *Psychiatric Foundations of Medicine*.

John R. Lion is professor of psychiatry, University of Maryland School of Medicine, and director of the Clinical Research Program for Violent Behavior. He has published numerous articles and books on violence including, *The Evaluation and Management of the Violent Patient*, Charles C. Thomas, 1972; *Personality Disorders*, Williams & Wilkins, 1974, and with D.J. Madden, *Rage, Hate, Assault, and Other Forms of Violence*, Spectrum Publications, 1976.

J. David Barcik is clinical assistant professor of psychiatry (psychology), University of Maryland School of Medicine and director of Psychological Services for the Maryland Division of Corrections. He has written a number of scientific articles on the contribution of limbic structures to memory and learning processes.

Barbara Hulfish is assistant professor of neurology in psychiatry at the University of Maryland School of Medicine. She has been particularly interested in the clinical evaluation of limbic system dysfunction and how this effects behavior.

Matthew McDonald is clinical assistant professor of psychiatry (psychology), University of Maryland School of Medicine and in the private practice of psychology. He is currently president-elect of the Maryland Psychological Association.

Duncan McCulloch is a research associate in Dr. Robert G. Grenell's Neurobiology Laboratories at the University of Maryland School of Medicine and is particularly interested in neuronal function and behavior.

David A. Paskewitz is assistant professor of psychiatry (psychology), University of Maryland School of Medicine. His research has been devoted to psychophysiology, particularly as measured by the electroencephalogram and to biofeedback as a treatment modality for psychophysiologic disorders.

Jeffrey S. Rubin is research associate in the senior author's laboratories and the only collaborator assigned full time to this project.